LONE WOLF

Manifesto For A Misled Youth

LONE WOLF

Manifesto For A Misled Youth

All rights reserved

© LONE WOLF & BEYOND

First edition published in the UK 2024

ISBN 978-1-9162839-0-9

Printed and bound by CPI Group (UK) Ltd

Artwork - Dean Mohr

Photography - Barnaby Newton

Wolf head graphic - Massimo Righi

www.lonewolfandbeyond.com

Be Curious.

Amy, Ben, Carly

and all the timeless ones,

forever keeping it real…

CONTENTS

An Introduction to a Lone Wolf

L<u>O</u>NE WOLF

The end is always the beginning   *1*

L<u>O</u>NE WOLF

(Ill)ogical progression   *33*

LO<u>N</u>E WOLF

Flatlining into oblivion   *99*

LON<u>E</u> WOLF

Getting real   *179*

LONE <u>W</u>OLF

Coming home   *229*

LONE W<u>O</u>LF

Hard wired   *279*

LONE WO<u>L</u>F

Tune in   *323*

LONE WOL<u>F</u>

The time is now (to bloom)   *389*

DISCLAIMER

While this documentation is an account of events as I recall them, certain names (including those that aren't distinguishable, along with locations and elements) have been removed or changed to respect (and safeguard) privacy. Any similarity to a name, character or event of any person, place or thing unrelated to this documentation is entirely coincidental and unintentional.

The words, viewpoints and general ramblings you may discover within these pages, are purely my understanding of 'the ways things are' as I see them. This does not make them true, nor does it mean I'm right…only what I think or perceive. In the grand scheme of things, I know nothing. I do not wish to position myself (or be seen) as an expert, nor proclaim to be a professional or specialist in any field, so please do not treat me as such. Some of what you find may be useful. Some of it perhaps complete horseshit. I'll leave that for your discretion to determine and interpret. Take what you need and leave the rest.

There's a saying - "Be careful what you read, you may die of a misprint." Hmm, makes perfect sense to me. Be curious. Be wise. Always question. Do not believe what I say, or anything else for that matter. Go find out for yourself through direct experience and investigation…and most importantly…

"Realise your own truth."

AN INTRODUCTION TO
A LONE WOLF

The following series of transcripts have been sourced from a personal collective memoir. Part historical account, part realisation...their totality have been previously spoken a thousand times over, to an audience of listeners worldwide. The sole intention of this book was to pass on what had been discovered, in the hope that others will benefit also. The message is clear. It is also pure. It is not written in the conventional sense, nor intended to be read in such a way, perhaps merely serving as a daily reflection for contemplative thinking.

From the very beginning, there was not one strand of intention to be told what to be, how to be, and more importantly who to be. For this very reason, the publication has been specifically left to be independent in its entirety. It was derived, written, designed and presented in the same spirit it was lived. If you have trouble with the fluidity and looseness of the dialogue, spelling, grammar, or simply feel it's not how it should be...well, perhaps pass this copy kindly on to someone who doesn't. No offence taken.

It is only through living the experience you find in these pages, that new beginnings of self discovery and a life beyond limitation and suffering became possible. The dedication to be open, honest, and willing as if my life depended on it, has helped empower not only myself, but countless other lives...who like myself once felt 'I am all alone'.

"You are not alone."

LONE WOLF

The end is always the beginning

THE END IS ALWAYS
THE BEGINNING

"How the fuck did it come to this?" I have no home, I've lost the girl I thought I'd spend the rest of my life with, I don't have a pot to piss in and I'm thousands of pounds in debt. To top it off, I'm constantly fearing the unknown, I can't sit with myself and I have an overwhelming sense of self-loathing. I owe not just the banks money, but friends, family and drug dealers…"For fucks sake, I just know this isn't how I'm meant to be living."

It's undeniable - I'm a hopeless wreckhead who's been self-medicating for the past two decades, yet I'm too scared to do anything about it. Somehow I've made it through my 20s and I'm now flatlining my way through my 30s. Life is passing me by and I honestly don't think I can take much more…"I am so god damn tired of this shit."

For as long as I can remember, there's not a day that passes where I don't feel the debilitation of my now, so called 'life'. Every night I lie awake and wonder…"Where the fuck did it all go wrong?" I try to avoid any kind of contact with reality by fantasising obsessively about dying. "I don't wanna die, yet I can't help but wish I was dead."

In my head I secretly plan the seating arrangement and playlist to my funeral. All my ex-loves will be there for sure, sitting front row exchanging amazing stories of how attentive and funny I was...but their laughter soon turns to hysteria, crying uncontrollably at their tragic loss, as Jeff Buckley's 'Last Goodbye' bellows out as a haunting homage to how wonderful I was.

"In all reality...I've become a narcissistic sociopath and a complete wanker."

ELASTIC RUBBER BAND

I see it like this. If life is an elastic rubber band, then my rubber band was 34 years old when it had its last twang, finally snapping one hot summer's night in July 2009. It was worn out and could stretch no more. Done. I'd been stretching that rubber band progressively harder, faster, longer...tweaking it in all different directions since childhood.

That's a long time to be putting pressure on something so precious. It wears thin under the strain to the point where it just ain't gonna wanna be stretched no more.

"The disillusion of how 'well' emotionally, mentally and physically I'd been was way past its sell by date."

Denial is a funny old thing. It's very personal our internal world. We protect it (and ourselves) vehemently. I know I did. I've heard it said many a time that change can be met with great resistance. Hmm, maybe…I guess that depends on what exactly you intend to change. I'd been carrying around this overwhelming sense in my body that I can only describe as a **black-hole-void-impending-doom-solar-plexus-fucked-up-I-don't-wanna-go-there-fuck-you-fuck-this-and-fuck-that** feeling. Or to put it another way…a constant fear of life. If you're anything like me you'll know exactly what I'm talking about.

It was there deep in my soul. In conventional terms, I'd say this sensation was more likely to be diagnosed as anxiety, stress or perhaps depression…but for me that was just the tip of the iceberg. Underneath the surface laying in wait was something far greater, and when it arose…holy fuck, it felt like it was gonna completely consume me.

"So what do we do about this unwanted fiend? I know what I did, and you're about to find out."

For many years of my life I was a prisoner to that tyrant called fear. The dictator whose every move was to cast me down to a whimpering mess, cowering in the shadows of life like a gutter rat in the big city. Life became for the most part, dreadful. The uncertainty of the unknown was a terrifying prospect to say the least. It's that debilitating irrational fear that seemed to punish me in so many ways that I simply could not defend myself against it, when all I really needed to do was tell it to fuck right off. That fear is a beast, and very different to the rational fears that are perfectly warranted in life, such as going on a first date, starting a new job or perhaps deep sea diving in shark infested waters.

Breaking away from the shackles of that misery and the self-absorbed-self-pity it creates is tough, and its existence is not worthy for anyone. It was a near on impossible nut to crack, or so I thought. The unimaginable life that awaited me seemed so far removed from my reality, neither did I feel deserving to even try. If you're anything like me, you'll understand when I say I felt an immense sense of anxiety and insurmountable levels of terror, at the prospect of even attempting to step out of my 'comfort' zone, which was in fact the complete opposite. I wasn't at all in any degree of comfort, I wasn't even close, using anything I could to far remove myself from the insanity and bewildering existence I'd found myself in. It'd been all I'd known for so long, and I simply assumed, or rather accepted, that this was my lot.

"Little did I know that beyond the walls of that prison lay freedom. Not just any freedom...it was mine, and it wasn't going anywhere, I just had to get to it."

Have you ever asked yourself..."How the fuck did it all go so wrong?"...or perhaps..."Why the fuck?"...Waking up in some strange mouse infested hallway with no clue to how or why?...then realising you're rolled up in a Moroccan rug like some giant sized sushi...or getting into the back of a police patrol car convinced it's a taxi whilst high on LSD. Those are such moments that led to my very own questions of utter bewilderment..."WHY?"

So where does this kind of carry on stem? For me, crazy ass shit like that always, ALWAYS happened when I wasn't paying attention, or in other words - I'd be off my nut, drunk, high or otherwise distracted and led astray like a famished little alley cat sniffing out some much needed lunch...and I didn't just wake up one day and think..."Hmmm, I know what, I'm gonna get into some right clusterfuck chaos today." Nope, it was a gradual slow burner, like a finely roasted tray of vegetables which was seasoned intermittently.

No one ever put a gun to my head (did they?) and said..."Do it, damn you, do it now!" Every single decision, action or consequence (conscious or unconscious), was a direct result of my dissociation, disconnection and unskilful doing. However, in my defence, there were certain conditions I encountered, which kinda made it a tad complexed to be skilful in my motives. Of course there were many ingredients to throw into the mix, such as certain learnt behaviours for survival, peer pressure, trying to 'fit in' and simply wanting to look cool as fuck...who doesn't want to experiment through trial and error?...but ultimately, I progressively fine tuned my skills of the unskilful in no time at all, and soon became a pro.

"In retrospect, I became the underdog very early on in life, blindly trying to figure out the coming of age process 'tuned-out' with my head up my arse."

The following documentation of misdemeanour, is a tale of how I slowly misled my better nature down a slightly precarious path, failing to pay attention and ultimately heading to a place of no return...

In other words - what started out as 'having a little bit of fun'...ended up going a little bit wonky.

SWEET SHERRY

My early years were spent growing up in a modest semi-detached house on a middle class estate, in a nice enough countryside town North of London. I always felt a little displaced from all the other characters in our household, those weird adult creatures. Dad was a teacher who became a headmaster in his late 20s and Mum was a nursery teacher. She actually taught me at pre-school.

Life from what I can recall always seemed strange, but I distinctly remember feeling in awe of it too. Early childhood memories are vague, and not because I'm some old codger who's gone senile and can't remember shit. Nope...it's just that for me, there's a sadness to that time. Now don't get me wrong, it wasn't all bad, I do have fleeting memories of innocence and the love of a family, I've seen the photos...a butter-wouldn't-melt-blue-eyed-blonde boy, wearing a Kermit the frog teeshirt with my red wellies on...and the token cowboy outfit...but it's as though I'd dissociated myself from that time.

"I just felt so awkward as a kid."

As time went by, any marvel I held progressively dissipated by the dysfunction of the world I'd found myself in, and led to the eventual disconnection from who I once was. I was 7 when Mum and Dad separated and soon after divorced. Dad maintained a weekly contact, however in my tiny mind my beloved Father had gone forever. I guess at that young age you just don't understand the complexities of love between two people. The only thing I could comprehend was a sense of confusion, separation and loss. I took it all very personally and just internalised my emotions.

"My world had fallen apart and it literally crushed my spirit."

Early signs of resilience meant I created a world of fantasy from which I could exist (hence the cowboy outfit). I did what any other kid does and I'd go explore hidden hideouts, be it the physical realm, or cocooned in the private confines of my expansive mind. For me, fantasy meant escape.

At that precise time, I had two really significant and juxtaposing dreams which I never forgot. I believe I had them in close proximity to one another, almost as though to counter balance the other. The first, was an incredibly vivid dream where I was straddled upon a mighty white horse in a sprawling field like meadow. The sky was electric blue, and I could sense the summer breeze as I rode that mighty white horse with confidence and marvel. It felt like this was how it was always meant to be, and I could feel pure euphoria and the joy of existence. Nice.

The second was gnarly. I was with Mum, Dad and a man who I did not know. The stranger was asking Mum and Dad if I should be taken to the gallows to meet my maker. They seemed unsure and indecisive. I was pleading for them to save me from my untimely demise, but they could not convince this man to pardon such action. Needless to say I was petrified.

I believe it was no coincidence these two apposing dreams were revealed to me at this precise time in my childhood. Caught in the crossfire of my parents divorce...I was trying to process both my external and internal worlds, but I didn't have a hope in hell. Feeling a lack of security to me resulted in being in a state of fear. Or to put it another way...

"I had no faith in the situation I found myself in (story of my life), therefore I felt trapped with no way out."

That sense of powerlessness would perpetuate throughout my life, and it all started right there at home. I can only presume I dreamt of the mighty white horse to reassure me that everything would be ok. I held on to that dream in the hope that it would. I never forgot. As for the gallows...well, likely that's precisely how I felt. Perhaps even an early warning sign for what was to come? Crikey...a prophecy even?

I looked up in a dream book the supposed meaning of a white horse. Apparently it represented something along the lines of...'A harmonious life with prosperity and purity'. Sounds bloody marvellous, but at that time I simply could not comprehend what that entailed. Now if a child psychiatrist had dissected my inner workings at this point, they may of uncovered a series of episodes that'd played out like a worn out record, precisely at a time when I was most vulnerable.

"I had absolutely no clue that what came swiftly after, would continue to reinforce that sense of powerlessness and define the shape of things to come."

There was this kid at school. In hindsight he was more foe than friend. The one thing we had in common was our parents divorce. I'd been invited to go to Smuck's house one Saturday to play. We watched a pirate copy of the newly released film ET on his Mum's video player, and after went outside to play in the garden out back.

I remember feeling sad that day, not only because of recent events at home…but because I'd just watched the tearjerker ET. I guess on some level I connected to the isolation and confusion of that poor little Alien. To top it off, Smuck was a selfish little sod. Narcissist to the core. The garden had a caravan parked on the side of the house, the type you take on holiday. Smuck led us there, opened the door and in we went, immediately closing and locking it from inside. He then made a forceful and very deliberate statement that I'd not be leaving anytime soon, going on to say I'd never ever see my Mum again.

"Fuckin' ell Smuck…chill out dude."

Not sure how that sounds to you?...but for me that was fucked. For a wee nipper who's feeling a tad fragile anyway, having seen ET say adios amigos and go home (take me with you), then being taken captive by a psychopath...and...to top it all off, add a nice sprinkle of nasty bastard behaviour and being told you're never seeing your beloved Mother again...well, it's simply not cricket. It seemed like an eternity before I could make my exit. Thankfully the snakes mum came looking for us, and I was able to escape his evil clutches. Remind me never to go camping with that family.

Around the same time as the caravan incident, I was hit with another sucker punch to my already diminished esteem, and incident numero 2 incurs. It takes place at the junior school I attended, where sitting all sorry for itself, was an old abandoned fire truck located within the playing fields. It was a total health and safety hazard, yet remained there for us young hoodlums to make use of because they couldn't move the damn thing.

One lunch break, as usual I'd been out in the fields playing and I ended up at the truck. It had side shutters to the rear where they used to store hoses and whatnot. I'd climbed in there with some other kid. Now I'm not sure whether I signed up for this, but someone decided to pull the old rickety shutter completely down... total blackout, jamming it with a stone. Seconds turned to minutes, and minutes seemed to turn to hours. Panic set in as our attempts to open the shutter were to no avail. We could hear what seemed like efforts to get us out with the clattering of the heavy metal shaking away, then a voice of a teacher reassuring us that we remain calm and help was indeed on its way.

"The irony...we're stuck in a frickin' fire truck, and Fireman Sam's probably being called to jack us outta here!"

When you're a kid, time takes forever. It felt like we'd been trapped for hours, when all of a sudden the first burst of daylight shone through from under a small gap. As the shutter slowly edged its way back up, we were greeted with the mixed reception of roaring laughter and jeering from literally the entire school. It was horrendous. The sheer humiliation was debilitating and hideous. The smart arse that'd jammed the shutter was apprehended, it was in fact the school's caretaker, not Fireman Sam who jacked us out, and everyone had something to talk about for a while. Nice one.

It wasn't long after those humiliating episodes of entrapment and powerlessness, that I began to succumb to the allure of a certain majestic, sparkling glass decanter, which I knew was stored in a wooden display cabinet in the lounge at home. I'd seen it there, shimmering, as if to wink at me with its hypnotic seduction. It was filled to the brim with a liquid, that unbeknown to me would go on to hold so much power over me...the sweet taste of sherry.

"It was a power which I now understand to be the potency of chemical enhancement. The intrigue alone was the catalyst for this soon to be ritualistic experimentation."

Naturally as a young boy I'd studied ritualistic habits from my elders, call it learnt behaviour. Both my granddads were smokers. One an avid pipe smoker, the other loved a roll up. I'd often sit at the feet of these elders as if I were a student of their craft, kinda like a young Luke Skywalker watching Obi-Wan Kenobi master the lightsaber. I'd watch transfixed as they carried out their beloved ceremony, the lighting up and watching it take a hold, satisfaction washing over their entirety upon that first inhalation.

I was especially captivated by Grandad on my dad's side, who'd sit in his favourite armchair chugging on the pipe. I'd sit there idolising him as he prepared that pipe, eventually taking out a single pink tipped match from the box and striking it ablaze. The smell alone, a combination of the match and the first burn of the tobacco as it sizzled, was an aroma that seemed to have me hooked.

Anyway, I can't remember what exactly was the defining moment I first locked my homing device onto that majestic decanter, all I know, is it would'a been due to a sheer moment of complete desperation to avoid my then reality, which was becoming increasingly unbearable due to my anxiety…and I just wanted out. It makes total sense I discovered a way to change the way I felt…my survival instinct had kicked in.

"I needed to escape…the 'fuck it' button had landed."

I still to this day remember vividly kneeling in front of those classic 70s style cabinets, with wooden slacks that ran across the front of the doors. They had brass hooped handles which you had to pull firmly to open. Once in, sitting there, placed like the Crown Jewels all regal and mighty, was the glass decanter.

Now, I'd never up until this point even held it, let alone opened it. Its round top had to be pulled quite firmly from the body, just like pulling a plug, or a cork from a bottle, POP! I remember the sheer thrill of potentially being caught at any moment, but I was far too crafty for that. The adrenaline sensation of intrigue was the trigger. Once pulled, that initial rush fired the shot…the bullet piercing any doubt that the potent allure, intoxicating and forceful as it was, could momentarily take me away from my otherwise painful reality.

The first time that warm, sweet taste of sherry hit my pallet it was like I'd found home again. Momentarily, in that instant I was safe. I'd realised with just a mouthful, it was like having a big spoonful of syrupy medicine, the kind that instantly makes you feel like whatever sickness you're suffering from...that everything's gonna be alright.

"I was lit up like a lightsaber...in fact, that electric buzzing sound it makes, that fiery crackling sensation fuelled my very being in those moments when nothing else could."

So that was it. Unbeknown to me at the time, those 'little' incidents (caravan/fire truck) were in fact humongous poison thorns that were now deeply embedded in my psyche...and at such a young age I'd discovered this 'on-a-needs-to-do-basis' ritual, one that was very secret. Every time it was just a mouthful, just enough to take the edge off. My escape, my comfort, my other world...and like so many of my yet to find rituals, it was an almighty ceremonious affair in times of need. It enabled me to get through those early years, and unsuspectingly, shaped the way for the future.

ALRIGHT DAVE?

1982, or thereabouts...Punk was still having an influence on society as an anti-social rebellion, and somehow it managed to intertwine its subculture anarchism into my tiny little noodle.

"I was just a wee nipper when my world collided with our hometown's very own Sid Vicious. It would serve as a profoundly defining moment to my life."

Me and Mum were standing in the queue of our local newsagent waiting to be served. Mum had a 70's style ultra-tight-perm-hairdo (you don't forget those minor details in a hurry)...and me, with my favourite dark blue tee shirt, with my name DAVID printed across the front in light blue letters. So I'm standing there, as I so vividly recall, this squirt of an introvert, when suddenly I set eyes on the man who's just entered the newsagent. Now this ain't no ordinary chump off the street, this dude was like a frickin' freak of nature. His hair was mental, a brightly coloured sky high Mohican, resting atop a skinhead like nothing I'd seen before. He was decorated with piercings, tattoos and dressed in a mash up combo of distressed leather and denim, all ripped, savaged with metal zips, chains and whatnot. He looked like a true warrior of life.

"I reckon his name was 'Danger' or 'Axe'...whatever, it didn't matter, he was simply mesmerising."

He walks by and immediately joins the queue beside us. Now, I'm standing there staring at him, catching flies with my jaw wide open as he's gazing down at me. I see him scan the letters across my top.

In that moment he then looks at me bolt in the eyes and says in a really gnarly way (as one might expect)..."ALRIGHT DAVE!?!"

BOOM!!! In that instant I had landed. I'd found my tribe, my people, dammit I finally felt tuned in to someone and something that understood my internal world, who got it, really fuckin' got it. It was like some cosmic telepathic frequency shit that I didn't need to understand or make sense of, it just felt so right. He saw me...it was as though he'd been sent from another galaxy - Planet Gnar...his spacecraft had landed and he was here to take me back to wherever the fuck I came from.

From that very day, I became DAVE, the DAVE punk arse Danger Axe saw. It was like some kind of rebirth, a metamorphosis even...out with the old and in with the new. I'd been granted permission by Lord Axe to be a rebel and follow his path as a way of life. In my tiny mind, an outlaw was born that day. This pierced, spike haired street walker had tripped me out and I was thrust on a trajectory quest for an alternative way of life. Breakdancing, graffiti and skateboarding all followed, serving as a means to an outlet way outside of the conventional realms. It would be a posse of fellow skaters where I'd intuitively gravitate towards and finally feel part of something for the first time.

"The misfits, the outcasts, the pirates. It gave me a greater purpose and a sense of belonging."

Skating became my religion. A fellowship where I could be a Lone Wolf, free to express myself unconditionally without rules. It was perfect. My skateboard was now my companion, my confidant, my saviour. Like the sweet sherry, I could lose myself, endlessly escaping the confines of my emotions without a care in the world, with the added bonus of smashing myself to pieces every once in a while to feel alive. Unbeknown to me at the time, this would be my introduction to 'self-harm'. Unprocessed confusion, angst and anger all equated to…"Let's crunch some bones and bleed…ahhh… TEAM PAIN!…where do I sign?"

A duality of personalities coexist for the first time I can recall. On one side of the coin I'm timid, shy and ever so polite with absolutely no indication whatsoever of my woes…however, flip that coin over and you've got a snarling, secret identity beginning to create all sorts of mischief. It was early days, but the storm was brewing.

"This newly embedded 'flip' identity of an anarchic rebel, somehow embodied the mantra…"Fuck you, fuck me and fuck 'em all!"

It was an attitude that just wanted to show the world who's boss, so ridding myself of the ever so holy David for a more fitting Dave, I thought to be just the ticket. There was a time I went to Sunday school…but I was turning against the conventional stream. A sensitive kid, aloof and perhaps a tad misunderstood even, yet deep inside I had this seething discontentment which I didn't yet understand, let alone know how to manage.

My curiosity was already starting to expel any limitations of an ordinary life, and perhaps the taste of danger was now beginning to get the better of me. Isn't this just what kids do in childhood? I'd always perceived the Indians as the good guys, my kind of people… "Fuck those Cowboys…where's Chief Firestarter?" There was something deeply ingrained in me that just saw the world differently, and unbeknown to me I was desperately in need of some kind of connection.

I'M THE BADMAN

Anyone who knows the concept of a stereotypical superhero, will know there's usually a tragic backstory. Born out of a necessity to survive, with an insatiable desire to take on the bad guys, an alter ego is created. Their suit of armour, a thick layer of double-hard-bastard-you-can't-touch-me-muddafuckers…and when worn makes them appear to be impenetrable, masking any trace of weakness. Sorted. Sounds rather frickin' ace to me, think I'll have some of that.

Having suffered a fatal blow at the hands of this dastardly strange thing called life…what do you think I did?

"Yep that's right…I sure as hell weren't facing the world without no badass, alter ego superhero shit!"

With the insecurities I bestowed, acute anxiety and vulnerability at an all time high, there's no plausible way I could possibly enter any social situation without donning that superhero outfit, metaphorically speaking of course. Don't matter where I went, or what I did...put it this way, I weren't leaving home without no armour on. "I'm the Badman." Reinforcement to the max. Zip me up and away we go, whatever the occasion I'm covered.

Through my desperation I'd already intuitively discovered the emotional crutch of escapism. That'd served me well up to this point. Creating worlds within worlds of unlimited potential of fantasy always seemed to distract from reality. My survival instinct homed in on that sweet sherry as an additional tool to my artillery, throw into the mix my rights of passage with Danger Axe the badass punk, this wee dude was now becoming well accustomed to deflecting any unwanted adversity, by simply blocking it out as a default setting.

"If I can't feel it, it ain't there...right?...creating a force field of armour, making sure no fucker was ever gonna penetrate it."

In hindsight, the price that came with that was losing the ability to express myself emotionally. My truth didn't count, I couldn't change anything so what's the use of having a voice? There's no feckin' way I'm allowing myself to cry…"What's that? My beloved parents are divorcing…don't matter…I'm the fuckin' Badman mate." Lord Axe had well and truly reinforced that sense of warrior ego in my tiny noodle…there was no going back now.

FOOLS RULES

School was challenging to say the least. Starting life in pre school and junior school seemed relatively ok, compared to attending a 'prestigious' all boys secondary school. In fact it terrified me. Similar to the likes of an old English traditional Hogwarts institution, this ancient relic took its toll. It would be this archaic monstrosity of an educational prison, that would be the setting for such horrors as mass ridicule, bullying and all manner of other nonsense…and that was just from the teachers.

"Those stiff upper lip teachers. We abused them, and they in turn gave us our dues. It was riotous behaviour you'd expect from a bunch of boys."

To begin with I kept my head down. Badman at the ready. An ex-choirboy who became captain of the school cricket team and a reluctant fly-half in rugby. I triumphantly won the infamous first year cross-country run, aptly named cow-pat-corner. Shows I had sheer determination not to be beat (go underdog) amongst a whole year group of about 120 boys. It kinda summed up my attitude towards school...I could achieve no problem, when I wanted to, but it would always be on my terms. So like most things at that time, a cows turd was precisely what I thought of representing the school's cross-country team, and after only two Saturday morning fixtures, I decided I'd rather spend my days shreddin' my skateboard, than hiking my arse through muddy fields in the lashing rain.

I showed early signs of ability, not only in sport but in the academics, however, I simply felt uninspired mostly by the rather bland teachers. Sorry, but if you're gonna learn something it's gotta be remotely interesting. I loved music, but our teachers looked like they'd been dug up from the neighbouring graveyard. At that age I wanted to learn how to play Led Zep not frickin' Mozart.

"Once again, I'd rather go skate than listen to the screeching coming from my violin."

As time went by the strain of the system wore me down. Home life was tough, but any kind of distraction that school may of served soon disappeared without trace, like dirty dishwater down the plughole. Just getting about the vast network of decaying corridors without a dead arm, a wedgie or a chalk dick and balls drawn on the back of your blazer was a serious military mission. Everyone seemed to be a target, a wild-west-bar-brawl-free-for-all. I found myself on more than one occasion swerving the meatheads, Johnny Big Bollocks and his not so merry men...the parasites who seemed to have a hard-on for me and vie for my blood.

"I made the mistake of thinking the toilets was a safe haven from the jocks, until I discovered it's the very place these venomous critters congregate to smoke crafty cigs and exchange dick size."

Bullying became a serious issue for me, both in and out of school. Somehow I'd picked up another couple of enemies from a neighbouring housing estate. They'd taken it upon theirselves to have an ongoing vendetta against me, simply for breathing the same air. I never stood a chance. To the outside world I'm the Badman, but when it comes to the crunch, I'm just as vulnerable as any mere mortal. It seemed my once steely armoured suit was beginning to show cracks for the first time.

It got so bad I began to swerve school. When you receive a punch on the nose, it really does mess with your mind. Mum was called to the school for my increasing absence and the bullying. Due to my anxiety, I was chaperoned to and from school, as I was in such fear over my safety. At one point it got so bad I resorted to hiding on the backseat of Mum's car under a blanket whenever we went out.

"Hmmm...a feeling of powerlessness and entrapment once more."

Body image was a real problem for me, as it is for anyone coming of age. Only later in life have I realised I wasn't alone. Countless young lads, from all walks of life hitting puberty, have indeed a similar struggle with these exact insecurities. No different for you ladies and everything in between. Body dysmorphia is ripe amongst us. It ain't the minority, you ain't a freak, and it most definitely ain't just you...it's more common than not. We are not alone.

I was a skinny arse matchstick, so boys were picking on me left right and centre because I didn't look a certain way, or my voice or my frickin' balls hadn't dropped yet. Other lads were well developed and looked like they belonged on a building site…proper full blown moustaches and shit, and you can imagine how Johnny Big Bollocks looked to someone like me. I felt disproportionate and feminine in comparison. It crippled me.

"I was called names like faggot and all the usual jock bullshit you'd expect from a bunch of Herbert's."

It didn't help that at that time in the late 80's, skateboarding was seen as being for losers in the eyes of mainstream society. The UK wasn't like America where it's part of their culture and seen as cool as fuck, so as a known skater at school I stood out as a minority. We were the geeks, the weirdos, the outcasts. It didn't deter me though, because those connections made it count…and kept my head above water, just. I spent every moment possible skating. The minute school was out, VROOM!…I was off in search off something far more exhilarating. Those school holiday's were spent lost in a world of escapism at a secret skate spot deep in the shadows of a remote woodland. A group of older local skaters had built an entire half-pipe ramp there, made out of wood. It felt like we were doing something completely unique and separate to everything else at that time.

"Going to school felt so unnatural to me. I'd often think...'What's the point in all this anyway?"

Academically I felt I'd failed already, so I decided to just comply and do what was needed to get the job done. I was more than capable in most subjects. Being a creative, the arts and sport were where I remotely came alive for a while....and I was certainly more interested in creating masterpieces of graffiti than learning the square root of 64 from dear old Mr Bore. The rest of the time I'd stare out of the classroom window lost in the dream realm bubble, wishing for another existence to come swallow me up.

"Escapism was always the remedy in any situation."

For me, I couldn't sit for shit. A total sense of discomfort in my own skin and my thoughts running riot, so I'd always try to change that in any way possible. I'd discovered the wonderful art of putting-ya-hands-down-ya-pants as a really quick remedy to satisfy this discontentment. Like most young lads hitting puberty...'erotic fantasy' became a regular go-to in any tortuous situation one could find themselves in. I picked up this one from the playground banter amongst my peers. We certainly didn't have the internet back then and I'm pretty sure I didn't learn such antics from studying my Grandad's.

I'd also learnt about the workings of the birds and the bees in the playground, because I didn't pay attention to the awkward robotic teacher doing his damn best to make it sound remotely exciting in the classroom. My curiosity and desire for sexual exploration was honed, by carefully tearing out pages from the women's underwear section of my nan's catalogues when we'd go visit her, folding them into tiny squares and stashing them to savour especially for these sacred moments. Gents I know I'm not alone here, am I?

"Sorry Nan if I ever deprived you of acquiring that sexy see-through bra and knicker combo. I can only presume I got far more use from it."

Anyway, cheap frills and erotica aside and back to the mundane of prison. The feeling of being unfairly governed by these ancient fools was intolerable, and I certainly didn't want to abide by their unreasonable rules. I think my anarchic…"Fuck you and fuck the world"…attitude kinda kept me in the mindset of …"Sod this horseshit!" It didn't help that there was an apparent hierarchy amongst my peers, especially with the older lads. I lived mostly in fear, which was induced beyond measure when us fresh bate sprogs, the newbies, were subjected to the threats of certain pastimes of tradition. Such antics, which to me, seemed to be on par with borderline psychotic, were initiation rituals like the rather formidable and aptly named 'soggy biscuit'.

"I never had the honour of being subjected to such atrocities (thank God), but the myth seemed to echo along the stoic corridors of this unforgiving place."

Now, if you're not familiar with soggy biscuit, it comprised generally of the school's toughest and most popular kids, with prominence they would choose their victims (the schools meekest). Congregating inside the old rickety cricket pavilion at the depths of the playing fields, far from view of prying eyes, the boys would all gather in a circle, inward facing with a single biscuit placed on the floor at the very centre. The last boy to unload his man goo atop the poor little biscuit would indeed have the pleasure of eating it, hence the name. I'm sure it would much prefer to be dunked in a nice cuppa tea.

Increasing peer pressure and my internal angst, led to my one and only fight in the final art exam. It was with a kid who I used to hang around with out of school. I'd often go to his house as a means to escape the isolation I felt at that time. His dad was rumoured to have the best porn stash in an undisclosed part of the house. There were many undercover operations with failed attempts to sabotage by means of deception. It became a challenge to find opportunities where one might have just enough time, to dash into a room and dive under a bed to rummage around for the sacred treasure chest of smut. It was whilst on one of these scavenger hunt missions that someone uncovered matey's dad's other hidden secret, a Smith and Wesson handgun which was stashed under his bed.

"Perhaps his dad was onto us and decided to up his security."

Anyway, it wasn't until I became older and wiser, that I finally came to understand the true nature of bullying. It makes perfect sense to me now, why Johnny Big Bollocks would want to throw his weight around. I mean don't get me wrong, I'm not condoning it, nope...it's just I realise now how someone like Big Bollocks junior is quite possibly being subjected to the same emotional, physical and psychological torment from Big Bollocks senior behind closed doors.

"Hurt people, hurt people...as they say."

Only once I'd become a target for the bullies, did I become a bully myself, hence the fight I'd started in the art exam. You can't beat 'em, join 'em. A bully has more than likely been bullied as well...

and when you've got a whole load of pain you're lugging around, you're more than likely gonna wanna off load some of it, right?

Somehow I scraped through school without being suspended or thrown out. I'd already checked out anyway. Attendance was poor, but I didn't care much for that. I left by the skin of my teeth with only A grades in the creative arts. I didn't revise, I couldn't focus or sit still long enough, let alone care...so I failed everything else. I guess one accolade worth celebrating was evading soggy biscuit for 5 years straight.

LONE WOLF

(Ill)ogical progression

(ILL)OGICAL PROGRESSION

Coming of age is like walking a tightrope blindfolded. Well, it was for me anyway. With an attitude of defiance and a slightly broken moral compass…it's like trying to head North but you keep ending up way down South. I'd been raised to know right from wrong, however, my mind was already starting to create distortion, and I was developing a stronger sense of rebellion with every turn.

"Fuck it, it'll be alright…anyway, it don't matter, you only live once and all that…ain't worth worrying about, right?" That was kinda how it was for me, as I slowly edged my way along the narrow cliff edge of my teens, a misled youth thinking he knew best, even when all the evidence was already starting to stack up against me that I didn't.

"Stuck in a groove, and unbeknown to me the rhythm I now play is one of dysfunction. My body holds pain, whilst my mind secretly maps out a coping strategy."

THINK YOU KNOW?...YOU DON'T

You know when you're pointing out to a friend something you can see they're doing, which in fact isn't helping them much? Something like..."Mate, you know that's not gonna work if you do that?"...to which they may reply..."Yeah I know"...as you witness them carry on regardless. It's just like that mishap character Andy Pipkin in the British TV series Little Britain.

It's a classic response I seemed to have ingrained as a default setting, when someone was telling me information, regardless as to whether that information would be beneficial to me or not. I could be about to dive off a cliff into a deep ocean of shark infested waters, you could see the shark fins piercing the surface below as I'm about to jump off as you say to me..."Dave man, I don't think that's a good idea, you know there's big-arse sharks in there right?!"...and I'd still blindly say to you..."Yeah I know"...as I'm leaping off to be shark food.

So where does this viewpoint stem from? Is this attitude just part of our DNA? I can't possibly answer that question for anyone else. What I do know, is for me, that outlook on life was held before I learnt to let go of pride, to rid myself of an unhealthy dose of irrational fear, and to smash through the solid brick wall of denial, hiding the very real fact that I was not ok.

Reality - Just 'FINE'...equalled Fucked, Insecure, Neurotic and Emotionally inept. Thinking I knew best was a habit I'd got into pretty early in life..."I'm a Lone Wolf, the Badman." More like Captain Blunderclutz! It comes with a warped sense of perspective...thinking the world s against you, and you're at war with yourself and everyone else that comes anywhere near you.

"Typical teen angst syndrome perhaps? Or was that just me?"

It's an attitude, more commonly known as 'victim mode'..."If you felt like I did, you'd be a cunt too!" Oh boy, the woes of feeling misunderstood. That angst came from feeling like the underdog all the time. I needed to prove myself and be in control (or so I thought), always having to be right no matter what. That pride, my steely arrogance, and a whole bunch of ignorance led me to believe I knew best, always. I was stubborn...a Taurus, so a hard nut to crack. A wild Bull in a china shop whose constant desire to be right was always paramount. Even when I knew deep down I was wrong, I was right. It drove people mad, including me, because inevitably I'd always be in conflict with myself, something, or someone.

"Dave, I think you may get burnt if you touch that scolding hot fire"...and I'd be like..."Yeah yeah, I know I know"...As my hand catches alight and the skin starts to slide off the bone. Keeping up that false pretence that everything was ok regardless, was nothing short of lunacy. I guess it's a similar mindset to insanity...doing the same thing over and over, expecting a different outcome each time.

"It was 100% fear driven delusion, pure denial at its finest."

It's not just me, is it? This thick layer of delusion so deeply entrenched in everyday life. It seems to be everywhere for us all to act out on, unless we choose not to, no? I could look someone straight in the whites of their eyes and say to them, just like people used to say to me..."You know that thing? You know, the thing that's really fucked up crazy bad?"...It can always be met with a rather swift..."Yeah I know." It's like we just don't wanna see it, or maybe we're just not ready to admit it, and don't wanna be burdened with the responsibility of facing up to these inconvenient truths, that our loved ones so kindly point out to us. After all, it's quite nice to be blissfully unaware of having to make change, no? Especially when it might mean getting in touch with a little discomfort or two. Much easier to remain (un)comfortably numb. Ignorance is bliss…"I'm staying put thank you very much. Laters."

I know from my own experience and from what I see in others, that change only takes place when you really, truly, want to make that change. I never stopped any bad habit for any other reason, other than absolute determination, and the complete conviction of actually wanting to stop. I wouldn't stop for you, I certainly wouldn't stop just because someone said I had to, or for any other reason for that matter.

"Tell me to go left...nah, you're alright mate, I'm heading right."

Even if I'd originally intended to go left, the very fact you're telling me to go left means I'll automatically go right. Sound familiar? That decision to change didn't come anytime soon, and it certainly wasn't easy. It had to come deep from within my core, and I had to be ready to make that commitment. I believe there are no short cuts worth taking. For me, I had to experience life and make some seriously significant fuck ups to have any true realisations. Experience was indeed the best education I ever had.

Lack of will power and a disinterest in the 'good stuff', caused me a lot of unnecessary suffering. It probably didn't help I'd become self-centred, which meant zero accountability. For some, including myself, getting to a place of complete self destruct, oblivion and experiencing depths of despair, pain and unparalleled suffering…is the only motivator to trigger the process of positive change.

"If you're anything like me, first you've got to overcome immense resistance to get to the good stuff."

I needed hardened evidence presented to me in order to have any confidence to make change, and if I don't see that evidence, or literally taste it, then I'm gonna sabotage any further efforts to do so, simply based on my own assessment (or rather an inaccurate perception, or judgment) that it's simply not worth doing. Hindsight is a wonderful thing...I was just getting started.

STONERISM

Cheech and Chong, buckets and bongs....ahh the life of a fully fledged space cadet. I was 14 when I first smoked cannabis. I'd only recently had a toke on a fag, for which I thought was disgusting. The only reason I cracked on and pushed through that awful taste was to look the part, to fit in and be 'cool'.

There'd been a time I would of said…"NO." I was happy to just lose myself in skateboarding, to sit and sketch or play around with music...creative stuff, but that all changed. I guess a total lack of confidence and the pressure becoming too much, I wasn't strong enough to withstand.

"Through fear of being judged and not fitting in, smoking became force of habit."

Doing something you're not sure of over and over until eventually it becomes ingrained, for me this meant literally forcing myself to do it repeatedly until it stuck. Isn't that how all habits are formed? Just with cigarettes, I didn't like the taste of alcohol much either (sweet sherry the exception), when I first started drinking super strong ciders, beers and cheap vodka with the kids on our estate. I wanted to belong as much as revolt. It tasted foul, literally forcing that shit down each and every time. Cannabis was no different.

I started to bunk off school with my adopted crowd of outcasts, perhaps the commonality being broken homes and broken hearts? I wonder if we'd taken off the superhero masks and laid our vulnerabilities out to see and own, whether life would of been different for us all? It's a nice thought, but was never gonna happen in a million years.

We were skipping class, occupying the stone memorial in the very centre of the graveyard, a go-to spot for the smokers. When that joint came out and was passed around I knew I didn't want it, but I also knew I couldn't say no. If you're anything like me, saying no was admitting you're a pussy. Vulnerability is seen as weakness, and that couldn't happen, not with this lot. I want to belong.

"So I took a toke, coughed my guts up…which is the worst possible thing you could do, and proceeded to force myself to have another go."

From that day, progressively…it went from (nervously) only smoking it with others on occasion, using their hash, to slowly but surely smoking it on a regular basis. Ultimately, this lead to me buying my own supply and smoking it every day, eventually smoking it on my own. I didn't see it coming, and I certainly didn't plan becoming dependant on it. It kinda just happened organically over a period of time, the way habits are formed.

The sad thing is, the further into smoking I got, the less I'd do the things I used to love. It became my new 'thing'. I could feel myself slowly drifting, disconnecting from all my creative outlets, including sport...yet I simply could not stop as I continued to lose myself. For me, being a stoner meant procrastination came naturally. It was effortless to not want to do things. I'd start something, yet I could not seem to finish it…"Ahh, maaaan… naaah, fuck that shit…it can wait." With hindsight, it's easy to see the link between procrastination and (my) stonerism, but at that time I simply could not join the dots…based on the simple premise they were too spaced out!

"I couldn't comprehend how some stoners appeared to 'get shit done'…I certainly wasn't one of them."

We had some lads in our school who we could easily buy Hash from. Before I left that place for good I found myself buying LSD too. It seemed as though my new curriculum in life was the experimentation of mind altering substances. That's when my grades dropped and with it my attention span. "Pay more attention"…and…"Could do better"…became a regular statement from teachers on any given day.

"Fuck English literature, let's roll a fat one."

Once I'd pushed through the fear factor barrier of chemical experimentation, and desensitised myself to the taste, it was plain sailing. As for the affects of cannabis, well it was really simple… momentarily, depending on how good the hash was, I could be taken away from the otherwise discomfort of being me. It took me away from all my problems, relinquished all responsibilities, and as far away from the anxiety and pain as possible…and for that moment, nothing was wrong.

Being in so much turmoil, meant drugs had become a real solution to all my problems. Sweet sherry and the fantasy realm had been a quick fix early on, as was the staple art of hands-down-pants...but this worked just fine (I thought), the perfect tonic (I thought). I came to really enjoy that subliminal state of being, my other world. It became the norm, to the point where the rare moments I wasn't baked, well...those were the times when I had to experience how bad it used to be, prior to discovering my haven in cannabis.

"Wake and bake really was my mantra. I kinda enjoyed being a stoner, and in a weird way it gave me a sense of identity and purpose."

By the time I was out of school for good, I was waking and baking right through the day, each and every day until lights out, nicely cocooned for the night in a hedonistic blanket of mash up. It was a highly addictive cycle, and one to which I was blissfully unaware of.

The way I see it, stonerism, like any religion...is a place of refuge, a community, a safe place you can dwell (or in my case hide). There you will meet fellow space cadets, pilgrims on a quest to find the truth, the meaning of life (the perfect pot noodle) or the answer we're all searching for (I never found it)...and like other religions, it can give you a sense of hope, a sense of connection. My sanctuary of stonerism certainly brought me friendship, laughter, kindred souls who were on this blissed out quest to share the divine (mash up). It was our duty (we thought), to one day teach our kids to roll a fat one, to keep pet chimpanzees at home to make cups of tea on demand. A real life stoner chimp tea party, with the kids supplying the narcs…how cool would that be? (Errr)

"At the time it all seemed so harmless…and of course when you're convinced you're invincible nothing seems to matter."

I connected to fellow stoners like Betty, a girl I'd met in the local youth club. She became my confidant back in those testing times of adolescence, when nothing made sense, and all we had to cling on to for hope was a sense of relief and escapism that our beloved God, Marijuana, the almighty granted us. She'd often bare witness to my dark sunken moods of depression, where I'd tune-out emotionally and we'd smoke ourselves into oblivion. Bless you Betty for all those countless cups of tea and rounds upon rounds of glorious toast.

I tried my hardest to stay on the one-love frequency of the highs, because it wasn't all bad to begin with….but alas the wheels seemed to come off uncontrollably. I only wish I could of had the answers back then..."Why am I doing it?"...and..."How does it make me feel?" I mean don't get me wrong, I probably would of answered..."Because I fuckin' love it and don't give a damn"...and... "It shuts my head up."

"The reality - on one hand I adore getting high, on the other...I secretly struggle with my emotions and what's going on in my noodle, but I ain't telling no one through fear of judgement...so I remain silent."

On a subconscious level it changed the way I felt. I couldn't sit with myself and I didn't like my reality, so I found solace in changing it. Hash was the perfect tonic for that. It instantly slowed everything down. It got me out of my head and into somewhere less chaotic. Underneath my persona-stoner-chill, I was an angry raging typhoon waiting to wipe out any natural surroundings that got in its way. That unprocessed part of me scared me. I was developing a stronger sense of hatred with an anger fuelled by my past.

"Cannabis was spot on for keeping that beast at bay."

Spliffs turned into bongs, bongs into buckets. I'd always need more and more. Naturally when your tolerance levels rise so does your intake. Back in the early nineties hash was cheap as chips and everyone had bundles of it. I never had a job, no part time paper round or Saturday job for me. Nah, I was lazy...procrastination was the aim of the game, so I bled Mum dry of her already limited financial and emotional resources.

I began to steal. Naturally once I'd become a stoner with an unquenchable habit, it was the beginning of a very long harsh road of skullduggery. Dishonesty was beginning to creep in on every level to get what I needed, when I needed it. The 'sanctuary' of what I once sought as a means to escape, and the disconnect it brought to my true nature, was beginning to erode my soul like nitric acid pulsating through my veins. I'd cleared out Mum's bank account by the time I was 16. She entrusted me with her bank card when she was poorly, to go get essential groceries. I knew that pin and I knew where the card was kept. That's the harsh reality of substance abuse right there.

"Early signs of getting greedy and screw the consequences."

Whether I liked it or not, my moral compass was well and truly broken. I'm doing things to the very people I'm meant to care about, but every best effort seems to always fall short. The more I fucked up, the less I liked myself, and the less I liked myself, the more I did it. Nothing could stop me. I guess it was the perfect excuse to crack on and continue to get high.

21 CLUB

I was convinced I wasn't gonna make my 21st birthday. Similar to the lost souls of the infamous 27 club, a tragic tale of a life gone wrong, meeting an untimely demise. The school years had taken its toll. The lack of direction and any remote sense of who I was or wasn't had left me stumped. I felt like a square peg, at times the round hole. Rarely did I fit, if at all.

"Is it just me…or are we all a little bit strange?"

Mum informed me that a former friend had taken his own life. We sang together in the school play in Spanish, dressed as clowns. Apparently he'd found out his best mate had copped off with his girlfriend whilst away on holiday. Upon finding out this ultimate betrayal, he drove to a remote spot, where he proceeded to drink himself into a stupor before closing the final curtain. Adios amigo.

At the time of hearing this tragic news, I distinctly remember feeling nothing. I had zero emotion associated with the loss, just numb. I guess I couldn't get past the sorrow or sufferance for what I was experiencing at that time. I was 16.

Any hope of early life aspirations had slowly ebbed away, leaving me totally uninspired and hopeless. It probably didn't help I'd been religiously smoking cannabis everyday since the age of 14. Those days were dark. I felt truly miserable, depressed even...and worse of all I'd lost any sense of meaning. Looking back, I can see I'd already given up and checked out.

"I just couldn't see a future and was certainly not ready to go into the big vast turbulent ocean of life. To be honest it was bloody terrifying."

My artistic merits had gained me a place at Art college. That holiday period between leaving school and starting term, I continued to lose myself (and my mind). Trippin' on acid became a regular thing. I'd go on walkabout in the woods to escape reality, only to return home and lye on my bed for hours staring at the artex ceiling, watching magical kaleidoscope patterns take form and come alive.

I self-harmed in the traditional sense whilst on holiday with my closest friend at that time. It was also on that trip I remember gravitating towards another kindred spirit. Like the second coming of Danger Axe the punk, only this time there was a full squad. They stood out a mile amongst all the other tourists lounging poolside. A posse of outlaws. Older dudes, looking cool as fuck with the long

Kurt Cobain hair. He was on my radar at that time. You could say I found my Nirvana in Kurt. I felt he understood me, that pain, that rage...it was mine too. So when their music burst out onto the world it felt like a lifeline.

These dudes were all tattooed, drinking and smoking, looking like they didn't have a care in the world. To me that was extremely intoxicating, and in an instant I wanted in.

"I wanna be in your tribe. Where do I sign up?"

I decided to grow my hair long, seeking out my first tattoo as soon as I could, from a man who was rumoured to be going blind. They became a form of ritual, and like all the others I'd picked up so far, this one would also go on to be a coping mechanism. It was art right?...Expression? So it was justified. For me, they served as the ultimate commitment to my rebel status...

"Fuck you and fuck the system."

Anyway, me and my mate had been getting sozzled in a bar-restaurant, and I remember being in the toilet having one of those bloke moments we do when we're completely smashed. The one where your head's firmly fixed against the wall in front of you, propping you up whilst ya pissing to stabilise your otherwise bent-out-of-shape state. Always a true champ if you can get your piss anywhere near the target. I walked out from that toilet and straight into a barren kinda wasteland. It was still daylight, bright blue sky and it was roasting hot. I remember feeling totally lost. There I was, in a strange place where no one knows me. "I feel so alone, like I'm the only one who could possibly feel the way I do." I remember seeing a piece of broken glass just lying there sparkling in the sun. I reached over and picked it up.

"I ran that piece of glass along the inside of my right forearm until I drew blood."

In that moment I launched the glass in disgust. It freaked me the fuck out. No one had shown me how to do this and it scared me. That was the only time I'd self-harm in that way.

Back home and before the summer break was over, I had my first of many encounters with the police. I used to knock around with local lads from our estate. We'd dick about with lighter gas, set light to everything and all that kinda stuff. I always felt it wasn't really me, but of course I'm trying to fit in and not look like a pussy. When you've got zero self esteem and you don't like yourself much, seeking validation from a bunch of rascals just seems the 'norm'.

"We're all wearing our superhero masks, but really underneath all the bullshit we're just scared, insecure little Mummy's boys, no?"

Feeling the pressure to conform? Monkey see monkey do. "Set a tree ablaze?…Damn fuckin' right, I'm gonna light up an entire forest"…"Get high on lighter gas? Hell yeah, give it here…I'm gonna eat the entire canister muddafucker!" It's mental, but I lived my life by that code. Peer pressure at its finest.

We were in the playing fields up top of the estate where we used to hang out, minding our own business smoking dope, when in roars a speeding police car with the lights flashing on top and the sirens screaming out. Like a shot we bolted through a gap in the hedge, we didn't dare look back. I found myself alone down some narrow alleyway, hiding for ages until I dared to make my way home. Now at this time (1991), the government were seriously losing their shit over the legendary illegal rave and party/drug scene. It was a national epidemic and the establishment wanted to snuff it out. So unlike today, you lived in fear of being caught with drugs.

"It was literally cat and mouse."

As soon as I turned the corner into our street, I could see the police car directly out front of our house. "Shit!" As I turned and walked away my bro came steaming up behind me, grabbing me by the scruff of my neck. Quite rightly he was livid, yelling that Mum was in a right state. He drags my sorry arse back home after I give up trying to talk him out of it. I had to take the bullet.

Mum was in a complete mess. She'd already suffered one meltdown when Dad left. I'd helplessly witnessed the struggle she'd had to cope with her own sense of loss and grief. She did her damn best given the situation, bless her...but now this. It'd tipped her over the edge. I felt awful. A policewoman consoled our poor Mum, whilst a policeman took me upstairs to my room.

"They'd already had a good rummage before I'd turned up."

I learnt that a passer by walking a dog had smelt the 'fruity aroma' and called the police. Like I said, it was a big deal back then. One of my so called 'mates' got caught in the chase, and when questioned, told the police I was a drug dealer peddling them hash. So they decided to raid the house. Luckily there were no drugs to be found. What they did find to my devastation, was my stash of 'erotic editorials'. Oh boy, the humiliation. I'm not sure what was worse, the look on the officer's face in disgust, or my awkward sunken feeling of being exposed with all those sacred images laid out for all to see.

"I reckon he'd done it on purpose to headfuck me. If so, it'd worked."

They gave me a ruddy good bollockin', and made me feel like shit for causing my Mother so much distress, declaring they'd be keeping a beady eye on me. It didn't seem to deter me much. In fact, it made everything worse. That shame and guilt I carried would not leave me, so I simply used more drugs to suppress it. The irony of this incident, is that approximately a year or so earlier, that very same police officer who gave me that rollicking, had facilitated a drug information workshop at our school, outlining the perils of drugs and the consequences to them. Didn't bloody work mate.

The week before I was due to start college we had an induction day. It was the day I had my first panic attack. We were all crammed into this classroom, I was stoned as per usual, when I suddenly began to feel an overwhelming need to get out immediately. There's the saying 'fight, flight or freeze'…I was stuck in freeze, like some freakish unseen entity pinning me down, rendering me defenceless. Every atom in my being wanted to get the hell outta there, but I was stuck.

"It was horrific…I had to endure sheer terror, pretending everything was ok."

It freaked the life outta me. "Something definitely ain't right in my head." My heart had been thumping like a frickin' champion prize fighter, literally up in my throat choking me trying to punch its way out. I thought I'd suffocate…"Death by asphyxiation caused by a dodgy ticker?" It was the first time I considered I may have a heart defect…"An irregularity perhaps?"

I'd been smoking a new strain of stronger weed…skunk. It was fuckin' me already, and I'm sure the LSD consumption didn't help. I keep the panic attack secret. "Much easier to keep schtum… besides, I don't trust anyone, and who's gonna understand anyway?" I was convinced it was just me…"They'll lock me up for being a crank!"

"Blimey, if only you knew what went on in my mind."

Manic meltdowns aside, college to begin with was exciting. I'd been to an all boys school, and now there were bundles of girls. I still had the confidence of a mouse, but my alter ego superhero was still a go-to. Asked if I'm ok (even when floored), my automatic response would always be a mighty…"Fuck yeah, I'm doing great man." In hindsight, there was a definite fine line between my inner and outer worlds at this time. That twin duality of my personas - 'I'm the Badman the invincible', seeking adrenaline fuelled excitement and euphoria...versus 'scared little David the mere mortal', suffering crippling anxiety and low self esteem. Social situations were met with nervous trepidation. There was no plausible way I could confidently talk to girls, let alone believe they had any interest in me, so skulling a few shots of alcohol or smoking a doobie was the only way I could muster the means to communicate...even if it did come out sideways.

"I had much to learn."

My ceremonious 'losing ones virginity', was off my crackers on Ecstasy at the break of dawn, whilst the homies were 'getting on it' next door...in a mates caravan, down the bottom of his parents garden. Pure class, who says romance is dead? Perhaps in some perverse way, it seemed to counterbalance the horrendous Smuck caravan encounter...and finally served as a rite of passage. Up until that point, I'd had to lie about the fact I was still a virgin, in fear of being judged and outcast by those who weren't.

Day one at college I landed a new partner in crime, Jimmy. Our first photography assignment, Jimmy recreated that infamous image of rock legend Jim Morrison with his arms out and top off. Perhaps a sign of things to come? I went to my first rave with

Jimmy. That night we lost ourselves on acid. It was rare if I took LSD and didn't lose my shit.

"Taking acid was the ultimate in escapism, it certainly expanded my mind, but it also created a lot of problems."

Once you're in a rave you're safe. You're with your people. The outside world doesn't exist. It's just you and your tribe, and in that moment nothing else matters...you just dive in to the expansive ocean of excess and leave all inhibitions at shore. It couldn't of come at a better time. I desperately needed to feel part of something. Drugs, girls and partying had taken me away from the skateboard community, my former trusted posse of outlaws. There was a gaping hole I needed to fill. That escapism, the excitement, a sense of fun and euphoria...if I didn't have that, then I'm not sure what I'd of done.

"I wanted to get outta my head, because being in my head was near on impossible. So outta my head I'd get... and as often as I could."

Our generation were all seeking the answers and connection. If pubs were our church, then raves were our cathedral. I was part of something extraordinarily special. It was the height of the rave counter culture movement sweeping across the UK like the plague, and I jumped in head first with my arms (and mouth) wide open. Hardcore euphoric dance music was our God...and taking Ecstasy was like having a direct line to the Almighty. Abandoned warehouses were used as temporary places of worship, organised dance events took place across the country each and every weekend. We were all disciples of this incredible movement, thousands upon thousands of us and we all had one thing in common...(Ecstasy)... seeking a sacred place where we felt understood, loved, connected.

"We were the jilted generation. A tribal gathering of 'truth seekers' who refused to live in the conventional way society offered at that time."

Coming out of a rave at the break of dawn on acid was entering paranoid city. The last thing you wanna see in that state is the police. Ecstasy however, you're more likely to wanna give 'em a hug and ask them home for a sleepover. Eyes like saucers, me and Jimmy made our way to a waiting taxi. As we sat there on the back seats, we heard a rat-a-tat-tat on the outside of the window. We wind it down enough to have a conversation. Cue a rather scary and towering cartoon policeman - "Excuse me gents, what exactly do you think you're doing in there?" He then opens the car door and asks us to get out. We had in fact cosied up in the back seats of a police patrol car. Lights on top. The lot. That's acid for you. Oh well. He then went on to say something along the lines of...

"If it's a taxi you're after lads, then I suggest you get in the one over there."

Throughout that first year of college it transpired I wasn't taking the academic side of it seriously. I was becoming more and more detached. Apparently (I don't remember this) Mum went to see the Head of year about my attendance and attitude. She disclosed I had some 'personal issues' and felt I needed support. They washed their hands of it, declaring it wasn't their responsibility to help. Thanks homies.

I vaguely remember not wanting to get out of bed or leave the house. Drugs were beginning to seriously fuck me in the head. Comedowns off Ecstasy and booze hangovers were a regular occurrence. Smoking the ganja somehow seemed to smooth the edges, but only just. This vicious helter-skelter cycle had now become the norm. Facing college was becoming a less viable option. I now held the ideology…"I am what I am, therefore I cannot change." I felt so powerless over my life, so I continued to keep my mouth shut and head down, through fear of being judged. I was in desperate need of a voice, to confide in someone the true extent of my low self worth, but I daren't. It's really hard not to slip into self pity and depression when you're feeling like that. Mum had on occasion suggested I talk to someone, a counsellor. Each time I refused.

"The thought of a stranger dissecting my inner most secrets horrified me. It ain't happening."

If I had seen a counsellor, they may of uncovered a series of events that'd already taken place, resulting in a devastating effect on my wellbeing. It wasn't just Dad leaving and the likes of Johnny Big Bollocks crippling me. Unbeknown to me, that perpetuating theme of entrapment from early childhood was casting a spell over me like an insidious curse...and I was about to encounter new levels of tyranny, furthering my seemingly downward spiral into the vortex of mental instability.

It was winter, as I remember it being fittingly stark, grey and dreary...the 'perfect' ambience for what was to follow. I hadn't seen my old nemesis Smuck (the snake) since the day we departed Junior school at the age of 11. So it was a surprise to seem him after all that time when we met at college. He hadn't changed. In fact, he'd become even more venomous. Like attracts like, so he'd acquired an equally psychotic new friend, Doosh.

"Smuck and Doosh, two egomaniac psychos made for each other."

On this day I somehow ended up with them. It was a case of…"If you can't beat 'em, join 'em"…and if you're anything like I was (defeated), you kinda just gravitate effortlessly towards negativity. We were doing the usual swerving a lesson or two…and instead, making the use of our time by experimenting in narcotics. I believe LSD was the order of the day, as was Hash. We'd decided to go check out an old derelict warehouse which was rumoured to be haunted. We got in through the boarded-up gaps in the doorways and found ourselves up on the higher level.

"It was definitely not safe, especially on mash up mind altering substances."

It was whilst up on the top floor that the two venomous amigos decided to strike, turning on me unexpectedly, subjecting me to what I can only recall as a tirade of verbal, mental, and physical abuse. They cornered me, not only physically but psychologically, making it clear I would not be leaving anytime soon. "What the fuck is it with this mentalist of a human being who gets his kicks from taking me captive?" First a caravan and now this. Is this some kind of weird freakish fetish? Hmm…makes you wonder. They decide to impersonate Llamas and spit at me (for real), taunting me whilst pushing me forcefully around and bating me like a cat does in duel with a mouse. It was traumatic as fuck, especially as I was sky high on acid and completely stoned. 'I'm the Badman?' Errr... he'd taken flight and left the building. To top it off, they insisted (thanks chaps) on giving me blowback upon blowback, continually blasting harsh plumes of intoxicating smoke for the entirety of a fat joint. I can't even remember (emotional blackout) how I came to leave that place...I can only imagine they became bored of their subject, just like any wild predator...

"It hunts its prey and keeps it alive just about long enough for it to have its fun, then it'll either eat it alive or lose interest and dispose of it."

That incident caused such devastation to my mental and emotional world. I just wanted to stay in the sanctuary of my bedroom and hideaway, never to be seen again. Jimmy would turn up unannounced some mornings to talk me into going to college. I'd reluctantly go on occasion, but as far as I was concerned I was done. It was over.

I continued to use Ecstasy even though it had serious side effects, but I had absolutely no will power to take care of myself. Instead, I convinced myself I was having the time of my life...

denial, fear and delusion at its finest. I just needed those highs, even knowing the darkest of lows would follow. Isolation became a thing, yet the lure of thrill seeking and pill-popping kept calling me. At times my only lifeline would be to sit in my room listening to the local pirate radio station, aptly named MAD FM...informing the disciples of Lord 'E' to congregate and hold mass.

"The religion of rave and drugs somehow kept me going. It was all I had."

It's so alarmingly obvious for me to see now, that I was already deeply entrenched in an addictive cycle of clusterfuck chaos, which I certainly didn't need in my life at that time, but when you're hopelessly chasing desire it's always gonna appear attractive, no matter what it is and to what detriment. That's how it was for me, as I slid precariously down the path towards oblivion. This misled youth was seeking a 'higher power' from something that wasn't sustainable...it could never satisfy me, yet I kept going back for more. The incredible euphoric highs of Ecstasy had now become the 'norm'...and it wasn't about to change anytime soon. Was I even aware of such catastrophic behaviour?...of course not, why would I?..."I'm having the time of my life!" There's no conceivable way I could stop now...

"Fuck it, I'm just going with the flow, right?...trying to find my way in the world."

Now, when you're traumatised and life has you beat, the last thing you wanna do is head straight back to another insanely reckless and damn right dangerous situation. That blasted chasing desire! Why do I not have an off button? (Attachment issues perhaps?)...and why do I not respect myself? (Hmmm, try low self-esteem & self hatred for starters).

The adrenaline rush that comes from risk taking is like a drug in itself...and I was hooked. As if Smuck the psycho terrorising me wasn't enough, perhaps an encounter with an axe wielding law enforcement officer may do it? Like the infamous "Heeere's Johnny!" scene from horror movie The Shining, I found myself 'victim' to equal measures of shock value...as it unfolded for all to see on a live broadcast for the news...

"Hi Mum, I'm on TV!"

Entering illegal warehouse raves always felt gnar to me, but I guess in numbers you kinda feel untouchable...teenage rebellion plus an unhealthy dollop of herd mentality equals 'I'm the Badman x1000'. "We're fuckin' invincible, right?"..."Errr, no son, you're just a dweeb who thinks he's the big man." Teenage delusion aside, I was at tipping point each time I ventured out, but nothing a magic pill couldn't fix, right? Outwardly I daren't tell a soul how scared I am, as I witness hardcore maniac party rebels barricade the doors of the warehouse.

"Fuck it, what can possibly go wrong? Well the answer to that is...plenty!"

Word started to spread the cops were on their way. Errr...a slight understatement, the entire North London Metropolitan police force to be precise. Plumes of tear gas entering the holes in the crumbling barricade confirmed this. Attempts to break through were met with resistance, but this only enraged the cops more. Me and my homies (aptly named 'The Lost It Crew') were at this point all cowering down, and in keeping with our namesake - were quite literally losing our shit. Helplessly, we witness the madness play out. Total pandemonium, as strobe lights momentarily lit up silhouettes of a full blown riot to the sound of the PA being destroyed...the bass finally cutting out, turning to a deadly backdrop of screaming and shouting.

Everyone's trying to get rid of their drugs...on the floor, up ya arse or down the hatch. I remember seeing a mate look at me in pure terror as he placed a tab of acid on his tongue to swallow, as we're subjected to the loudest noise crashing against the emergency fire door directly behind us. CRAAASH!!…as we witnessed the blade of an axe piercing through it.

"We froze in horror as the door slowly peeled away, and a mob of angry riot police crashed their way through."

It was like something out of a Wild West bar brawl gone wrong on a mass scale. We were marched out into waiting police vans… unbelievably, in front of TV camera crews capturing the whole damn thing. Now depending on your luck, determined whether or not you received the dreaded anal probe from a rather pissed law enforcement officer. The Gods were looking down on me that night, and I'm released a free man with my butt still intact.

So what does one do, having swerved any serious consequence to such antics? Hmmm…it's a nice thought, to think I could'a just snapped out of it and woken the fuck up…but alas it wasn't to be. It would take a lot more than a close scrape with an anal probe to be deterred.

"There would always be another rave, another warehouse, another night of thrill seeking adrenaline to be had."

Somehow I scraped through that year at college, but on the second year I dropped off the course, having been transferred to one which wasn't so advanced. It made me feel like shit…"What a failure!"… and the inevitable was soon to be, not long after I'd drop out all together.

As if it couldn't get any worse, it did. Later that year I found myself without a home. The terms of the divorce agreement, meant Mum had to sell the house once me and bro were out of education. So that's what happened. She couldn't afford a big enough place, so she moved up north to stay with a friend to figure out what to do. I hadn't spoken to Dad in years…he had no idea what I was up to. Mum did help out with a chunk of money, which I could'a used for a deposit for somewhere to live, but I didn't have a clue about that sort of stuff. Instead, I bought a pair of Technic 1210 turntables, a mixer and a load of vinyl. Safety in sound.

"I had absolutely no idea how to do adulthood. Fuck man, I couldn't hold down a single day without getting high, let alone organising this grown up shit."

Once more I felt displaced, with my insecurity at an all time high. I spent the final days in that family home alone. It was just me and our beloved cat Sophie. I took that place hostage like a glorified squatter and I certainly wasn't leaving without a bang. One last stand before handing the keys over to the estate agents on the day they arrived.

Over the years my frustration and anger had taken care of smashing holes in doors, wardrobes and the walls. It also needed fumigating. I'd blazed defiantly, plumes of smoke in every nook and cranny. I was utterly devastated when I had to leave. The final farewell took place in the back garden, saying a heartbreaking last goodbye to Sophie, who was staying with neighbours.

"All that pain and angst I'd bottled up exploded as I huddled over her and I burst into floods of uncontrollable tears."

My only option was to move in with my girlfriend, Alabama. She was slightly older and had her own place. Alabama certainly had her work cut out with me. We were both complicated people trying to navigate our way through life. We had some amazing times together, and some dark shit too. She knew my pain. She felt it, as I did hers.

"Funny how two lost souls find each other."

The effects of paranoia from the constant chemical intake was turning my mind to jelly. I was beginning to feel like I was losing my shizzle, crazy thoughts and voices would sabotage that space between my ears. Dark, intrusive imagery would manifest, playing out horrific sequences in graphic detail…always ending in carnage. How delightful. I developed alternative 'coping' strategies in an attempt to combat these incredulous thoughts. Obsessively 'scanning' registration plates of passing cars became a staple go-to in times of need.

On occasion, I'd stare intently in the mirror, transfixed… glaring into the darkness of my pupils, trying to figure out who was in there. "Mirror mirror…please explain, why is my mind so frickin' strange?…will I one day be clinically classified as mentally insane?…or will I die, similar to the lost souls of the infamous 27 club, finally meeting my untimely demise?" No one had a clue what was really going on for me, least of all myself.

"Although unsettling, I kinda liked the idea of being a tad weird. I secretly became attached to that identity."

One night, back at the apartment with Alabama, I had my second, and worst panic attack I'd ever had. We'd been smoking skunk and my brain just couldn't cope with it. It hit me in a split second whilst lying in bed. No warning. WHAM!! Like a defibrillator shock of 50,000 volts…I shot bolt up right and gasped for air, like I'd been deep underwater holding my breath for too long. I thought I was having a heart attack (again), this time for real. The more I panicked, the more I couldn't breathe. It was like there was no oxygen in the room and my chest felt like my heart was going to thump its way outta there.

"Fuck man, that heavy weight prize fighter is back with an almighty vendetta."

Alabama was trying to calm me down, but the more she tried, the more I panicked. I made a beeline for the back door. It was cold and I could feel the icy air hit my senses, but it didn't help. I scurried frantically up along the pathway and into the street out front. I paced up and down trying to draw breaths, but nothing seemed to work. It went on for what seemed like an eternity. I cannot remember (emotional blackout) how I managed to level out, but eventually I did. That night I couldn't sleep…instead, I lay awake in a state of worry. It'd freaked the life out of me, but this time it forced me to take action.

I made an appointment with the doctor that very day. He asked me what was wrong. I told him I thought I'd had a heart attack. I was 18. He looked at me with confusion, and with obvious concern. He reached down to his desk draw and pulled out a sheet of paper. It was a questionnaire form. On it were the following questions...

- **Do you smoke?** If yes, how many cigarettes a week do you smoke?

- **Do you consume alcohol?** If yes, how many units a week do you consume?

- **Do you take drugs?** If yes, what drugs? How frequently? Etc etc...

I read through those questions, marking a big fat 'NO' to all of them. I didn't realise this at the time, but I didn't trust him, and the shame and inadequacy I felt was insurmountable. I went to him for help, for answers. Maybe I expected him to read my mind, to reach deep into my soul and see what was lurking there, to tell me everything was gonna be ok, perhaps even give me a massive hug...but the bottom line was, I simply wasn't able to trust him. I didn't trust anyone. I had lost my voice. I couldn't speak my truth. I didn't know how to.

"I was probably screaming inside..."Help me please, somebody, anybody, please, I need help!"

He gave me a diagnosis for my suspected 'heart attack'. He explained it was probably a symptom of my anxiety and stress levels being a tad higher than average. He went on to say I had in fact experienced a panic attack. I don't recall him offering me any advice worthy of my attention…or maybe I just didn't hear it. Either way, I walked out of there convinced more than ever I'd be dead by the time I was 21.

THE ISLAND

I made a somewhat serious attempt to stop smoking skunk and any other headfuck chemicals, but I just couldn't stick it. Instead, I picked up an additional habit along the way, cocaine.

I first knew of cocaine back in those early college days when it seemed to be dabbled with only on special occasions, such as Christmas or Birthdays. Alabama would treat herself on such occasions, but I was always like…"Nah, no way man, that's the real deal, big boys shit." So I made my excuses and always shied away. Deep down I was scared shitless, I kinda knew participating was stepping it up a league…"We're getting into drug addict territory here, fuck that shit." The irony.

The only way I was gonna stop smoking skunk, was if I dedicated my focus to drinking, and with it came the cocaine. It was the only way forward. It didn't seem to mess with my mind so much, or so I thought…so I dared to investigate. Classic switching one attachment for another…aka 'cross-addiction'.

"All day drinking at weekends was the norm, and cocaine seemed to seep into the scene insidiously like a viral infestation."

The euphoria that came with Ecstasy and the rave culture died when cocaine came to the party. It went from 'hugs and one love'…to… 'thugs and fuck love'. It all got moody. Attitudes, egos and gangsta vibes. Wherever you went, no matter who you was with, there'd be someone getting bang at it on cocaine. The white stuff was to all day drinking what the Spice Girls was to 90's pop culture. It was screw 'GIRL POWER'…I've got 'POWDER POWER!' Very quickly the inevitable happened and I gave in. The pressure of fitting in had gotten the better of me (again)…plus, once I'd sampled it…I realised in that very moment, it had given me unparalleled confidence…

"Fuck Badman, now I'm muddafuckin' Tankman."

My relationship to Alabama was always destined to be in ruins. When fuelled with such toxicity it's likely to implode. Drugs, self hatred and a loss of direction were all it took on my part. I'd dropped out of Art college, so the only thing I felt I was good at I'd already fucked. I ended up working at a supermarket, great if that's what you aspire to do with your life, not if you're an accomplished artist who's just shitfucked their college placement.

It was soul destroying. I was left with no real desire to do anything, and I sure as hell didn't know who I was. I literally bounced from pillar to post, all over the place, trying to figure it out. Alabama could see this (as could everyone else). She had many failed attempts to help me, but I wasn't prepared to help myself...I just didn't know how. A prime example was the time she set up a 'trial' day for me, working as a labourer for a roofing firm.

"It filled me with absolute dread taking responsibility, let alone work. Slap bang in winter, and I hated heights. Fucks sake!"

The stupidly early morning of my first trial day, I didn't feel so great. In fact, it felt so unjust, and in my opinion, total bullshit. I was subjected to passive-aggressive, toxic-testosterone coming from all angles. Big burly meathead geezers all givin' it the large. I was being loaded up with feckin' tiles and expected to walk the spines of a god damn roof, on my first day. "Are you shittin' me!?!

That night Alabama was so proud of me. I just contained my angst and directed the anger inwards at myself. The next day, I walked to the yard, but before I got there I'd done the right thing by me and talked myself out of it. I wasn't happy. So I swerved it. I pretended to go to that job for days before Alabama realised.

"That would be the first, but not the last of many 'experimental' jobs."

The first proper job I landed, which I kinda enjoyed and seemed to slot into, was working at a local design studio. The boss was a legend. He knew I had issues and helped endlessly. At the same time though my drinking and coke habit was escalating, and I was becoming a bit of a cocaine wide-boy. He showed me boundless patience and tolerance, but I was a complete dick and deserved to be sacked. It was a series of fuck ups, one after the other. Doesn't everyone treat their work premises as a glorified place to party?

"He used to pull me on the white powder residue, which I'd carelessly leave on the desk tops...ain't me governor."

I stole from work to feed my 'secret' habit. It started by 'skimming' cash from the till, until one day I dared to take money from the cash bundle. What the fuck was I thinking? What a wanker, so god damn low. The further I got away from the real me, the more dishonest I became. Getting the sack and losing the partial sense of direction, security and sanity it seemed to provide really spun me out. It was apparent I could not hold down a job any more than a relationship. It was like everything I touched turned to shit. I cared more for the party life, than the mundane inconvenience of taking responsibility or working a traditional 9 to 5. This here pirate wasn't made to stand in line and be told what to do. I'd rather walk the plank into the unknown, than be subjected to the monotony of doing something I despise. Anyway, this was now the tone of things to come. Tankman was on a mission.

"With my self-esteem on zero, and an inflated ego of a superhero, I was landing myself in a right pickle. I'd act first and think later. Hmmm...not necessarily wise."

Around this time of not really knowing what direction to go in life, I'd struck up a friendship with a beautiful young woman who I'd met through a friend of a friend. She had long red hair down to her bum and big blue eyes. She was funny, drop dead gorgeous and we became best of mates.

One day Red announced she was off to sunnier climates to go live abroad. She had decided to try out the party island life, and go work and play hard in the all year sun. Marvellous, where do I sign? Without having to be asked (or think) twice, I was on a plane heading out with her, having booked a return flight for a weeks holiday in the sun. Sorted. Now, in hindsight, it's fair to say that after all that'd been going on recently, my best use of my time and energy, would of been better served seeking some form of therapeutic support, a spa break perhaps, or even a good ol' traditional bit of self reflection to re-evaluate my life. Hmm…that was never gonna happen. Why?…"Because I'm having the time of my life, that's why."

"Crazy arse delusion…ESCAPE!…ESCAPE!… ESCAPE!"

Life on the Island would prove challenging. It would also serve as a metaphor to that time, because an Island was precisely what I'd become. Unbeknown to me, I was knee deep in a savage cocaine and alcohol dependency. Well actually let's get it right, I was knee deep with anything and everything. It was my early 20s and it was already at tipping point. I was on the run from that **black-hole-void-impending-doom-solar-plexus-fucked-up-I-don't-wanna-go-there-fuck-you-fuck-this-and-fuck-that** feeling, which at that time in my life was really prevalent. Saying that, I was also doing a Little Britain's Andy Pipkin, convinced that it was ok, that I was ok, when in fact…"Yeah I know"…is a definite…"NO I FUCKIN' WELL DON'T!!" Denial is a serious problem man.

I was not only on the run from myself and my emotions, I was also in a shit ton of constantly escalating debt. I owed money to too many people and I could not control it. Most, if not all, was owed due to my reckless behaviour and party lifestyle. I always scraped the pound coin somehow, but I mostly borrowed because I just couldn't manage my finances. More importantly, I could not manage my emotions, which is why I was getting drugged fucked to try and contain the perpetual mess I always found myself in. Everyone could probably see this except me.

"It was never my fault. It was always you, ya Mum, ya Mum's dog, ya Mum's dog's pal Stanley...but never me...avoid avoid avoid."

It transpired I wasn't the only one fleeing to the Island to evade life back home. It was a common theme that seemed to run through the veins of this pulsating beast of a place, like a deadly venom slowly dissipating its inhabitants. Just as soon as they came, they'd go. One by one people disappeared never to be seen again. They'd either burn out from partying, or they'd upset the wrong person and have to get on their toes pronto.

That week's holiday turned into an extended break. In fact, I was still in the madness of that 'holiday' four months later. It turned out to be some of the maddest, darkest and most traumatic times I've ever experienced. My increasing paranoia distorted reality, so I saw things through the eyes of a warped sense of perception. What was actually happening, and what I thought was happening, blurred...like my own secret Jekyll and Hyde existence of duality. Sleep deprivation and 'blackout' oblivion with daily marathon cocaine and booze benders, all contributed to my distortion of events. "Am I really seeing the things you'd only expect to see in a battlefield?" Very 'real', serious shit went down, or so I thought... and my naive, impressionable noodle got to witness every last drop of menace...even if it was a vague figment of my chemically enhanced imagination.

"Did I just see that man in the shadows wielding a machete?...Did that baseball bat just open up someone's head like a boiled egg?"

The weeks turned into months, and the 'partying' seemed to turn into survival. Just getting a bed for the night was a challenge in itself. I'd often find myself trying to get some much needed shut-eye wherever I could, be it some randoms bed, a hotel lobby or poolside under a sunshade. At times I'd have the luxury of using an inflatable li-lo on a dining room table.

"Always the creative."

Food deprivation meant I'd lost a lot of weight. One night I threw up so violently there was blood in it. It scared the hell outta me, convinced my liver or kidneys, or both were about to give up and tell me to fuck off. That very night there was a total eclipse of the moon. I'm lying there unable to move, whilst this incredible spectacle's taking place, and I couldn't even muster the strength to lift my body enough to look out the window. Kinda symbolic really - darkness had truly taken over my sorry arse.

Although I didn't realise it at the time, chemical dependency meant I couldn't stop what I was doing, even though it was caning me. One night I remember Red hopelessly pleading with me, literally begging me to stop what I was doing to myself. She was crying and really upset. I remember so vividly just saying to her… "I'm sorry, I can't." We didn't speak for weeks after that night, and things just got worse.

Work out there for me entailed being one of those pesky little blighters who got up in your grill, annoyingly and very persistently insisting you come drink in the wonderful and most prestigious club on the Island. 'No' was not in our vocabulary. I could not of done that job in a million years if I hadn't been fuelled by a gallon of booze and a pile of coke each night.

"I was out on those streets in my own warped fantasy thinking I'm some double-hard-bastard tough guy…

...in all reality, I'm some little dweeb who can barely grow stubble."

This ideation was only enhanced due to the fact we had the right people behind us. We were just a bunch of minions trying to make a bit of money and having 'fun'…and just like those cartoon Minions, I too was recklessly bouncing around all over the place getting into mischief. A Benny from the Bronx wannabe, frantically running around like a madcap Benny Hill impersonator on speed. Jeez…

"It was always gonna go tragically wrong."

I was pissing more and more people off. Owing people money. The wrong kinda people. I was used to this kind of bollocks back home, but I was a little fish in a bigger pond now, thousands of miles from home, slowly getting out of my depth. Craving and delusion was making me careless and greedy. I didn't know it at the time, but that's the nature of it. Give me an inch, take a mile…right? "Oh you wanna buy some drugs?…"Sure, give me ya money and I'll go get you some"…that's pretty much the gist of it, as unsuspecting holidaymakers came to us streetwalkers for their party prescriptions. As a crafty fiend, I naturally learnt to skim either money, drugs or both in order to feed my own increasing habit.

"Why wouldn't a greedy little monster take more each time?…My dependency was entering a new level of powerlessness."

It all came to a head when some dude took a rather disliking to me. To be fair, probably didn't help I was bumbling around all over the place like Captain Blunderclutz! It was enough to earn a stern warning…which came in the form of him thrusting me up in the air in a Darth Vader death grip to my throat…bloody impressive, but in all seriousness it scared the living daylights outta me. So much so, I convinced myself it would be off with my head. My boss stepped in and told me to leave. I was only too happy to go. I was done.

What happened next, illuminates the ferocity of what I experienced in the full scale horror of my escalating dysfunction…

Now it wasn't that simple for me to just up and leave. I didn't have my passport, work had it. They took your passport when you owed them money as insurance. It wasn't a lot, money I'd borrowed for taxis here and there…but in my mind (paranoid/neurotic/psychotic), I was convinced something really bad was about to happen. In reality - I was a scared little Mummy's boy pretending to be a big shot, who perhaps needed a little slap to be taught a lesson. I could simply go and pay back the money, say thank you, get my slap, say thank you, get my passport and away I go. Everyone's a winner. Instead, I did what I always did…fight/flight/freeze…this time with an impulsive flight. If only an airplane…nope, I ran away and took 'refuge' in someone's apartment, through fear of confrontation and excepting responsibility. It would be there, I'd take myself hostage in isolation for days on end. I was so terrified of being seen, I'd stay below window level at all times. My head was falling apart with the uncertainty of the situation. A constant feeling of catastrophic, insurmountable nausea…

"I could not sleep, fearing someone would break in and harm me."

The reality - I simply owed people money and I didn't have it, yet in my mind they're gonna torture me in some medieval public exhibition. Completely unbeknown to me, I was deeply traumatised by past events, experiencing unmanageable levels of insecurity, and reliving terror over and over, putting myself in volatile situations with the exact same outcome - an overwhelming sense of alienation, entrapment and powerlessness.

I managed to make a phone call to Mum back home. She was well versed in my pleas to be bailed out and would always help no matter what, but at that time, her then boyfriend, who had an equally pain-in-the-frickin'-arse son, encouraged her to do the tough love thing. The very next call was to my estranged Dad, who I hadn't spoken to for a decade. He answered and I could tell he was really upset. His Father, my Grandad, the pipe smoker, had recently passed away. I felt awful, because I was so detached from the emotional feeling of having any kind of family bond that I knew I needed and wanted, but was unable to sustain because I was a fuck up. We both remained on the phone crying. I was crying out of sheer exhaustion. I was tired of this shit. This life. The excessive drinking, the drugs, the lack of sleep, the disconnection from any kind of reality. Dad wired the money into a Western Union account the very next day.

That night I returned to work and collected my passport in exchange for the money I owed...no slap required. Now that should of confirmed there was absolutely no need to worry, yet my mind was causing catastrophic consequences that hadn't even happened yet, projecting horrific sequences that may play out.

"Sleep deprivation and drug induced psychosis makes the mind seriously delusional."

All I wanted to do was see Red and make up. We met, and after a few drinks I slipped away to do a final lap of honour...one last dance before I go. I caught a taxi and headed for the airport in the dead of night. I arrived exhausted, high as fuck, down as fuck, excited and nervous all in one big pot of stewing emotion. I headed to the first booking counter and asked for the cheapest and next flight home. I sat anxiously in the airport departure lounge until we boarded. It was only once I could feel the wheels leave the ground, that I did a secret imaginary victory celebration. "Thank fuck I'd made it…get me the fuck out of here!"

EASY SNIDER

Like most young guys coming of age, I too had a pack of mates in the fold. I knew a lot of people through partying, it's what happens when you're a 'face' about town. Some were mere associates, fellow wreckheads I graced one random night in some strangers kitchen (why is it you always end up in the kitchen, or was that just me?)…and some were in the inner sanctuary of my world at that time.

Jimmy'd always been there since college, as had a dude called Fuzz, who I'd known since school. I'd also picked up a couple of other colourful characters along the way…Itch and Bumble. Itch was flat out on another planet. As for Bumble, first time I clapped eyes on him he was facedown unconscious, clutching an empty bottle of vodka like his life depended on it. Kindred spirits. He also had a strange desire for the undesirable.

"Eating dead bumblebees high on dope just came naturally to this maniac."

It came with great apprehension on my part, when we all decided to go away on a 'lads holiday' to an Island not too far from the one I'd just evaded. Primarily, based on the sheer fact my last jaunt away to a 'tropical paradise' nearly cost me my life (or so I thought), plus, I knew what we were capable of when we got together. Once again I keep my mouth shut and say nothing. I didn't dare tell a soul the full extent of my misadventures on that Island, and I certainly wasn't about to get real about my progressively declining mental health.

Being on that godforsaken Island taught me the art of street warfare…but I'd yet to learn my lesson. You'd of thought having a face off with Lord Vader may of made me change my ways. Not so…instead, it had left a lasting imprint, deluding me into thinking I was still some kind of invincible wide-boy gangsta. Yep, remember that ruddy Benny from the Bronx wannabe? I'd brought him back with me…but sure as hell, it was always gonna be that Benny flippin' Hill impersonator causing havoc.

On the first night we were nearly deported. Somehow, we end up in a drunken poolside altercation with the police, who threatened to drive us back to the airport and put us on the first plane home.

"Isn't the definition of insanity - doing the same thing over and over and expecting a different outcome?… Hmm."

Far from deterring us, the next day we continued to drink to our hearts content, and as per usual I was starting to want chemicals. Why is it that each time I consumed booze, I'd have the unrelenting urge to do more? Easy to answer that now…powerlessness. Before I'd gone away with Red to that Island, I was under the impression I was just 'experimenting' with cocaine. I was already an established big drinker, but something had changed on my return. I've heard it said it takes a certain amount of time to form a new behaviour/habit…hmm…well, I'd been flat out bang at it for as long as I could remember, and there wasn't one single day where I hadn't sniffed a bit of gear or drunk my own body weight since leaving for that Island.

"What did I expect?"

There's a certain air of restlessness and a distinct feeling of discontent that comes with constantly craving. The concept of simply relaxing by a pool in the blazing sun was always a nice idea, yet it never really surmounted to much, due to the overriding agitation and boredom I felt deep in my soul. The only thing that could remotely relieve that incessant bore, would be to either power drink my way through it, or go on a mission to find some relief. My destructive mind was now well accustomed to the art of plotting.

Before the second day was out, I'd convinced myself I needed to go on a mission. We were staying in a quiet fishing village miles from anywhere, and that meant zero chemicals apart from booze and hash. The others were reluctant to share my enthusiasm, seemingly more intent to do what I couldn't, chill…but persistence pays, and I persuade Bumble to join the crusade.

"The plan was to hire mopeds…ride to the main resort, find drugs and come straight back."

Hmmm, a nice intention indeed. After a long, adrenaline filled ride we arrive at the resort. Being a fiend is like being a Jedi. You have special powers. You have an unseen skill to be able to detect a fellow fiend. It's unspoken, and I still have that ability to this day…it never leaves you. We immediately homed in on Vinny. Vinny was this dude sitting on a wall no more than 20 yards from us. We knew he was our man. I was that guy back on the other Island. Before we knew it we're bundled into Vinny's motor and whisked off to a nearby apartment.

Now in all fairness, we should of stuck to the plan and returned to base camp straight after the pick up…but greed and desire has other motives. It wants to play. No matter what the right thing is, you ain't gonna do it. You ain't capable. Even with every best intention, the self sabotaging mind will create a million reasons to sidestep the issue and have its way. "Go on, you know you want to!" Cunning little fecker and a selfish little sod. Before we knew it, we're sitting in a pizza place with an ice cold beer overlooking the ocean from the balcony.

"Everything in that moment was just 'perfect'...or so we thought."

Now, the thing with drugs, especially if you're greedy fuckers like me and Bumble, is that you just wanna dive straight in. If you're holding, you ain't likely to sit out the time it takes for a pizza guy to whack and roll the dough, prepare it so it looks all pretty and pop it in the oven to bake for 20 minutes. It ain't happening. At the very least you've skulled your ice cold beer, bolted to the nearest cubicle and you're hoovering up a fat line of the 'white stuff' before the shrooms are brown. "Eating's cheating"...and..."Fuck it, it'll be alright. Right?"

There's a saying - "One is too many, a thousand never enough." I mean come on, you don't need to say any more than that. For me that encapsulates the unquenchable first perfectly. Whether it's booze, weed, cocaine, food, gambling, hands-down-pants, shopping, gaming...once you start, that is it, you are off and running and there is no off button. I now know that's addiction, plain and simple.

"Did I actually know this at the time? Nope. Did I even care? Hell NO! I'm having the time of my life, aren't I?"

So me and Bumble broke the seal, the 'One is too many, a thousand never enough'…"Maybe we could just have a cheeky one?…and then bid farewell and have a nice leisurely cruise back down to see the homies?"…Haha yeah right. With every best intention we decided to have a gander down at the beachfront. We could see a bunch of hotties playing volleyball nearby, so we take a seat whilst Bumble rolled a fat one. I was still having a love/hate relationship with smoking hash and weed because of the panic attacks, but I'd always fold to peer pressure. Not that anyone ever put a gun to my head. That pressure came from myself. Our party prescription also provided a bag of pills…"Just the one won't hurt." Once again that cunning craving fiend was exceedingly good at the art of sales.

"I'd taught it well."

When I first started experimenting with Ecstasy, like Acid, I was a little nervous about losing control. I'd heard and seen too many horror stories. People losing their shit or dying. I was scared. I secretly used to take a tablet, snap it into quarters and do it bit by bit. Over the years I'd end up diving into a bag and wouldn't think twice to bosh a whole one, or two and I wouldn't stop at that. Not only had my tolerance levels increased over time, but the quality of the drug had decreased. Overriding all of that though, was the fact I was experiencing more and more self-loathing. I was inadvertently self-harming using drugs. I had some close scrapes on more than one occasion, using a cocktail of ecstasy, speed, ketamine, cocaine and alcohol. I would most certainly consider these to be 'accidental' overdoses.

"I'll save you the gory details, but let's just say each and every one of them I'd consider to be a near death experience, praying to a God I didn't believe in, pleading for me not to die in my mates bog hole!"

Back on the beach and we were starting to feel the affects of the 'tester' pill. I can't remember how long we stayed there, but eventually we agreed to get back before we start hugging palm trees. We found our mopeds and headed up the main stretch next to the promenade along the beach front. It was always in such moments I'd have a heightened sense of invincibility...like I was unstoppable. I was high as a kite, feeling the euphoric warm sun (and love buzz from the pill) penetrating every atom in my body. We were just coming off a bend in the road, when a car suddenly pulled out from a parking bay and reversed straight into me. WALLOP!! The impact sent me flying over the front of the bike and I landed on the road side. The driver comes to my aid, as I bounce straight to my feet and immediately scan my body for damage. Unbelievably I was unscathed, apart from grazing the side of my right leg.

"Fuck me, I AM invincible!"

The accident hadn't gone unnoticed. We were greeted by an almighty roaring cheer from the pissed up punters from the bar opposite, who found the whole incident remarkably entertaining, as did Bumble, who just sat there on his moped with a big Cheshire Cat grin on his face, buzzin' his tits off. Maybe it was the 'love buzz' and the alcohol that enabled my body to relax upon lift off... who knows, but I'd somehow managed to get away with it.

It was pitch black by the time we finally arrived at the resort, having spent an eternity precariously navigating our way back, whilst intermittently stopping off for a roadside 'top-up'. We sheepishly found the others, who were drinking and playing pool in some back room bar. They only had to take one look at us to see we'd been greedy little feckers. Needless to say they were seriously pissed...but they knew what we were like. We'd spent their money, and consumed the entire supply of narcs. I for one would go on to deliver what I thought to be a very fair and plausible reason to why we'd done such a treacherous act…but it was no use.

"They were right. We were selfish, lying fiends who'd go to any lengths to get what we wanted…if only I shared their enthusiasm for such observations."

This secret squirrel behaviour always seems to come with having a destructive habit. You lie. Period. You forget your lies, the sneaky bullshit stories you create to cover your devilish tracks…and you forget which lies you've spun for each of the given snide moves you've made. Deception and betrayal is the nature of the beast. I used to get into such a pickle over my storytelling, and the drivel that seemed to flow quite effortlessly from this mouth of mine…and to add insult to injury, I'd vehemently contest anyone who dared to challenge me. "Nah, I swear it wasn't me…honest to God, you gotta believe me…besides, how dare you even think it was me!"

Drinking and cocaine had now become a staple habit I'd forged, and like all my others, it was at mine and others detriment. Prior to that first try of cocaine, I'd go on marathon booze benders, always ending up in a drunken stupor, unconscious and incoherent by late afternoon. Once cocaine arrived, I suddenly realised why others who danced with the devils dandruff, could quite literally have limitless bouts of booze fuelled extravaganzas, if you can call them that.

"Cocaine simply gave me that kick, the turbo...the twin pipes wide open with a 10,000 Horsepower smashing the fuck out of it."

Once this becomes the norm, there's no turning back. It didn't matter where I went, be it some dodgy nightclub, dinner with a girlfriend or round someone's house for a movie…I'd always have a couple beers and be on the phone to a dealer without hesitation. Acquiring such fanciful tastes, only results in needing to pre-order, to absolutely guarantee your 'holding' before even having your first drop of booze. Well, that's how it was for me anyway. The dance with the devil…'gettin' on it'. It manoeuvres like this...go to pub (or maybe we're starting off at home?), crack on with your first drink, maybe two, have a cheeky livener, feeling a tad pranged?..."Fuck it"...smash three or four drinks, pronto..."Ahhh that's better, levelling out a bit now"...continue to get marginally more drunk... "Ok, now I'm feeling a little bit smashed"...go for another blast, nice fat one. "Fuck it, double barrel"...now we're flying, and on it goes…

"That perpetuating chase of the 'getting it just right'…"

I was either too pissed up or too pranged out, continually trying to counter balance the other to make the perfect cocktail. Looking back, it's true what they say - you never recreate that first initial hit of a drug. Any substance I tried, I'd always seem to relentlessly chase that initial super-charged-buzz. So why is it that each time I consumed booze, I'd have the unrelenting urge to do more than just drink?" Well, unbeknown to me, I was quite possibly at the mercy of a wee little gremlin called Cocaethylene. Apparently, Cocaethylene can be formed by the liver, when cocaine and ethanol (alcohol) coexist in the blood. As I continued to guzzle booze with cocaine, the addition of Cocaethylene was quite possibly forming in my system, potentially producing harmful effects that are much more powerful than the effects of alcohol and cocaine alone. If true, this reaction was creating an addictive pattern all of its own, which would explain why, once it became habit, it was near on impossible to not use one without the other. Kinda makes sense to me.

If I'd known that to stop this gremlin I'd need to cease drinking, or stop coke, or both…would I of stood more chance of breaking free from that cycle? Hmm, not sure about that…for me, alcohol always made me flick the 'Fuck it button'…and I certainly wasn't about to stop 'partying' just yet. Cocaethylene was potentially increasing my heart rate and blood pressure more than cocaine was alone. Besides the panic attacks, I was already aware of chest pains and occasional heart palpitations, but I just ignored them. Fuck man, I may of been impairing the ability of my poor little ticker doing its job.

"For all I know, I was heading for a significant heart defect, and ultimately heart failure...yet I was totally unaware."

Seemingly, life was continuing to get uncontrollably worse for me. I didn't just wake up one day and become a full blown wrecking ball...yet alarmingly it appeared to be that way. That line I said I wouldn't ever cross, evidently I was crossing it, breaking boundaries effortlessly along the way. Those close to me would pull me on my behaviour and challenge it...and would always be met with a swift and (not so) sincere..."Yeah I know, I know...I'm sorry, really I am"...yet I'd carelessly fuck up again...different day, another calamity. Captain Blunderclutz strikes again!

Denial meant I kept moving that line, and I kept crossing it each time. I'd say..."I'm never ever gonna do that"...and then one day it just happens, and when it does, it just gets buried like all the other bullshit. I was well and truly caught in an endless, self critical tirade of feeling constant shame and guilt. I wasn't proud of all the awful things I carelessly seemed to do, fuckin' myself over, and anyone who got in the way. Numbing it out, convincing myself it doesn't exist...but it does exist. Momentarily, I might stop to ponder...

"Why the fuck am I harming myself and others this way?...Why can't I just stop?"

Every day seemed to be a struggle, yet I put on a brave face and continued to pretend all was dandy. "I'm the Badman!"...and... "Fuck it, it'll be alright!" In all honesty (which I was losing all sense of), underneath all the bravado and superhero cape bullshit I was screaming for help.

LONE WOLF

Flatlining into oblivion

FLATLINING INTO OBLIVION

Life has a habit of serving us 'inconvenient' curveballs as a means to learn. Thing is, if you're not paying attention and oblivious to this notion, then you're caught in a perpetual cycle of dysfunction until you see it.

The trouble with delusional behaviour, especially if you throw in a splash of chemical enhancement and a sprinkle of narcissism (all of which intertwines rather effortlessly), is you become accustomed to it. That's how it was for me anyway. The further into the abyss of the darkest ocean I got, the harder it was to drag my sorry arse back to the safety of the shore…and just when I thought it couldn't get any worse, guess what?

There are no limitations to just how bad things can get, it's simply a case of how much one can endure and how much you're prepared to sacrifice. The lines get blurred. Gone are the moral standings I may, or may not of once been taught as a child, and gone is the ability to even care. For me, I'd slid so far past the point of caring…I had tuned out, bouncing around in a trance like state from one catastrophic disharmony to another, regardless of any consequences for my actions. Gone was any concept of taking responsibility for myself or these erratic behaviours, and worst of all it'd become standard...convinced I was playing the greatest symphony of my life.

"I think I'd resigned to the simple conclusion that I'm not able to change, or maybe I just wasn't ready yet?"

50 POINTS X3

One of the recurring themes (apart from powerlessness and entrapment) to my seemingly downward spiral, was to end up either in a doctors surgery, a clinic, a police cell or a hospital. I'm forever thankful I didn't end up in a mental institution, prison or as ashes scattered out to sea. All of which I constantly feared would happen sooner rather than later. I was convinced I was slowly using up my jammy dodger credit, and would be met with an imminent end to all this madness.

"Somehow I always landed on my feet, even if it meant another visit to the hospital."

I'd managed to evade the A&E department so far with my mindless acts of buffoonery, but my recklessness was about to catch up with me, and alas..."Oh fuck, I think I need to go to hospital"...was about to enter my vocabulary for the first time since my days shreddin' a skateboard. The following escapade is an idiots guide of caution - and a moral tale to always, ALWAYS pay attention. Easier said than done, especially if you're anything like I was…and you can't.

One of the many jobs I found myself doing was driving. I wish I could say a stuntman in the movie business or an F1 driver. Nope. For me, it was as a courier. I loved that job. It suited my lifestyle ('functioning' wreckhead) to a tee. Everyday was different, a certain air of independence and freedom, and it was always spontaneous, which meant it remotely excited me somewhat. Each morning, I'd get a phone call stating where the first collection was, and the day would unfold from that point onwards.

"No sitting in an office with people I don't like much…it was just me, a bag of dope and the open road."

The 'party' lifestyle had now become a kinda 'semi-professional' career…or perhaps you could say I thought I was a rock star. Thing is, I wasn't in a band, I was more Keith Lemon than the Keith Moon persona I portrayed. I mean, don't get me wrong…I was tearing the arse out of it in a truly rock 'n' roll, reckless kinda way…but as for my musical merits, I was no more a drummer than Keith Moon's persona was a Saint. There was a time I'd submerse myself in mixing vinyl…and I used to pick up guitars and begin to learn, but I could never really sit long enough to actually do it. I think a big part of that was the snarling beast of low self-esteem. I did however, self appoint myself as the unofficial roadie for Jimmy's band. We'd traipse the length of the country together. Me, Jimmy and their keys man, a Scandinavian equivalent of Scarface, were the deviants that would endeavour to fulfil the role of touring rockstars.

"They'd be up there on stage living their dream, and I'd stare on in envy from the sidelines, paranoid to fuck and wishing it was me."

Anyway, at this time I'd been staying at Mum's boyfriend's house. I'd ended up there having spent some time at Dad's. I tried to rekindle our estranged relationship after the SOS call from that Island, but I just could not seem to do it. I didn't realise this at the time (or perhaps I did)…but there was a monumental, emotional block I just could not get past. From the moment I arrived at Dad's, my alcohol intake went through the roof, masking my inner turmoil. I somehow managed to stay off the powder for a few weeks, but the insatiable cravings got me in the end.

My 'relapse' on cocaine, came when I received the inheritance from my Grandad who'd passed. It took approximately 4 days to 'party' away the 2 grand so generously given in his memory. The shame. I finally left Dad's one morning at the crack of dawn, without even saying so much as goodbye. I'd always felt alienated since Mum and Dad's divorce. He'd married the woman he left Mum for...and, as my mind always perceived...'gained a new family', which he had. His new wife had sons from her previous marriage, so in my tiny noodle I was never gonna fit in. If I'm honest, I wasn't prepared to either, and I guess that defiance had caused me to be a Lone Wolf ever since. Over the years my sadness had turned to anger because of the betrayal and disconnect I felt. I didn't consider he might of 'fallen out of love' with Mum, but the bottom line was, he'd fallen in love with someone who wasn't Mum...and that broke my heart. A fatal blow to my esteem, fuelling the insurmountable suffering. It was now who I'd become...and with it came an insatiable desire for self-hatred and oblivion.

"I've heard it said, that holding onto resentment is like drinking poison and expecting others to die. Well I was livid, I had my poison, and others did suffer...but ultimately I was the one dying inside."

Like most things, I just could not seem to sustain any meaningful relationships, including the one to my estranged Father. My stay had expired, and true to form my immediate thought was..."Fuck this!"...so I started to pack in the dead of the night. Next day I was gone. "WHOOSH"…I'm off. It would be another decade before we'd speak again.

Back at my new digs, and like clockwork I received a call with the first collection point. Our boss would always instruct us to get lively and be on our way sharpish…if he were a dog, he'd be a Pitbull. On this particular morning (hungover to fuck) I stepped out the front door, only to find the van wasn't there. "Oh, bollockchops!" I'd left it in town somewhere. Knowing I'd be barked at with a follow up call, I got lively and began to make a run for it. I was sprinting down the road along the pathway, and as I came hurtling through the clearway from the estate onto the main road, I slammed straight into an oncoming motorised mobility scooter, which was whizzing down the pavement towards me. WALLOP!! The impact, which may I add frickin' blindsided me big time, propelled me straight up and into the path of an oncoming car, WHACK!!…

"To my disbelief, I found myself sitting in the middle of the road, facing the car that'd just hit me."

The old boy on the scooter was still in his seat, even though it'd flipped on its side. "Fuck!" He looked completely out of it, his big rimmed glasses all crooked and broken. I felt mortified. The car that'd hit me had a smashed windscreen. "Fuckin 'ell!" Passers by came to my aid, my elbow hanging out of its skin, with nice blobs of blood filling my left hand which was cupping it. A girl I knew, Angel, appeared quite literally like her namesake. She was holding my mobile phone, which'd flown out of my hand and landed on the pavement on the opposite side of the road. It was ringing…she took the call from my yapping boss, informing him the only place I'd be going today was the hospital.

"As I sat there, I could hear the distant screeching sirens of an ambulance."

Humiliation washed over me. "Jeez man, what a shit show." I was more worried about that poor old guy than my own welfare to be honest. "Perhaps deep down I'm not so self-centred after all?" If only my efforts to say sorry were acknowledged…he didn't even know what day of the flippin' week it was. "Fuck!"

At the hospital, it was straight in for a clean up and a nice row of stitches, whilst staring at a picture of Homer Simpson on the wall…kinda symbolic don't ya think? "Doh!"…as they stick a giant needle in my arm to relieve the pain. As soon as that juice hit my veins, I melted into the bed with a nice blissed out grin on my face.

"Incredibly, I had not one broken bone. I was shaken, sore and bruised, but nothing major."

Two police officers turned up asking for a statement. An eyewitness backed up my story of it being a freak accident. A case of being in the wrong place at the wrong time. The cops were still pissed at me. They said the old boy, who was 87, was lucky to be alive. He'd received a nasty shock and was extremely fragile. They went on to inform me that the driver of the car was an elderly lady, her passenger being around the same age…both in shock. Someone was looking over me that day…my saving grace had been their dedication to the speed limit.

"Any faster and I'd of been a cropper."

The cops actually did ask with all seriousness…"Have you got something against the elderly?…You've managed to take out not one, but three OAP's today." I was told to pay damages towards the old guy, which I willingly paid, enabling the repair of his scooter and glasses. I'm not being funny, but I swear that scooter was pimped. Still to this day, I have never seen one go so fast. I never did get to say sorry to those two unsuspecting ladies. I really wish I had.

Years after that incident, I attended a funeral of an old school mate. It was there I learned from a mutual friend of ours, that it'd been her dear old granddad I'd knocked off his scooter that day. She went on to inform me that he'd been on his way to lay flowers at his son's grave. "Fuck man!" It ruined me. These endless stupid acts of idiocy. Consequences to my mindless fuckin' behaviour. Why am I such a dick? It never felt good, which is why I'd bury it every time.

"I was stretching that elastic rubber band even harder, yet it always seemed to somehow retract back and remain intact."

That visit to the hospital, was my first real introduction to prescription drugs for pain relief. The question is though...was I medicating on the physical pain I was putting myself through? Or, was I in fact medicating on the underlying emotional pain and turmoil? Hmm...hindsight is a wonderful thing.

These car crash moments (literally) were the pieces of evidence, bit by bit, that, unbeknown to me were drawing me closer to a final verdict of..."Guilty as charged your honour"...on all counts, that I needed to stop what I was doing, otherwise it was highly likely I'd meet my maker prematurely. Will it be off to the gallows?...or death by stupidity?

DAYLIGHT ROBBERY

Like most jobs I did, I couldn't seem to hold them down. I lived, worked and breathed to party. Gettin' wrecked was all I could think about. The way I saw it, work was an inconvenient but necessary evil, a means to an end…and the end was always oblivion.

I'd blame anything but me for their inevitable demise, and like most things in my life, I was in constant search of 'that thing' that would make everything ok. "How can I fill this void that I feel?" I'd always be discontent, with an underlying sense that I wasn't meant to be doing what I was doing, that I was destined for much more. That dream of riding a mighty white horse, and the (inconceivable) feeling of immense joy was always in the back of my mind.

"When will I find what I'm looking for?…I always just assumed it would fall into my lap."

My (dys)functioning demeanour was destined to fall apart the day I landed a job selling office equipment…or to jazz it up a bit - 'innovative office solutions'. It was my girlfriend, Tasha, who stated the obvious - "Dave, you're not surmounting to anything, you need to sort your shit out". To be fair, we had moved in together, so she was right. I needed to buck up. Bollocks.

I'd met Tasha via my ex Pitbull boss. On one of the very first days, I'd been with him loading up the van, when a beautiful girl walks by about 20 yards from us. Being a young, hot blooded wide-boy, I naturally turned to my boss and quipped…"Blimey, look at her!"…to which his speedy growlin' response was…"Oi! Don't even think about it, that's my daughter!" Oops. Well, I did think about it, and alas I got the girl. Sorry governor.

I started out doing telesales for the sales team, which I was darn good at. A somewhat audacious master manipulator by means of deception, my natural ability to trance the 'gatekeeper' in any given situation, had not gone unnoticed. I quickly learnt the basics of the game, and eventually worked my way up to sales. We'd go under the title 'Account Manager', or in my case, 'Unaccountable and Unmanageable'. My job interview was more like an initiation test. It consisted of me getting and supplying a bag of cocaine for the Chief, Billy-Bionic, whilst out for our initial 'meet and greet' in a local bar. Of course I thought this was epic.

"Bionic had earned his superhuman ability to party, however…he would in fact end up on the road to redemption shortly after."

There was a woman who worked there called Velma. She never knew this, but she planted a whopping great seed in me. In brief, when she wasn't dealing with the day to day business, you'd find her practising Reiki at home. I'd heard about Reiki, Mum had talked about it, and a friend I knew was into it, but I'd never given it much thought. Velma offered to do Reiki healing on me, because I'd told her of a severe trapped nerve in my neck, something of a regularity throughout that time in my life. I never really knew or understood why, until she told me.

One lunch break she took me into the conference room to perform the healing. She explained I had all this trapped tension in my body, but went on to explain how my 'energy' was all over the place, causing my physical body to have an adverse reaction.

"So I'm getting crippling neck, back and chest ache because my 'energy' is running riot?"

After that session, although a little apprehensive, I was curious and wanted to know more, so Velma invited me to her house one day after work. I think it was on the second or third visit, that no sooner had we started, she announced…"Dave, it really would help if you could attend these sessions without being high on drugs." My immediate response was…(shut the fuck up!) "I'm not"…to which she replied…"Dave, come on, you don't have to pretend to me, I know you are." For a split second I dropped my guard…"How do you know?"...Velma then calmly said..."I know because a while back I used drugs in the same way, so I just know."

Blimey. Her response kinda took me by surprise and removed the sting out of being rumbled, so we continued to talk openly for the rest of that session. I still wasn't skilled at articulating how I felt, but I was able to ask her more on how my 'partying' lifestyle was effecting me, not just physically, but mentally and emotionally. Although I couldn't quite comprehend it at the time, she outlined how, until I stop doing what I was doing to myself, it was likely I'd continue to not only experience the same ailments, but they'd progressively get worse.

So that was that. Call it a brief encounter with someone who knew better. Velma had perhaps presented a good case for me to go away and rethink my life. Maybe on a subconscious level I did, but...unfortunately, it ended right there. Looking back, I can say without any hesitation, I just wasn't ready to give it all up yet, no matter how bad it was getting.

"Fear was still running the show, and my denial as strong as an Ox."

Working as a hooky salesman not too dissimilar to Peckham's very own wide-boy Derek Trotter, meant wearing designer suits, nice bling watch, Italian shoes and all the trappings you might expect.

Unlike Del Boy, I got to drive around in a lovely Mercedes Benz (on tick). Saying that, I couldn't even afford to fill it past the quarter marker on the fuel gauge, yet I'm acting as if I own an oil firm.

"In my mind I was the Don, but in all reality I was falling apart just like Del Boy's three wheeled van."

All these external 'things'...I now know could never make my internal world complete. In reflection, it was complete madness. I used to drive around in that Merc, thinking I was some gangsta caught up in a rather fancy, and dare I say it, romanticised fantasy. I was this outlaw you see. "Can't touch me. No one can fuckin' touch me." That's what cocaine did to me. It gave me a false sense of grandiose. The once reliable mask of 'I'm the Badman', had morphed into some kind of mutation of itself. I believe it all started when working those streets back on the Island, when I got caught up in that world. A by-product of the environment I'd been exposed to.

Eventually Tasha moved out of the apartment we'd been renting, having had enough of my unmanageability. Smart cookie. It wasn't long after, that I too needed to vacate. I'd been hanging on by the skin of my teeth. It was the story of my life. I seemed to have this reoccurring habit of...need home...find home...move in to home...don't pay rent/royally fuck landlord off...be evicted from home...no home. You could replace the word 'home' with 'girlfriend'...it was all the same clusterfuck to me. It was relentless and altogether soul destroying.

"I just could not seem to hold it together, and it really got me down."

I'd always end up at Mum's, who'd lived on her own in a one bedroom house since moving back to the area. My 'room' consisted of a space on the floor in the front lounge area. I would often wake up having not much sleep, if any at all, get up outta my makeshift bed on the floor, roll it up and store away in the under stairs cupboard. Like Groundhog Day, I'd go upstairs to have a shower, usually having to direct hot water from the hose, blasting it up my nasal passages, washing away any crusty remnants of cocaine from my pipes.

"I would often stand in that shower thinking..."Jeez not again!"

My suit would always be hanging on the door of the under stairs cupboard. Once suited, I was The Don, ready to leave the house. I'd bleep the Mercedes, in I hop...tunes on and I'm off to do it all again. As often as I could I'd stay out at someone's house. Anyone who'd have me. Usually someone I'd convinced into getting drug fucked with. Partying on any given night didn't really matter. The amount of shame and lack of self-respect I felt was astronomical. Essentially, I didn't really have a place I called home. It was Mum's home, but I didn't belong there. It wasn't Mum's fault. She did everything beyond measure to make me feel welcome and cared for. It was me...I just could not seem to be at peace. Not with myself, in relation to who I'm with, or where I'm at.

A typical day as a salesman would consist of me reluctantly driving my sorry arse to work, and, on occasion, getting entangled in a kamikaze road rage battle with a complete meathead (like you do). Evade getting my skull cracked. Safely arrive at the office. Usually, if not always, composing myself before entering, having to suppress that immense sense of underlying shame (and dread), due to my secret life back 'home'. I walk into reception..."I'm the Don"...and step onto the sales floor.

"In my minds eye, that designer suit...it'd become my new coat of armour. My conceptual barrier to ward off any unwanted entities."

I'm an introvert at heart. Somewhere lying beneath the false exterior of pride and ego, the joker's grin, the mask, the bullshit and the whoever the fuck you want me to be...was a very sensitive and desperately kind natured young man. I was scared and vulnerable, no different to a small child left alone in the supermarket by his Mum. To cap it off, I was still emotionally stumped, and a very petulant and seriously angry teenager…at worse a pure raging bull. Although no one really saw that side of me apart from girlfriends and Mum. All smiles and "everything's cool."

Finding myself surrounded by all these intimidating 'mature' adults, was both terrifying and overwhelming. With work colleagues such as Bomber, Tommy Steals-a-lot and Killa Ken, it's no surprise I felt a tad overwhelmed. Certain sales environments can be savage. They're not for the meek. I found that if you're too nice you'll be slaughtered…so you've kinda gotta be a cunt, or at least pretend to be one. That was my experience anyway.

"No different to school, for me, the work place can be just as fucked up."

I now see it takes a certain kind of character to be in those environments. Survival of the fittest. If it weren't for my steely alter ego, I'd have been gobbled up alive. I gave as good as I got. Underneath it all I knew I was way too timid to be doing the job, but I'd become a bit of a cocaine wanker. Can't beat 'em, join 'em. Sheer audacious arrogance, damn good for getting what you want.

"Thing is, what I thought I wanted, and what I actually needed, were completely muddled."

Needs vs wants - At this time, I thought my basic needs to live and the things I wanted were...

Needs - Money (lots of) / girlfriend (or) beautiful women (bundles) / sex (keep it coming) / partying (always).

Wants - More money (lots of) / girlfriend (or) beautiful women (bundles) / sex (can't get enough) / partying (can't and won't stop).

In reality - This is how they should of looked...

Needs - Financial stability and management / a good nights sleep / healthier lifestyle / honest livelihood / positive outlets / be kind and loving to myself and others.

Wants - Peace of mind / security / to help myself and others / to be open, honest and willing / to know true freedom / to experience unconditional love (you get the idea).

I believe I was conditioned by the world around me from a very young age, led to believe that being academic was all that mattered, institutionalised into thinking superficial material things will make us happy. Maybe momentarily they will...but by the time I left school and attempted this fucked up thing called life, I was perhaps mind fucked into thinking we gotta chase the dollar, the pound, the paper, we gotta get to the top of the fuckin' stack man...

fame, fortune and power…otherwise we're nobody and nothing. Get the right status, the perfect grades, the perfect partner, the big monster house, the fat cars, the right clothes, the right music, best gadgets, hairstyle, body, bling, blah blah fuck you blah…in my mind it's simply bullshit and not true, it's a lie.

None of it made me happy. None of it fixed that **black-hole-void-impending-doom-solar-plexus-fucked-up-I-don't-wanna-go-there-fuck-you-fuck-this-and-fuck-that** feeling. None of it. I tried. It didn't work.

Aside from not owning the perfect grades or the monster home, I seemed to acquire most other material things. I could potentially earn chunks of sizeable money, but never did I save it. It would all disappear as quickly as it came, buying designer clothes, drinking fine wine and champagne, dining in fancy restaurants and generally behaving like an entitled, selfish little prick…who, may I add, was deluded into thinking I was 'living the dream'.

"Monte fuckin' Carlo mate…yeah right, more like Monty friggin' Python."

I'd be lucky enough to have gorgeous girlfriends like Tasha, to cruise around (on the red) in my Merc, and sniff shit loads of coke day and night. So what was the problem? I'm happy aren't I? In all reality the problem lay within. Underlying everything was an

insanely insecure and cunning addict persona, creating problems...
and with it immense self loathing. Give me a bucket full of coke,
and I'll have a go at emptying it up my hooter, just because I don't
know any better.

That was the problem right there. No amount of money, or
any other superficial 'thing' could save me from my thinking, my
ignorance, my self destruction or my not taking fuck all
responsibility for my actions. It all took priority over my basic
needs. Tasha actually served me an ultimatum - "Either sort your
shit out or I'm off!" I couldn't even do that. I considered her to be
the love of my life, yet I had to watch her walk away time and time
again, because I could not change who I was (or so I thought).

Back at work...and the immoral compass that seemed to serve
as perhaps an indicator to just how fucked things were heading.
Unbeknown to me, I was stretching that elastic rubber band closer
to breaking point...

"Could this finally be the wake up call I so badly needed?"

Dishonesty and the desire to not be caged in the office, meant I'd
always make spoof meetings with potential customers. I was damn
good at doing this, both lying and legitimately getting my foot in
the door. Addiction is a fiendish enemy of the mind, however,

directed in whichever way you choose fit, it's been my experience it will usually deliver the goods. Master manipulator - if you can persuade a hardened drug dealer to give you more narcs when you're already up to your eyeballs in debt, you can quite easily 'ask' Mr Collins over at Speedy Print to sign his name on a moody lease contract for some heap of junk photocopier.

I had a wingman. Now he was as smooth as they come, and just like me he loved guzzling copious amounts of everything. In my mind we were Tubbs and Crockett from Miami Vice. In all reality, the only thing we had in common with those dudes, apart from our sharp suits, was the way we'd infiltrate unsuspecting 'opponents' to get what we wanted.

"We learnt how to execute many deviant scams with precision, most if not all from rogue, wide-boy-sales-goons."

The crux of it was smoke and mirrors. We had to be Harry fuckin' Houdini to get what we wanted. We'd often get retainers for large sums of money, in exchange for finance approval checks being cleared and a signed doc on a Sales Director's desk. For me, it was an 'ecosystem' based on chasing the deal, and just like any drug, no deal was ever enough. My entire existence of perpetual needing, meant I was a famished little vampire, drooling at the prospect of a feed, gasping at any opportunity to strike. These 'daylight robbery' activities were nothing short of a glorified, egomaniac adrenaline junkie, driven by an insatiable lust for more. More money, more power, more whatever the fuck I can get my hands on. MORE MORE MORE.

A greedy feckin' rogue 'executive', sucking the life outta all existence, for my own gain. No wonder I'm losing sight of my moral high ground and shoving as much coke as I can up my beak, in order to suppress the truth of the matter. Tear the arse out of it, reap havoc, then scram. "Deal of the fuckin' century? Nah, really you're gettin' ya pants pulled down mate."

"Not exactly classy, but still, the power buzz I'm gettin' is worth it, right?"

The following, is one of a chain of events that unbeknown to me would serve as a catalyst for my eventual downfall...

Summer days like these always enhanced my mood when nothing else could. We'd done the usual doing a hooky deal in the morning, making a beeline for the nearest establishment serving food and more importantly, alcohol. We were looking sharp, the wine was flowing, and we'd already made a pit stop on route to grab some marching powder for dessert.

"I remember distinctly thinking in those moments, that it all seemed to be getting way out of hand."

We got progressively more sozzled, whilst I hurriedly shoved food into my belly, because my eye's on the prize...dessert. As soon as the food's done, whoosh!...I'm off like a firecracker to the gents... "Wallop!"...a 'straightener' to stabilise my daytime drunkard demeanour. May I just add - that false sense of grandiose, a plethora of exuberance like no other, was not only a cunning ally wreaking havoc, it was making me increasingly agitated and paranoid. Where as before I felt invincible, now, as soon as I did it, I'd automatically go into psycho(tic) mode...and what I mean by that, is I'd have this overriding urge to get away from absolutely everyone. An insatiable need to be on my own and in my own oblivion.

My crank behaviour didn't go unnoticed. I actually picked up the nickname 'back-door-Dave'...because I'd suddenly disappear without trace...'POOOF!'...gone. My phone would be off in an instant. I'd walk out of a busy bar or house party with the phone stuck to my ear, waffling away to an imaginary friend like a loon. As soon as I'd got around the corner, 'VROOM!'...I'd disappear like a fox in the night, never to be seen again.

This day was no different. It was a military operation being back-door-Dave. "Phone? - 'check'...wallet? - 'check'...gear? -

'check'...keys? - errr, hang on a minute. Fuck!" Angel had them. Yep her again, my guardian from above. She'd been dining on the table opposite. She was worried I was gonna drink drive. "Fuck it, it'll be alright, can't go back now."

"With my in built sat-nav set to 'nearest off license', I go grab a party bag full of booze. Sorted."

Now, not having my keys, meant I couldn't go back to Mum's. Isolation was the number one priority, so I made a quick calculation in my scrambled mind of 'go-to' places. My immediate thought was the place I used to go when I was young, the secret skate-ramp-oasis deep in the shadows of a remote woodland. There were only two ways to get there, depending on which way you came from. I used to walk down the track between the football club and the stables. The other, was to cross a river by stepping precariously over these sketchy big ol' pipes that made a makeshift bridge. On this occasion I chose the track between the club and the stables. As I swaggered along in my fine suit, with a bag of booze clattering around heading into the wilderness, I distinctly remember the feeling of not belonging there. In fact, I felt like I didn't belong anywhere. I was beginning to have notable dialogues in my head, discussions...

"What the fuck are you doing?...What is the point in all this anyway?…Why are you even here?…Why?"

I'm there, but I'm not there. My body, skin and bones are without a doubt there, but my soul, my spirit, that'd fucked off a long time ago. I was surrounded by nature, the sun blazing down on me, but I just could not feel any of it. "I'm dragging my sorry arse along this path, but for what reason? I'm not entirely sure?" The only plausible answer was to further remove myself from anything real.

Eventually I arrived at the spot where the ramp once stood. All that was left in that old bunkered crater was literally a piece of timber, just poking out from a bunch of overgrown woodland. It was symbolic of an old shipwreck debilitated on a deep sea bed. The eeriness creeped me out…it was like I was experiencing the death of something beloved. So many fond memories to my otherwise fucked up youth. Perhaps this served as the perfect metaphor for my incapacitated sense of self. I bid farewell and scarpered the hell outta there.

As I headed back onto the main pathway, I found myself on the track which led to the river. As I approached, I came across a clearing within the woods. I could see a fallen tree, it felt isolated enough for my needs, so I parked up and proceeded to tuck into the remainder of the booze and cocaine. I have no real idea how long I remained in that spot…all I know, is I could not settle, and this rang true to literally every situation I found myself in. There was always that underlying sense of agitation, a restlessness.

"I could not sit with myself. I didn't like me. I wasn't comfortable with me, this person I'd become. Who the fuck is this alien fiend inhabiting this body of mine?"

Did I even know, that underlying feeling, the discomfort of that **black-hole-void-impending-doom-solar-plexus-fucked-up-I-don't-wanna-go-there-fuck-you-fuck-this-and-fuck-that** sensation, was in fact unresolved, unexamined, and yet to be processed trauma I'd experienced from a very young age? Trauma that had rendered me dysfunctional...in all my relationships, be it my own sense of authenticity to self, family, friends, girlfriends...and this equalled disconnection, rejection, loss of self respect and hopelessness. I was carelessly putting myself in dangerous situations, with consequences becoming worse. It'd all been building up to a huge surge of toxic tension within my gut. My nervous system was failing me, and all I could do was try to fuck it off, by numbing myself with anything I could...but nothing was working.

My mind had become volatile, with depression, paranoia and panic attacks normalised...I felt psychotic, disempowered and completely trapped with no way out. I simply did not want to feel like that anymore. I was desperately alone, hoarding a secret, my other life, the dark side. Suicidal thoughts had now crept in, and for the first time in my life I seriously consider these options...

(a) Continue this path of self destruction and oblivion in complete denial, experiencing a very slow and painful existence with the constant feeling of death ever-looming.

(b) Kill myself.

(c) Don't kill myself. Consider getting help. (This option has a limited window of opportunity, before I talk myself out of it and continue with option 'a').

The once oh so trusted allies of my existence, hash and weed, stopped working long ago and became my enemies. Even my old friend alcohol was failing me. I'd saddled up with a new allegiance, cocaine and ecstasy, but for all the love in the world of doing it, they too had ceased to work. Unbeknown to me, this 'cross-addictive' behaviour of switching one drug to another, was still enabling the dysfunction to flourish, and all the destructive emotions that came with it. I was entangled in a perpetuating cycle of suffering I was far from ever getting away from.

Fear of the unknown had created an attitude of ignorance/arrogance/pride, with an absolute refusal to except responsibility for anything in my life. Through my defiance and 'Fuck you' attitude, I'd taken myself hostage and wasn't going out without a fight.

People who cared tried to negotiate my freedom, but there was no way of surrendering (or so I thought). I was well and truly stumped. Addiction had me by the balls…and with it denial and a very warped sense of perspective…

"I'm a wreckhead who gets high to relieve the burden of life, yet has the burden of life because I'm a wreckhead who gets high."

The Buddhist word for this malarkey is 'Samsara'…which means… "The endless cycle of birth, death and rebirth." The perpetual cycle of life. These bald headed dudes say a life filled with unskilful acts of ignorance and delusion, will create bad karma and an endless stream of suffering.

"Fuck it…does that mean I play a part in creating my own suffering?"

Sounds about right to me. Fuck me I could'a done with that there wisdom to awake my displaced mindset…but alas I wasn't ready to hear it. Not just yet…"I'm too busy feeling sorry for myself, so fuck you!"

Having thought about my options (thinking of death alone scared the life outta me), I decided to get off my sorry arse and walk. I vaguely stroll through the clearing and back onto the pathway, finding myself at the river's edge looking across at those crusty ol' pipes. Now, I know in theory I could cross that river. I'd done it before, granted (a) I was younger and braver, and (b) I wasn't bent out of shape back then. "Fuck it, it'll be alright"...that engrained, worn out mantra I thought still served me so well, was ringing out.

"If only I'd had the common sense (or sanity) to take my shoes and socks off, before stepping nervously onto those rusty old pipes."

The combination of the three pipes was no wider than your average treadmill. To make it more challenging, the pipes weren't flush. Instead, the middle one stuck up more prominently. Having somehow managed to negotiate the first few steps, I paused momentarily, trying to compose myself, before impulsively making a scrambled effort to scurry across. In doing so, I lost my footing, attempting a half stay on/half lunge for the bank. Neither worked. Instead, I did what I can only describe as an 80s flashback-crazy-legs dance move, as I tried desperately to stay on. Before I knew it, I'd slammed against the river bank. Half my body (one arm, leg and part body) on the bank, the other submerged in the scuzzy dirty water. "Fuck sake!" If it'd happened to anyone else I probably would of pissed myself laughing.

"I drag myself up and out. Thank God no one was around to see what just happened."

My suit was drenched with the dirty remnants of underwater scuzz. "Jeez, what a dick." Sitting there on the riverside, I realised I had another hurdle to overcome...a big old iron clad security fence, about twice the height of me, running along the entire length of the woodland. On the other side was an industrial estate, which was the only way out. "There's no way I'm scrambling across them frickin' pipes again." The only option was up and over. My primal childhood tree climbing skills kick in, and I find myself on a branch, with one foot placed between the sharp spikes on top of the fence. With all my effort, I focus as best I can...and launch.

As soon as I hit the ground, 'CRACK!'...the impact shunted me bang onto my arse. Immediately I could feel it. I've broken bones before. Being a skater it comes with the territory. "For fucks sake!" It's almost comical. I didn't know whether to laugh or cry. I did neither. I just sat, in seething pain...not just my feet, but my entire being.

Now, any 'normal' rational human being, given the exact same circumstance, I'm sure would simply make a phone call and ask for help. That was the problem right there…I mean, come on… who in their right mind would allow such a clusterfuck to happen in the first place? "Back-door-Dave ain't switching his phone on for no fucker!" after all…

"I'm the fuckin' Badman, right?" No dude…you're Captain frickin' Blunderchops!

After a mammoth 'hike' I arrived at Angel's. Praying my keys are there, I nervously knocked on the door. May I just add - I say 'pray'…to put it into context - I thought God was a punishing, narcissistic psycho. "If there's a God, why the fuck is the Almighty playing such ridiculously cruel jokes on me?" After a few moments, her Mum answers…"Oh hi, erm, I left my keys with Angel, is she there?...I've come to collect them." She wasn't, but to my relief her Mum hands me the keys with a look on her face which I could tell was one of…"What the fuck have you been up to chump?" I grimaced, said thanks, turned around and did my uttermost best to walk away as if I'd been to a health spa for a week. Instead, I made my exit waddling off like a rather cheap Charlie Chaplin impersonator high on drugs.

"A swell of shame overcame me…"What a fuck up I'd become. Jeez."

I found myself sitting on a bench in a nearby graveyard. "Will anyone notice if I disappear into the ground with the rest of these dead corpses?…just a little snuggle and a spoon." In all seriousness, the will to carry on had definitely gone and joined 'em. I remained there until nightfall. Once again the thought of those three options plays over and over, and I keep asking myself…"Surely I'm not meant to be living this way?"

Eventually I got up and made every effort to get 'home'. Once back, I hoist myself up the stairs and ran a hot bath, thinking that'd be the perfect tonic. I remember taking my shoes and socks off and to my horror, clapped eyes on my feet. "Holy feckin' shit"…

"My once slender feet now resembled two swollen aubergines."

I tried to block out what I'd just seen and slid into the bath. The heat seemed to make the pain intensify, so I clambered back out. At this point the shock overrode me, and the comedown from the adrenaline used to fuel my journey, plus sobering up, meant I finally acknowledged I was in a bit of a pickle. I edged my way back downstairs rather precariously to set up my make shift bed, where I lay for the entire night in unbearable seething pain, whilst trying my damned hardest not to think of those blasted aubergines on the other end of my body.

My bloody inability to ask for help...always keeping it zipped, no voice, no confidence...too engulfed with shame, pride and stupidity. The self-decimating, intolerable pain of my throbbing aubergines needed assistance, so a house call from a doctor was inevitable. As soon as the doc laid eyes on my swollen beauties, I could see he was a tad surprised to put it mildly. He asked how I'd done it, and when I was honest enough to say I'd jumped from a high whilst inebriated, late afternoon the day before...his jaw dropped in absolute disbelief.

"He said I must go to hospital immediately, and suspected my feet were broken. No shit Sherlock."

Still too ashamed to call for an ambulance, I called my mate Disco, a wild child who'd had his own fair share of scrapes in battle. He came in an instant. In true commando style, he hoisted me over his shoulder and carried me to his van. On arrival at the hospital, Disco grabbed a wheelchair and left me in the waiting room, called me a twat, wished me luck and off he shot to work. Years later, Disco confessed he'd always suspected I'd lied about that incident. He thought I'd been beaten with a baseball bat for an unpaid debt or some crazy shit. Although his suspicions may of been warranted, on this occasion it was simply a case of me acting like a bellend.

Once seen by the nurses, I was reunited with meds. "Lovely, let's skull a load of painkillers!…Fuck your peppermints doc, just give me the pills!" Co-codamol, Codeine, Tramadol…any Opiate will do, and if you're lucky, get some Benzos down the hatch. "Hmm, Valium." Always the perfect lubricant.

"They were moreish, and just like everything else I used, they took me somewhere that wasn't here."

The X-Ray's confirmed the obvious…I'd successfully broken the left metatarsal bone in my left foot, with additional fractures, and had splintered my right heel. The specialist doctor explained that due to the flat leather soled shoes and the high impact landing, I'd ruptured the base of my heel…and, if I'd in fact been more rigid on my landing, I could of possibly damaged my spinal cord. "Yikes!" My left foot was cast in rock hard plaster, a boot for my right…I was handed a pair of the NHS's finest crutches (???) and a taxi was called.

Those following weeks that ensued, I was laid up in an extended psychedelic fuzzy haze of yumminess, all wrapped up in a warm blanket of Opiate bliss (Kinda). A few days after leaving hospital, Mum found me laid out on the sofa practically unconscious. As I came around, I vomited my guts up...a common occurrence I was well attuned to. It's what happens when a greedy fecker over prescribes the stated dose.

104 MPH

Have you ever felt as though life was passing you by at such a rapid rate, yet it felt as though time was standing still? Sounds like a bit of a contradiction, but that's how it was for me. My persistent nature meant I continued to battle on, no matter what life was throwing at me, hoping it'd all just get easier...but I was entangled in something far greater than my sorry arse. When you encounter addictive behaviour, you're kinda entering an unspoken agreement with your worst enemy. What that entails, is you're at the mercy of their unforgiving control 24/7.

"It's like being stuck in a relationship with someone you dislike...and just like all unhealthy relationships, we love to hate them, right?"

I'd managed to vacate Mum's house, and had acquired a decent enough apartment by the skin of my teeth. Me and Tasha had been seeing each other again, but it all ended in tears and we finally broke up for good. Her Mum actually intervened and said I needed to back away, as I was causing her daughter distress. It killed me. Her Dad the Pitbull wanted to, and I didn't blame him.

Only a few weeks after our final split, a mate of mine disclosed that Tasha had met a guy, and was now engaged to be married. "What da fuck!?!" I just could not believe it. It destroyed me. In fact, the mere thought of her being with someone else was so gut wrenchingly awful, it forced me into a downward spiral of merciless self-pity and medication more than ever.

"Those feelings were so prolific, I just could not be with myself."

I'd been rather 'enjoying' the isolation of living on my own, but that rejection from Tasha and her new fella was fatal. My entire existence polarised from that point. I took myself hostage, holing up in that apartment hiding away from the world, living a secret double life. On the outside everyone thought I was a social butterfly (which I was), a complete extrovert wearing a guise of many masks, but on the flip side, I was hiding a very secret, sordid, dark persona. A life of depression, suicidal thoughts and addiction.

On top of losing Tasha, I lost my driving license. I don't mean down the back of the never regions of a couch. All 12 points penalised, in separate offences, all for speeding. I hadn't opened mail for as long as I could remember. It was never good news. I was in a constant state of angst over anything that remotely resembled taking responsibility. I owed over £30,000, which had accumulated over the years. I kept it secret. From a very young age I'd installed a strange concept of money. The basic premise that, when you attain credit, you're actually meant to repay it, was completely out of my psyche.

"Tick was made for people like me. No need to worry, just keep on ticking and it'll all be ok, wont it?"

I had unpaid bills dating back not just months, but years. I'd ramp up my mobile phone bill, then switch service provider and not even notify the old one. "See ya!" As for bank loans and credit, well, I'd rinse as many as I could, different banks, different loans, different overdrafts, don't matter. "Next!" I simply did not pay what I owed. On top of all that, I owed friends, family and pretty much anyone I came into contact with. I had absolutely no financial control and was a complete liability. I hated myself for it and always felt a lot of shame, inadequacy, frustration and desperation…ultimately creating the belief that I was somehow the victim in all this.

I was still working, selling moody copier leases, so I was earning, I just couldn't manage it. My unhealthy lifestyle was outstripping my resources. I was in an endless cycle of craving. My tick extended to maintain my image and the 'swagger' of a nice Mercedes, designer clothes and watch.

"I could and would go out every afternoon and into the night partying, champagne, coke and cocktails, but in reality my soul was as empty as my fridge."

Spiritually bankrupt as I now know it, I lived in fear with the blinds shut, secretly coexisting in that duality…a false external existence based on lies and inauthenticity, of which I somehow maintained my 'wide-boy' facade, "I'm the Badman"…yet my internal domain was desolate…a baron world of emotional poverty, with only isolation, paranoia and dysfunction to feed on. My ego was so defiant at those times of despair, there was no way on earth I could ever get past my pride and ask for help. "Fuck it, it'll be alright… right?"

Rewind to a few months prior. I'd been partying with Disco and his girlfriend at a holiday park up country. In short, I'd unexpectedly driven up there straight from work to help them out… his girlfriend had locked the car keys in the boot, so I'd brought them a spare set and decided to stay the night. True to form, we sat in the bar lounge until last orders, getting truly annihilated whilst watching some ABBA tribute band bang out classics. The next morning I awoke abruptly to a blistering gale force wind. I was on the top bunk in some pokey, kids sized cabin room in a flipping caravan miles from anywhere. Suddenly reality hit me. "Fuck, I need to be outta here, I gotta be somewhere for work."

"So without making a sound, I slipped out and made a run for it."

It was starting to get light and I was feeling like shit with the worst hangover imaginable. It'd become a standard procedure to 'wake up', usually with fuck all proper sleep, get in that car of mine and do the drive of shame. Blackout drinking had long been a staple practice. The weirdest places I found myself…waking up in some strange mouse infested hallway with no clue to how or why?…then realising you're rolled up in a Moroccan rug like some giant sized sushi…all fairly 'normal' behaviour on any given day.

In a mad hurry to get back, I was 'zippin' down the motorway…overtaking, undertaking, and as I flew past this particular car, I could see in the rear view mirror the blue lights flashing in the front grill. "Fuck! Bollocks and cunt!" The car gets right up my arse and forces me to pull over. My heart's in my throat and I start to think I'm done for. "How am I gonna wriggle out of this one?"

"In my wing mirror I see the officer getting out of his car and start to walk towards me. He's on his own. Bonus."

As he's approaching, my brain's scrambling to find a suitable 'get out of jail blag'…"I'm on my way to the hospital officer, I'm not well in the head, honest!" He comes to my side and requests I put the window down. "Do you know how fast you was driving young man?" I'm not entirely sure what the correct response to that question would be, so I go for a cheeky…"Erm..." with a slight humoured tone to it, in the hope that he's down with the satire. To my surprise he is. In the words of the Fonz..."Ayyyyy!"

He was one of the good guys, not a little fascist abusing his power. He informed me I'd been doing 104 mph, clocked on the inboard camera. Had I been going 110 mph, I'd have myself an instant ban. I very apologetically explained that I'd in fact been doing a good deed for a friend in need, and as a result, I'd been late to get back...blah blah.

"He wrote a ticket and said…"Take your time young man, don't be rushing back." I said thanks and goodbye, before slowly edging away feeling like the luckiest cat alive."

Fast forward to the first week in the new year. It was a Sunday evening and I was at Mum's for dinner. I was downstairs when the phone rang. Mum answered from her bedroom upstairs. I heard her distant muffled voice, then silence. A few moments later, she appeared at the top of the stairs and whispered, in an urgent and worried voice..."David, it's the Police."...I can honestly say I couldn't think of a single reason why the police were asking for me. "I was no saint, but why on earth would they be calling Mum's to speak to me?" I genuinely believed I had nothing to hide, so I told Mum I'd speak to them. "Hello"...I nervously answered the phone. It was met by an officer from the main Police HQ in our area, explaining they had a warrant for my arrest. Apparently they'd been trying to track me down for some time. "What da?" I held back from stating the obvious, that they'd not exactly done a good job of finding me up until now.

"I thought it strange to be calling, rather than knocking on doors...not that I was complaining."

He explained I'd been issued not one, not two, but three Magistrate Court Orders, regarding a driving offence dating back to last year. "Oh shit!" It all came flashing back to me. "How on earth did I not think to sort that ticket?" I hadn't opened mail for an eternity, so I knew I couldn't grumble and sidestep this one (although I tried my damn hardest to begin with). The simple fact was, I was burying all my problems. Anything remotely a burden, had to be buried and fast. The officer on the phone appeared to be one of the good guys. He told me the seriousness on a scale of 1 to 10, was a 1...to 'pop down' to the local Police Station and all I had to do was fill out a form. I asked if I could go in the morning...he insisted I go now.

Now at this time I was attempting to do a detox 'dry' January. I'd previously attempted these but always fell short. A day here, a day there...my experience of detox, was that it was hard as fuck. It felt painful as it did scary. Withdrawals always left me feeling raw. Emotions surfaced and I didn't know how to manage them. "That's what chemical enhancement is for right?" So I always failed. My first ever attempt to give up an addiction was cigarettes on my 18th birthday. With every best intention, I was convinced I'd do it...on the very morning of my 18th I 'relapsed'.

"I'd tried on multiple occasions thereafter to abstain from various substances - all failed attempts. Zero will power."

In hindsight, it was nothing short of a miracle when I finally managed to somehow detox through two entire January's with total abstinence. It was still fiercely hard for me to achieve, literally 'white knuckling' every single day...but I did it all the same. I believe those moments, gave me a tiny whiff of hope and a taste for what was possible (empowerment)…and for someone like me, it was an incredible victory.

"I now know my elastic rubber band at those times was getting increasingly weaker…and I stronger."

Anyway, back to the Police Station. I'd told Mum I wouldn't be long, as I wanted to come back and eat dinner. On arrival I was instructed to sit and wait to be seen. Not long after, the waiting room door swung open and in walks two uniformed officers. I instantly see one is holding handcuffs. "Muddafunk!" It was one of those times when I'd lose my shit completely, and the maverick outlaw would just boil over. With hindsight, I now know it's the fear of not having control in my life, that was masked by those snarling outbursts. Add a pinch of…"Fuck you, fuck the system and fuck authority"…and you've got an anti-establishment rebel on your hands.

They'd well and truly tricked me into handing myself in. Maybe I would of done eventually (hmm), but I just know it wasn't done on my terms, which infuriated me. I would of at least liked to of eaten a nice home cooked meal first. "Maaan…the injustice of it all." They read my rights, handcuffed me and lead me to a cell.

Every single time I've occupied one of those skanky concrete 'tombs', I've thought the exact same thing…

"I'm not meant to be here. This is so unjust. This isn't how I'm meant to be living…This isn't who I am."

They explained I'd be transferred shortly to another police station for the duration of the night, then first thing in the morning I'd be transported to a Magistrates Court up country, where the driving offence was committed. "What the fuck? That's frickin' miles away! All this for a driving offence. Come on, surely not?" What I came to learn, was that when you ignore the Magistrates Court, err, three times!…in the eyes of the Law that's a blatant…"Fuck you!" Oops.

I didn't spend long in that first cell. Shortly after getting acquainted to the pungent smell of the steel piss pan, I was transported to another Police Station in a neighbouring town. There, I spent the night. I didn't sleep. It was cold. I was also feckin' hungry. The whole time I was in there, I kept thinking to myself… "What the fuck? I'm on a detox, I'm not even off my nut drunk or disorderly…Why is this happening to me? It's just so unfair, so unjust!" At the time, I just could not see I was putting all the blame on everything and everyone but myself. I was fuming and feeling so damn sorry for myself, again. "I'm the victim here god damn you."

"I was still not ready to accept responsibility."

Reluctantly, I made two calls from the station. One was to a fully accustomed, yet justifiably hyper-anxious Mum, the other to my boss, Billy-Bionic. Both were well versed to my bullshit. Mum was as usual empathetic, Bionic simply laughed, called me a twat and hung up. May I just add...on occasion, I'd sit opposite Billy-Bionic in the office, usually on a Monday morning, looking like shit and feeling worse...and I'd ask if he'd allow me to go with him to one of his support groups he attended for recovering wreckheads. He'd always respond with a swift..."You don't wanna come to one of those, you're not ready" (he was testing me)...Each time I'd ask, he'd always reply with the exact same response.

"At the time I took it as a big 'fuck off'...in hindsight he was right, I wasn't ready. He could see it, I couldn't."

I was cuffed and led out to the station car park, where to my horror a prison security van was waiting...the ones you see with the tiny square blacked out windows on the back and side. I always wondered if you could see out of those tiny windows. You can. It's shit, because you're in there, and the world is out there. At this point I'm thinking this is deviating off piste a tad too much for my liking. I enter the van through a side door and go straight into the back holding cell. Door locked, hands through the tiny gap, cuffs off. Great. I'm then informed by the officer who accompanies me, that we're making a detour to pick up another 'inmate' from another Magistrates Court. "Hang on a minute chief, I'm just some regular dweeb who's got mixed up in a little 'administrative' technicality"...jeez man, this is getting worse by the second.

We arrived at the Magistrates after what seemed like hours. It was then down some stairs to an underground holding cell within the Courthouse. This time it's one of those big arse ones you see in the movies...you know, the ones where every goon and their dog is pacing up and down doing sit-ups and 'manly' shit. "Seriously, what da?" The minute I got in there I was pounced on by a skinny arse woman, clearly off her crackers. She got right up in my grill and was wittering on about god knows what whilst spraying my face with saliva. I'm all for socialising and having a bit of banter, but this was mental.

"The voice in my head is adamantly shouting..."Get me the fuck outta here! There's been a mistake, I'm not meant to be here."

Luckily the other 'inmate'...a young lad, had already been seen by the Magistrate, so it's back on the van and we're locked up again. It was that long drive to the Magistrates Court up country, that I had the most significantly profound realisation. I'd been complaining this was all so unjust. That I'd done nothing wrong. I mean, I knew I hadn't opened those letters, all three of them, but I didn't really equate that to the predicament I'd found myself in. I was also sober as a Judge (why do we say that?), had been for a handful of days... so I'm thinking..."I'm making a real effort to be a better human being, so why the fuck is this happening to me? Eh? Why?"

Obsessive, catastrophic overthinking had long been a commonality in my demeanour. I dedicated the entire last leg of that journey, to seriously 'contemplate'..."Why the fuck am I in this damn prison van?" I was also beginning to fear the worst. "Fuck man, I'm heading straight to prison...some mardy old fuddy duddy Judge, who couldn't care less is gonna make an example of me." Then it dawned on me, like a flash of brilliant white light. The answer to my predicament literally punched me on the nose, and for the first time in my entirety, I came to see the truth of the matter... "HOLY CRAP!!...it was all my doing!" I traced it back to where it all started. "NO!...it wasn't just me speeding."..."NO!...it wasn't just me not opening mail."..."Why was I speeding? Why am I not opening mail?"

"BAMM!...Suddenly I cut through the bullshit of me not taking accountability."

"OH MY GOD! I've been playing the victim. ME ME ME!"...I came to see it all stemmed from MY actions...MY drinking, MY drug taking, MY reckless partying, and ultimately MY unmanageability. Absolutely undeniable. For the first time ever, I'd put a huge dent in that almighty wall of denial.

I started to join the dots. To bare witness to the plain fact that ALL MY PROBLEMS, past and present, were a direct consequence of MY CONSTANT CHEMICAL INTAKE. I could see it light as day. If I hadn't been so self-absorbed, completely dependent, with an overwhelming desire to get wasted every moment of every day, then perhaps I'd pay more attention to the things I completely dismissed. The intensity of paranoia (at times psychotic) had rendered me so afraid of life, that a simple task like opening mail seemed incomprehensible. I have no doubt in my mind (with hindsight), that this realisation would not of happened if I hadn't had the clarity of being sober. I had an underlying sense for the first time, that everything may turn out alright. A glimmer of hope perhaps. That's all I'd ever wanted...and now I had it (just).

We finally arrived at the Courthouse late in the afternoon. I was famished, tired and hangry, with the feeling of uncertainty of my fate still hanging over my head...but I was holding onto that tiny slither of hope. I was put in a cell and awaited my request to see an on duty solicitor.

"I was relieved to finally see one, and granted a few moments to plead my frustration and sheer horror at being in this situation."

She was amazing and very empathetic. By a scrape, we just managed to catch the last slot of the day with the Magistrate. He was, as I feared, a rather old and grumpy sausage, yet surprisingly he turned out to be rather forgiving. He read the charges and asked what I had to say for myself. If it hadn't been for my earlier epiphany, the pathological liar in me would of quipped some malign protest of injustice and made matters worse. Instead, I was willing to own my shit. With an unfamiliar sincerity, I found myself apologetic, and for once…honest about the circumstances laid out before me, as somehow these words left my lips as I nervously announced - "I'm truly sorry for breaking the law…I have a drink and drug problem and I think I need help."

"BOOM!! There it was. A confession. I'd grassed myself up, and was at last getting real…guilty as charged your honour, on all counts, including substance misuse."

Fuck, I dunno where that came from. Unbeknown to me, this major realisation was an almighty seed of truth, having a monumental effect on breaking the spell, that'd cast such a monstrous curse over my entire life. Without me realising, that confession had also started the eventual downfall of my denial.

Before the Magistrate released me, having served a sizeable fine and issuing a full ban on my driving license, he encouraged me to seek help immediately, which I must admit sounded like a ruddy marvellous plan at the time…"Yep, will do your honour, anything you say." Thing is, I kinda needed someone to take this bull by the horns and literally do it for me. Is a judge, the prospect of my consequences or the constant weight of angst enough to pull me out of oblivion? A window of opportunity had presented itself…all I had to do was seek help. Did I even consider to ask…"How? Who? Where?"…before the gravity of my self sabotaging ways pulls me back to my ego's dictatorship.

"These fleeting moments of realisation don't come around too often…act now or forever be enslaved to this god damn curse."

GUNS, GIRLS AND GETAWAYS

Since the psychotic episode on that Island, I'd done a grand job of 'functioning' as a wreckhead…or so I thought. Delusion has a cunning habit of convincing you all is well, when the reality is - you're completely nuts. In my experience, us 'functioning wreckheads', are usually feckin' delirious behind closed doors. Secret psycho squirrels, suffering in silence. The psychosis I encountered came in waves...usually in heightened pangs of danger. Well, I was about to have one last round with that champion psychotic beast, when a bunch of us boarded a flight to an unknown destination for a weekend of debauchery. It filled me with dread (again). I wanted off that rollercoaster of madness, but I just didn't know the million dollar question - HOW?...so I did what I always did...smiled (grimaced), shut the fuck up and cracked on.

Jimmy was getting married. Everyone around me seemed to be doing 'normal' shit. You know...career, mortgage, marriage, dog. "Fuck man, I ain't got shit to show for nothing." This thought'd always demoralised any sense of esteem. Deep down I'd always considered myself a failure, which only fuelled my glorified sense of self pity and kept me on the floor, beat.

"If only you knew what it was like to be me."

It was Jimmy's stag do and I knew the drill and what to expect. Depending on the company you kept, determined the probable outcome to such weekends. Now, if you're with a posse of hellraisers, it's highly anticipated that someone, or something, would implode. I knew this would be no exception. The mere task of getting from point A to point B proved to be a test in itself. The night before we flew out we'd all met at a hotel for a pre-trip meal and drink. I didn't sleep that night. In fact, I hadn't slept the night before either. Instead, I was up all night sniffing coke. I had a full blown panic attack sitting next to Jimmy on the flight.

"We hadn't even taken off and I was already wanting to call it a day."

On such trips, you're often greeted by a 'fixer' on arrival, who will lay down very specific guidelines as to the dos and don'ts, and the importance to take heed to them. This time, the standout, absolute don'ts were...

1 - DO NOT go off alone, safety in numbers.

2 - DO NOT ask a taxi driver to go find drugs or women.

3 - DO NOT go to any remote 'clubs'.

These guidelines are more like lifelines. Ignore them at your peril. We'd arrived in a foreign land, somewhere in the arse end of nowhere. Having heard tales, true or not, didn't matter...when you're all together getting mashed, it quickly becomes obsolete. The signs were there...the hotel we stayed at had a security door with a buzzer system for entry. Not to be perturbed, we went straight out for the first days session of 'fun and frolics'. We end up in a boozed up mess in some retro 80s rock nightclub. Bon Jovi and Whitesnake were booming from the gigantic PA system, whilst scantily clad women wearing sweet FA, poured neat vodka from giant bottles, directly into the mouths of eager punters.

"It's the only vodka I ever drank that I could only imagine tasted like actual rocket fuel."

The next day we're all driven to a waste ground, where it'd been arranged for us to shoot AK-47s, Glocks and pump-action-shot-guns. To think we actually did this whilst still inebriated with fuck all sleep is nuts. It's a miracle no one got hurt. Our instructors for the shooting party were two ex-militant meatheads. One of the renegade lumps had a monster scar on his neck from ear to ear. "Better make sure I don't break his precious toys!" His advice, in broken English, was animated by him sticking a Glock to his own head, then shoving it into his equally scary comrade's head, as if to say…"Do not shoot!" I remember thinking…"Right, got it."

I now truly understand why guns bestow such power to those who use them. It's seriously intoxicating. There's an incredible surge of adrenaline that hits you so unbelievably hard when you hold one. A pure rush of invincibility when you pull back on the trigger, as you watch in anticipation hoping your target will explode on impact. In our case, human bodies made out of wood, fixed on posts in the ground. High from the buzz of it all, we head straight back out to the bars and clubs. In hindsight, we were stereotypical British drunkards, staggering around like numpties without a care in the world, thinking we're untouchable. Thing is, when you're inebriated, you just kinda naturally hit the fuck it button, don't you? "Guidelines (lifelines), what frickin' guidelines?" It was on this night, our final leg of the onslaught, that the golden rule to any Dodge City was broken...

"NEVER, EVER get in a taxi and ask the driver to take you to find drugs or women."

We ended up in some seedy club. I was sitting next to the not so Saintly Sid, one of Jimmy's old pals from New York. He turned to me, and mumbled in my ear..."Let's get the hell outta here." Without a second thought, 'WHOOOSH' we were gone...back-door-Dave had a wingman. Going against everything we knew (?) NOT to do, we jumped in a taxi - "Driver, drugs and beautiful women please." Fuck man, might as well of been our chauffeured ride to go see the grim reaper for our inevitable fate.

As we slowly navigated our way further away from the hustle and bustle of the city, it began to feel a tad sketchy. I could feel that heightened sense I knew too well, yet always ignored...unrelenting, unadulterated dread...and that equalled paranoia and psychosis. The driver announced we were nearly there, as we pulled into what I can only describe as an industrial area. There was absolutely no one else around and it seemed intensely dark and forbidding, with only silhouettes of these long, warehouse units dotted all over. We turned into a road which was even more desolate, and down a dead end, where standing before us was a lone unit. "Fuck, what have we got ourselves into?" The driver signalled for us to get out and follow him.

"Nervously, we hopped out and walked with him to the door."

Now, at this point I'm already fluctuating between panic and a full blown meltdown. No matter what's happening, my mind's already creating a catastrophic agenda all of its own. "Uniformed blacked out cars and 4x4's parked out front?" Back on that Island, they were a familiar mode of transport, and I knew precisely what cats used them. I immediately wanted to get the hell outta there and as far away as possible. I could sense Sid felt the same, but it was too late, the driver had already hit the intercom buzzer on the main entrance door. "Fuck."

We were greeted by what seemed to be a fairly harmless man, he looked smart, and signalled for us to enter. I'm secretly projecting a potential hostage and massacre scenario as we walked into the reception area. The taxi driver took a seat behind us near the door, and we're escorted through to another large door, similar to the ones you find in large recording studios. A hefty, deadweight security door, that when shut behind us, felt as though it'd quite literally sealed our fate.

"Yep, we're fucked, we're gonna be butchered...I just know it."

As we stepped through into the main area of the 'club', it was obvious we hadn't entered the Ritz. To our left was a half moon sofa with a dance pole slap bang in the centre, with a cluster of women sitting around it. They looked more like Mrs Lovett than Miss World. Gaunt sullen faces and dishevelled hair. "Who's more wasted, them or us?" I don't think those poor souls intended to be there any more than we had. "Fuck"...alarm bells were seriously ringing at this point, as my paranoia went from nought to imminent death in a blink of an eyelid. We'd been warned about these places. Drink and party to your hearts content without putting your hand in your pocket, then get 'asked' to pay an extortionate amount of money or 'pay the price'.

"I'm in a fucked up movie and I already know the ending!"

To our right was a table with a low ceiling lamp coming down, lighting up four men sitting there playing cards. Now, in hindsight, perhaps this served as a suitable metaphor to The Four Horsemen of the Apocalypse. Like a scene from a Scorsese movie, they were suited, drinking and smoking, and in my mind it had gangsta written all over it. Straight across the dance floor was a bar area. Behind it, was what I can only describe as an André the Giant impersonator on steroids. At this point I could feel the oxygen disappear and my throat and lungs tighten. "Fuck, please don't let me have a full blown panic attack...not here, not now." I'm not sure André and The Four Deadly Horsemen would see a shmuck like me having a panic attack, and necessarily think..."Ooo, quick, get that young man a glass of water and some fresh air!"

"Fuck, do we ask politely if we can leave?"..."Hmm, not sure about that." On one hand they may just say..."Yes sir, of course, sorry it wasn't to your liking, have yourselves a lovely evening"...and on the other, well...those tales of paying a grand for a shot of vodka and a bowl of nuts didn't quite take our fancy. Sid took the lead, ordering me to go to the toilet and check for an alternative exit. "A window, anything, just get us the fuck out." Without hesitation, I followed my nose, trying to casually meander past the four dudes without letting on I'm losing my shit. My heart and gut somersaulted when I entered the toilet...nothing but walls! Not one single window.

"My mashed up brain tries to calculate a way out...but I just couldn't think straight."

All I could think of, was we're in the middle of nowhere, and there wasn't one person who knew where we were. That's the price you pay for being back-door-Dave. There wasn't even a single other punter in that place, just us and the cast of Sweeney Todd and Goodfellas..."Will it be a bullet to the back or a blade to the throat, demon barber style?" I was trying to think rationally, but nothing was working..."I can't just hide in the loo...or could I?...Maybe I'll have a go at flushing myself down the toilet?" I knew I had to go back out.

Without daring to get eye contact with anyone, I walked straight up to Sid, who was deep in negotiations with the man who'd originally escorted us through. "We'll be straight back, our mates will love this place, just gotta go get 'em." Somehow, the now, ever so Saintly Sid, a true archangel if ever I saw one, was looking to be our saviour and was indeed about to lead us to the pearly gates of freedom. The Gods were looking over us that night. The guy folded. He lead us back through the holding door into the reception, where we urgently signalled to the waiting taxi driver, that we're leaving pronto. As we're reversing back out along the driveway to the road, one by one André and The Four Deadly Horsemen came out of the club and stood there staring at us.

"Me and Sid literally screamed at the driver to floor it."

Having made a getaway, my neurotic membranes were still fizzing with paranoia. "Did that really just happen?"…"Are we actually safe now?" Sid experienced the exact same scenario, so were we both delusional, or had it really been that extreme? I'll never know, because firstly, I was sleep deprived and intoxicated, and secondly…I was having an episode of pure terror where the mind escalates uncontrollably, so whatever the fuck was going on it ain't registering properly. Call it a 'manic blackout'.

It's a sobering experience facing extreme danger, whether it's real or not. I quietly considered my actions and sanity once more… "Fuck man, how much more do I have to endure?…seriously, I'm done." These precarious situations always occurred through a total disregard for safety, and in my case, the inability to say "NO!"… another example of…"Fuck it, it'll be alright"…and…"Yeah, yeah…I know, I know." The truth was blatantly obvious now…

"Drugs, risk taking, chaos and drama. I have to find a way to stop…somehow, I've just gotta do it."

SOLO (SO LOW)

Having originally convinced myself I'd be dust particles by 21, I got to celebrate my 30th birthday with work colleagues in a karaoke bar. Elvis and Oasis songs were murdered, whilst attempts to skull 30 shots of tequila were made high on some of the Med's finest cocaine.

It really hadn't been that long since I'd faced the judge in that courtroom, confessing to him (and myself) that I had an issue, yet my powerlessness (and insatiable appetite for destruction) still outweighed any hope of finding a way out.

Life seemed to slowdown to a grinding halt in those moments of despair. That constant feeling of dread...the **black-hole-void-impending-doom-solar-plexus-fucked-up-I-don't-wanna-go-there-fuck-you-fuck-this-and-fuck-that** feeling was not seeming to wanna leave anytime soon, so I continued to put on a brave face and numb it. The following three or so years blurred into a vague travesty of irrelevance...and just like the dissociation of my childhood, the avatar of my existence dissipates as I continued to flatline further into oblivion.

Since Tasha left, I'd used sex as a means to distract myself from feeling so miserable and alone. Desperate for attention, love even...but no flippin' clue how to do it, associating fleeting moments of gratification for what I thought to be love. I begun a web of 'interludes' with multiple lovers, including some I considered (as did they) to be 'exclusive'. I could be lying next to a girlfriend or 'lover'…and I'd be desperately alone. I was extremely insecure and fearful behind that Romeo mask…yet asked if I was ok, my default answer would always be a steely…"Hell yeah, I'm cool."

"Some of my darkest moments were in isolation…but for me, isolation didn't necessarily mean physically being alone."

Everyday we step out into life and hear the most commonly used dialogue…"Hey, how you doing? You alright?" with an answer of… "Yeah really good thanks, how's you?"…with the response of… "Awesome, yeah, all good here, thanks." Now, if that's what's really going on then bloody marvellous. My reality. Not so. Asked if I was ok?…of course I'd answer with that same default response. I'd even do it with a skip and a smile on my face, and a wink for good measure…but inside I'm dying. What I really wanted to say but couldn't, was…"No, I'm not ok actually. In fact, I desperately need help and I'm suicidal."

"I didn't wanna die...god no, I was just scared and stuck in a cycle I couldn't get out of."

The frustration of my torment underpinned the anger which was starting to bubble up to the surface and be more evident to Amba. She always said to me..."You've got serious issues." I'd always look at her in bewilderment as if she were bonkers, defiantly protesting my sanity and putting it back on her..."Nah, you're the loon love." Sound familiar? She was right though. All that pressure over the years had been slowly building up, an almighty mass of toxic tension that I just didn't know what to do with, was about to explode. I was finding myself more and more ill equipped to deal with the extremities of my existence. No amount of chemical enhancement could tame the beast that lay in wait, striking at the first sign of weakness.

"For me, anger (rage) always stemmed from pain, powerlessness, shame, and the frustration and fear of entrapment."

The following incident, would prove to her that I did indeed require some form of psychological help...

I'd been round Mum's for dinner. Salmon and steamed veg was about to be served up, and just as I was placing something in the bin, I noticed the 'use-by-date' was out by a couple days. I said to Mum…"I can't eat this Salmon." I'd had food poisoning not that long ago from some dodgy Sea bass (or was that just another moody hangover?), so I was a little apprehensive to say the least. Mum calmly replied, simply saying…"David, it'll be fine, it's ok." I just couldn't let it go. Cue the snarling beast - I saw red and began an argument which resulted in me shouting and erupting with uncontrollable rage. My poor Madre. Something snapped in me and I lashed out, punching the solid oak staircase with the full force of my fury.

"CRACK!!'...as soon as my fist smashed into that beam, I didn't just hear, but I could feel the bones snapping."

"Arrgghh, for fucks sake, now look what you've made me do!" Being the twat that I'd become, I had the sheer audacity to proclaim it was Mum's fault. I took one look at it and quickly buried it deep into my armpit, not only to hide it, but to somehow comfort myself from the agony. Mum was in a state, so I scarpered to go meet Itch, who drove me to the hospital. What a dick. In all reality, I just could not manage my emotions, and the anger I felt would often boil over.

"The more I did it, the more I loathed myself."

The X-Ray revealed broken bones, (no surprise) to the extent that the two outside knuckles on my left hand had collapsed downward by approximately an inch. I was given a nice dose of Morphine (perks of being a twat) and was told I'd need an operation to have a metal rod inserted to restructure my hand. They put a cast on it and I was prescribed more opioids for the pain. Unbeknown to me, these opioids were rapidly becoming a more permanent fixture in my chemical dependency.

The night before the operation, I stupidly disregarded the importance of going back to the hospital the following day, choosing to attend a Halloween party at Amba's brother's University, nearly 200 miles away.

"I spent that entire night bouncing off the walls on a cocktail of booze, cocaine and opioids whilst dressed in fancy dress as a hit-and-run-victim."

By the time I managed to finally get another appointment for an operation, my hand had deformed. I awoke from the op on a Sunday afternoon feeling groggy. I had a whopping great cast covering my entire hand and forearm, and was left to recover in bed with a Morphine drip. I rinsed that drip to the hilt. I was meant to stay that night, but I signed myself out of hospital and was collected by a very reluctant Amba. Dumb move. In the middle of the night I awoke to a raging opioid withdrawal and a savage post-op-comedown, with the searing pain too much to handle. As soon as I could, I insisted on Amba driving me to get more meds, and just like every other time I had them, I abused them like my life depended on it.

The months that proceeded didn't get much better, as I continued to nosedive mentally, emotionally, and I guess I can now say, spiritually. Whilst all this played out, unbeknown to me, my elastic rubber band was becoming increasingly weaker, in fact…it was about to finally snap. "Hallefuckinlujah!"

My 34th birthday…I'd found myself alone, staring out to the vast ocean, having driven to the coast in a desperate bid to escape reality. I sat, wishing for something or someone to intervene and just take me away from this hopelessness. "If only a beautiful mermaid could scoop me up and save me!"

"Perhaps the 'big blue' could put me out of my misery?"

Days after, I sat with Jimmy at a friends apartment. I recall him looking over at me and saying with all seriousness…"Mate, are you ok? You look like you're dead." I couldn't even respond to that, I simply acknowledged him with a vacant glance. I was so low, so empty, my soul, my spirit, my very being was gone. There was nothing left.

"What have I become?" The shame I felt living at Mum's, I'd yo-yo'd back and forth with no real stability, bed hopping with different 'lovers' to try and satisfy my own selfish needs, sheepishly kidding myself and poor Amba that we were exclusive. I was a liar and a cheat. The anger and frustration of an absent Father in my life had clearly never left me. Instead, it'd stripped me of any true chance of happiness. I'd lie awake at night off my nut with incessant thoughts of insurmountable fear and regret. It's as though the truth that hid away in the subconscious world, the secret life I lived, it only surfaced when I was left alone with myself.

"The same dialogue played out, over and over, night after night and I just could not escape it anymore..."

"How the fuck did it come to this?" I have no home, I've lost the girl I thought I'd spend the rest of my life with, I don't have a pot to piss in and I'm thousands of pounds in debt. To top it off, I'm constantly fearing the unknown, I can't sit with myself and I have an overwhelming sense of self-loathing. I owe not just the banks money, but friends, family and drug dealers..."For fucks sake, I just know this isn't how I'm meant to be living."

It's undeniable - I'm a hopeless wreckhead who's been self-medicating for the past two decades, yet I'm too scared to do anything about it. Somehow I've made it through my 20s and I'm now flatlining my way through my 30s. Life is passing me by and I honestly don't think I can take much more..."I am so god damn tired of this shit."

For as long as I can remember there's not a day that passes where I don't feel the debilitation of my now, so called 'life'. Every night I lie awake and wonder..."Where the fuck did it all go wrong?" I try to avoid any kind of contact with reality by fantasising obsessively about dying. "I don't wanna die, yet I can't help but wish I was dead."

In my head I secretly plan the seating arrangement and playlist to my funeral. All my ex-loves will be there for sure, sitting front row exchanging amazing stories of how attentive and funny I was...but their laughter soon turns to hysteria, crying uncontrollably at their tragic loss, as Jeff Buckley's 'Last Goodbye' bellows out as a haunting homage to how wonderful I was.

"In all reality…I've become a narcissistic sociopath and a complete wanker."

I could feel the heaviness of my pained body, a dead weight slab of meat, pinned to the mattress of the makeshift bed at Mum's. That's where my existence had got me in those final days of despair. I'd feel the sheer brute force of my empty soul, overcome with an irretrievable sense of self pity and void like I'd never felt before. I'd dare to close my eyes, only for it to feel like I was being sucked down a long, dark, bottomless tunnel into a vortex with no return. Insomnia had become the norm, and it terrified me each and every time I had to prepare for sleep, because I knew what awaited me. That was the place I was forced to face myself, and I'd do anything not to have to go there, but ultimately I had to. I think I'd gotten to a point where I felt so depleted, it didn't matter who, what, or how many people I was with...

"I was now on a solo mission for survival."

The following chain of events, results in what I believe to be a visit from the lord of death himself, Mr Reaper...and a final face-off with the Devil. Little did I know this last dance with insanity, would in fact be a pivotal moment in time, changing my life forever.

The last weekend in July, 2009. Early Friday, I did the usual morning ritual of rinsing out my nasal pipes, to wash away any remnants of cocaine crust from the night before. That day I was attending a works do at the races. A coach load of wide-boy salesmen on a jolly...aka...annihilation. My work buddy and fellow caner G picked me up. Perhaps 'G' stood for 'Get on it'...or...'Go all night'...because that's what we did. Before meeting the others, we deviated to find the nearest pub to open.

"I remember the short drive back from the boozer. We listened to his favourite Johnny Cash, the song 'Hurt' plays out and serves as a metaphor…whilst I sat quietly and internalised the dread of what I knew awaited."

It was utter carnage. We were there representing the suppliers and entertaining our clients. The only thing I entertained was getting more fucked. From what I recall, someone pulled out a bag of pills and that was the end of that. Blackout as standard. I always assumed a blackout was when you're out for the count, unconscious, sparko, kaput. Not so. The lights are on but no fucker's home. I could be in any social situation, surrounded by hundreds of people, off my chops, in full blown blackout mode and not remember a flippin' thing. I'd be walking around a festival, talking shit to unsuspecting punters, licking them on the forehead, doing gymnastics on the bar or urinating in some lovely ladies handbag, and I would not have a frickin' clue.

"I think we all know that someone, don't we?"

The morning after, I 'greeted consciousness' with a sudden shock of…"How the fuck did I get home?" Then panic ensued…"Fuck!" It was the day of my mates stag-do. What I'd do for a bit of sleep, to eat, then sleep some more. Ahhh boy. Instead, I call a dealer, grab a bag of coke and head straight to the city.

The very first pub we enter, first drink…everyone's getting hyped for the 'big night out'…when out of nowhere a colossal tidal wave of terror hits me like a freight train tsunami. "Uh-oh…fuck man, not here, not now!" With only a few moments to contain that beast monstrosity of horror, I make myself invisible and get the fuck outta there!

"Every cell in my body was reacting relentlessly as if to say to me…"Dave man, wake the fuck up…STOP THIS BULLSHIT NOW!"

Cue 'back-door-Dave'. I managed to stealth my way outta the pub, finding myself on the street in the city centre. "Fuck!"…it was a warm summers evening and bustling with people. The terror seemed to intensify with all the activity, plus it was still daylight. Hyperventilating uncontrollably through gritted teeth and wild eyes, ain't exactly a good look in public. Biting my teeth down hard, grinding them poorly pearly whites (stained and a tad eroded) was something I used to do when extremely high, stressed or anxious, and this was no exception.

"Feeling extremely exposed and volatile, I made a beeline for a restaurant on the opposite side of the street."

As I approached I could see it was fairly busy, but I couldn't stop gravitating towards the door. I entered the restaurant and was greeted by a rather disconcerting waiter, who could see I was in a pickle. He was quick to cockblock my efforts to use the men's room, stating it was for customers only. Understandably he didn't need a mash up situation to contend with…but persistence pays. I couldn't get there quick enough as I 'spun out' uncontrollably. I always suspected that physical reaction ('manic' hypertension) was a combination of no sleep, not enough to eat and too many chemicals. For a long time my body had been trying to tell me to slow down, to rest and stop. Back in 1991/1992 when I had the first panic attacks, 1999 vomiting blood, the liver prangs, kidney prangs, the heart palpitations and chest pains. The body has the intelligence to let us know when something ain't right, or if it needs something…even when we don't.

"I'd been ignoring those signs for way too long, and it was apparent it was losing patience."

What happened next will remain embedded in my mind for eternity. On entering the toilets I immediately saw a mirror above the sink on the left hand wall. I turned to face it, placing both hands on the sides of the basin to steady myself. As I looked up, what I saw staring back at me scared the crap outta me, more than I'd ever been spooked before…"Holy fuck!"…I can only describe what I saw in that reflection as what Jimmy'd seen just weeks ago in our mates apartment…I too saw death. A ghostly, haunting vision…a war-torn victim of life. My psychological state captured in a moments glare…grey, weak and dead inside. My lifeless eyes, a stark indication that my very soul had ebbed away, finally about to fade into eternal nothingness.

"There was nothing left, that elastic rubber band of mine had finally snapped. I was broke."

In that moment, I just knew I was heading for a certain early grave. No doubt whatsoever…it wasn't a question of if?…but when? I was slowly killing myself, abandoning all trace of authenticity, relinquishing my needs and giving up on life by destroying this body of mine. I knew that if I didn't get help, I'd be signing my own death warrant. With absolute desperation and a very certain knowing, I went into the toilet cubicle and closed the door. I sat on the toilet seat and prayed to a God I didn't believe in to save my soul.

"Once again, an SOS cry for help...but this was different. I'd reached bottom and there was nowhere else to go."

I believe (with hindsight) that final 'confession' to whatever the fuck I was pleading with...was my unwavering decision to flick on a switch, igniting a spark from within, serving as a final surrender to let go and allow something to happen. I had no clue to what could possibly restore me to sanity, but I just knew with more clarity than I'd ever known, that to begin with, I needed to stop what I was doing to myself. The coke, the booze, the lifestyle...it's gotta change. "I HAVE TO CHANGE!!!"

It took a while to decompress and compose myself, to slow my heart rate down to a place I knew was safe. That heart irregularity was something I'd become accustomed to. It's why I was so sure I'd keel over from heart failure. "Death by supersonic stress!"...I mean, fuck me...I was certainly flirting with it. Cocaine is killer...and just like extreme stress, a common cause of heart failure the world over. I was 34, yet my body felt as though I was 94.

I came out of that toilet and went back to the sink. As I turned the cold tap on and splashed my face to calm myself, I fixed my glare back at the reflection. Never had I envisioned such conviction to take action...

"I WILL conquer that person looking back at me."

As I walked back to the hotel through the busy streets, I noticed a strange, unknown calmness. I could tell the dialogue in my head had shifted tone, from the familiar punishing, hate fuelled tyrant bully..."You worthless piece of shit, you deserve to die!"...to a softer, more gentle voice..."Everything's gonna be ok man...you got this." Had hope arrived?...and with it an immense sense of relief? Well I can safely answer that now - "YES!"

Back at the hotel I sat in the bar and sank pints of the black stuff. For me, always a great leveller. I'd convinced myself a few years prior I needed to drink copious amounts of the black, based on the premise it was loaded with iron, ultimately making me stronger and healthier. I switched from beer to red wine on occasion, as red wine was good for the heart of course (?)...it's a grape, and ruddy darn sophisticated don't you know?...so loads of that then please. Unbeknown to me, the perpetual cycle of cross-addiction. Stop smoking weed and start drinking. Drinking too much vino? Fuck it, start drinking lots of beer. Drinking getting on top? Back to the weed then. Weed psychosis flaring up? Let's have another drink instead...

"Booze getting me down again? Where's that tub of ice cream?"

Anyway, I was feeling a lot more mellow sipping the black tonic, when in walks Jimmy and our mate Fletch. They'd decided to swerve off back to the hotel for a crafty session. I'd already reached the conclusion the night had ended, but after a couple more drinks at the bar I found myself heading up to Fletch's room. With every best intention, I wanted to swerve it, but Fletch pulled out some gear, and before I knew it I'm smoking the white stuff again.

"Muddafuck!...Literally moments ago, I was in that basement toilet praying for help, and here I am hitting the fuck it button again."

Somehow, after not too long...I mustered the strength to make my excuses and head back to my room. That in itself spoke volumes. I remember laying awake for some time after, going over in my head what'd just happened...and contemplated the usual options that'd been so prevalent throughout this battle of mine...

(a) Continue this path of self destruction and oblivion in complete denial, experiencing a very slow and painful existence, with the constant feeling of death ever-looming.

(b) Kill myself.

(c) Don't kill myself. Consider getting help. (This option has a limited window of opportunity, before I talk myself out of it and continue with option 'a').

Now, I couldn't help but think - "Fuck man, I accept option (c) is all I have...but I've gotta act on this shit immediately." I knew I didn't have the balls to kill myself, and I'd given option (a) a ruddy good go...but seriously, if I don't do something now I'm screwed.

The very next day, a Sunday, I was round Bumble's. Itch was there too. He'd been on the stag-do, but I'd kept my meltdown secret (standard). As per usual Bumble and Itch were chugging away, doobie after doobie. Whenever I was around these two it would always result in carnage one way or another. Our motto for every situation was always..."Fuck it, it'll be alright."

It was well into the afternoon, Bumble and Itch were getting more baked and I was drinking red wine, when out of the blue I heard myself say out loud..."Let's get some gear in"...which was met with a very rapid response of..."Fuck sake Dave!" It was the kinda response which would suggest it wasn't a good idea. The irony...I got these two mash heads telling me I'm a wrongen'. It's what we did. We'd always banter each other...I'd often call Itch a crack head (he wasn't) and they'd call me a smack head (I wasn't)…although I was partial to opioids. I had no doubt it was heading that way though. They were right, and I knew it, but it still didn't stop me from wanting it. It'd been less that 24 hours since I was staring at that deathly stranger in the mirror, having the very real realisation that I needed help. "STOP!…or meet my demise." Yet here I am, AGAIN!…just hours later, wanting, craving, needing. "Fuck me, if that narcissistic psycho…God…if real, was in fact a good egg after all, now was the time to prove it."

"I managed to get my head on the pillow that night without doing coke. For me that was truly remarkable."

27th July 2009. Monday morning. I awoke feeling distinctly clear minded about the events from the weekend. It was a kind of clarity I'd never experienced before. Knowing I needed to make a change right now, was still at the forefront of my mind, instilling even more hope and belief that I could do it. I remember thinking that I needed to stop drinking immediately. My theory being that if I could stop drinking, it's very probable I'd stop a hell of a lot more along the way. I felt lighter and more confident about this than ever before.

Later that day I had a tattoo booked in with a friend. Before I went in, I deliberated on whether to take a Valium. That in itself amazed me, the fact that I'd paused to even give it a second thought. At first, I decided not to do it, but I somehow ended up snapping it in two and doing just half. Still an improvement. I sat in the waiting room, and before going in to get inked, I swallowed the remaining half. Sitting on that bench having my shin etched was immensely enjoyable that afternoon. I sat calmly and gazed in a blissed out state of fuzziness, with an ever so slight feeling that everything was gonna be ok.

LONE WOLF

Getting real

GETTING REAL

So, is this it? Time to finally own my shit? Recent realisations, heightened (and unavoidable) awareness over some seriously fucked up situations, have led to the timely and inevitable conclusion..."I am not right in the head and I need help."

Now, if you're anything like me, pride and ego has led you to the point where your best thinking has rendered you not only a miserable version of your former self, but let's be honest...and I can only speak for myself...I've turned out to be a bit of a tit. Without a clue of what I'm doing in life and too damn proud to admit it, that crafty nemesis the ego has led me down a garden path and into the deadly brambles, where I've become a victim of my own demise.

"Time to brush myself down and pick out those poisoned thorns, and begin the arduous task of getting myself back on track. First things first, where the fuck do I begin?"

LAST NIGHT A DJ
SAVED MY LIFE

Ok...so, I've finally had enough and broke through the denial of 'everything being ok'. That blasted code of conduct..."Fuck it, it'll be alright"...

"NO. NO. NO. FUCKIN' NO. OH FUCK NO!...IT WON'T!!"

I was always a good natured, kind and caring person deep down. I'm damn sure I was taught right from wrong as a child, I'd just lost my way. Disconnected...I just needed to find my way back to who I really was. I'd become dishonest, immoral, selfish, and you couldn't trust me. I couldn't trust me. Reaching out, finding my voice and learning how to trust someone, to trust myself, was vital in order for me to rediscover who I was always meant to be, underneath all the bullshit that'd defined me for way too long.

That garden path of insanity into the deadly brambles...well, picking out those poisoned thorns from my past would prove to be a challenge. Unbeknown to me, time, experience and a shit load of humility, would evidently strengthen the character of who I'd become...a mighty-strong-bad-arse-muddafuckin'-maverick, boldly pushing on through to a freedom of unmeasurable rewards...but first, there was much to learn. Zero patience, resisting acceptance and an insatiable desire to control absolutely every god damn thing, were all major obstacles to overcome...and for me, it couldn't be done without some much needed guidance. Wasn't that bloody obvious!?!

"When the student is ready, the teacher will appear...as they say."

I will always treasure the chapter in my life when I first came to know Tony, a DJ from Manchester. I'd seen him around...and from what I knew, he was on the wagon. I had absolutely no idea he'd be such a significant piece of the puzzle, and would soon become my mentor, changing my life forever.

Rewind to the week before the stag trip, and my basement toilet meltdown. It was a warm summers night when me and Tony sat and talked for the first time. Call it luck, fate or pure coincidence, he entered my life just at the right time when I was at my lowest of lows. My vulnerability was so obvious to him. I was still completely convinced that, although I'm fucked, I'd somehow figure it out...but the curiosity of a sober DJ had me wanting to know more.

"A clean living DJ?...I mean what the fuck? How the hell does a DJ not get off his nut? I just could not comprehend it."

I'd been invited to a family and friends get together at a local campsite. They had a fire, the kids were having fun and everyone was hanging out drinking. Most of the evening I spent dipping in and out of conversation through gritted teeth (turbo-coke-head-waffle). Tony was there, but I hadn't yet said hello. Someone had told me he'd been completely abstinent from all drugs, including alcohol for a total of 5 years. Knowing this freaked me out as much as it intrigued me. I'd always swerved anyone who didn't do what I did, based purely on the warped attitude of..."Can't trust anyone who doesn't drink." I mean, what the fuck was I thinking? Me and my fellow wreckheads used to laugh and joke about people who'd been to rehab. "Rehab's for quitters!"..."Sober pussy's!" All that bullshit banter that comes with big-bollocks-ego. Complete madness.

"That attitude had not only kept me away from the solution, it'd also enabled that fiendish, greedy gremlin (ego) to remain free to reap havoc, regardless of any consequences."

That gremlin finds sober people an inconvenience. It feels judged, attacked even…and subconsciously, I hadn't been prepared to look at my own shit, therefore FUCK OFF! Something had shifted though, and it now blew my mind that anyone could refrain from touching a single drop of alcohol in 5 years.

Anyway, a little later, under the darkness of night, I found myself sitting beside Tony in front of the fire. The ambient glow and hypnotic dance of the flames, serving as the perfect metaphor to a burning desire laying dormant in my soul. We got talking and spoke of our shared passion for music. It was a long distant memory that I once aspired to be an artist, a DJ, or to play in a band perhaps. We talked about creativity, becoming engrossed in conversation over songs we liked. A spark of connection was all it took…the universal power of music was upon us. I didn't know it at the time, but something was beginning to reconcile a part of me I'd forgotten.

"There was a time when I was so connected to expressing my creativity. Music, drawing, skateboarding...I used to do that stuff. Where had it all gone?"

That night we arranged to hang out at Tony's place, where his decks, mixer and a fat collection of vinyl awaited. I felt a tiny spark of excitement, inspired even…but most of all, I sensed I could trust him. He was different. For starters he was sober, which meant he was safe. It was also unconditional. He didn't want anything from me, and you know what, for the first time in as long as I could remember, I just knew I didn't want anything from him either. That in itself was invaluable…and at the time, I had absolutely no idea that what he was about to give me, was greater than any material worth imaginable.

Just as planned, later that week I went to see him. I remember calling on route to ask if he minded me bringing alcohol, as I respected he didn't drink. He was cool about it, so I bought a four pack, and of course I had a cheeky bit of gear with me, but I definitely didn't want Tony to know that. That's what blew my mind…he was sober, but he never once judged me for drinking. We spent the evening hanging out, mixing, talking. I'd snide off to his toilet to do a crafty line of coke, returning and trying to act like 'normal'. Still to this day he remains adamant he never knew. Damn, I must of been good. I must admit, I did have that 'flush-and-sniff' on lockdown.

"The following week I returned to Tony's. Same scenario, this time I didn't pick up any gear or booze."

Something had shifted. Unbeknown to me at this time, I'd already made a significant decision to change the outcome, a definitive realisation...and even if it hadn't been a conscious decision, it certainly came from a subconscious level. Was I starting to see a way out? A new found hope? A lifeline?

We spent more time out on his balcony talking than we did playing music. The conversation got deep. I made a confession to him, something I had not ever dared to do...I told him about my crank behaviour, the panic attacks, the psychotic episodes and my latest meltdown just days ago in the basement toilet of that restaurant. How I'd scared myself shitless and feared for my life... the desperation, self hatred and suicidal thoughts.

"He listened, and I could tell he got it, really fuckin' got it."

He responded, by telling me about the madness of his former life, the party prescription of class A's he used on a daily basis, the chaos, the drama, his dysfunction...we had different stories, but the similarities were undeniably real. Desperation, confusion and isolation. That's what did it for me. "Fuck me, he understood." He talked about himself as if it were me. He had literally described how I felt, and in that instant my fate was sealed.

He went on to assure me that his life now was incomparable. How it'd just got better and better each day he'd been 'clean'...and I could see this. It was just so alarmingly obvious how at peace he was. He radiated happiness and a sense of contentment…and that was bloody damn attractive to me. "I want what you've got dude… whatever the fuck it is…I am in." It was like he was filling my empty hope doughnut with gallons upon gallons of glorious jam (easy tigers)…and fuck it, a shit load of icing on top for good measure.

I'd dared to share the inner workings of my mind…I trusted him, I knew I could tell him honestly what was really going on for me. No more…"I'm fine"…I could finally dare to take my mask off, revealing my vulnerability in all its glory.

"I was now ready to be the student."

We're told constantly in society that vulnerability is a weakness, especially if you're a guy. Granted, if you dare to reveal your 'sensitive side' amongst the likes of Johnny Big Bollocks and co, you're probably gonna end up fish bait. It's bullshit, but it's just the way it is. The way I see it, Big Bollocks is flat out ego, pure and simple. It's not real, it's fake.

"Vulnerability is strength and courage. It's real and it's truth."

That night before I left Tony, he said to me…"There is another way to live your life ya know, if you really want it." I didn't have to think twice…"Holy shit, I DO!" He asked if I'd like to go with him to one of his support groups the following night, a place he called 'the rooms'…He told me it was a safe place, a community of like-minded people all striving for a better way of being. It didn't even enter my mind to say no. I was ready to start over.

As promised, the following night we went to that support group. The fact I stayed true to my word was a monumental achievement. I was scared of the unknown, but it somehow felt natural to do it. I didn't tell a soul I was going…"Might as well apply the same secret squirrel attitude in remaining covert"…it's just my priorities and moral compass had realigned.

"I was now seeking truth and sanity, not deceit and chaos."

I remember it like it was yesterday. We drove to a notoriously sketchy part of North London. One of Tony's mates, Ricky the Bricky, joined us. He sat for the entire ride up there on the backseat supping a can of beer. That in itself baffled me. I later heard that these 'rooms' held a strong belief that anyone is welcome…"You just need the desire to stop doing whatever the fuck it is you're doing." In matey's case, a desire to stop drinking, he just hadn't achieved it yet.

The meeting was held in a church hall. I gotta admit, that caused me some apprehension...but I ignored any doubts, based purely on my absolute desperation to find happiness. As we pulled up in the car park, I noticed a group of people all standing around near the doorway. I couldn't help but think..."Blimey, what a bunch of scallies"...but as we approached, I was greeted with the biggest warm reception. "Hugs not drugs"....hmm...I must admit I was suspicious, and a sudden flashback to the 'good ol days' of raving.

"Oh, hang on a minute, that's...hugs on drugs!"

We sat around on chairs in a circle, inward facing, with the lights low. I continued to feel decisively suspicious, whilst the guy leading the group began to read from a scripted card. At this point, I'm kinda half expecting a goat to appear for us all to slaughter in ritual. For the next hour or so I struggled to maintain any real focus on what was being said. Instead, I scanned the room, and one by one, made personal judgments and preconceptions of each attendee.

"Fuck me, I'm not as bad as him, he looks fucked!... Jeez, she's straight off the street, homeless for sure...and he's definitely still on smack, look at the state of him!"

In hindsight, my head was still really busy, amplified to the max with chattering and noise. I now know this crazy head takes a little time to quieten. A guest speaker was sharing his life story and how he'd found sobriety. I wasn't hearing any similarities to my own life, only differentiating myself to him. "Am I even this bad?...Do I really need to be here?" (Bloody ego - "Shut the fuck up ya little punk!") I actually did say to Tony on route, that I'd go for as long as needs be, perhaps a month, sort my shit out, and I'd be good to go...which in hindsight was naive on my part.

"Spoiler alert - the path of redemption aka truth, is not a quick fix...in fact, I now know it's a lifestyle...and one that requires discipline, dedication and heart."

It wasn't until the very end, when the last person spoke, that something happened that would cement my feet on this path I'd discovered. He was an older guy, looked a little bit like a washed out rockstar...I'd already made an assumption of him being a wannabe member of some supergroup from the 70s...perhaps his name was Warlock or something. Anyway, as soon as he opened his mouth, the words he spoke were to me, poetic. In the space of 5 minutes, he described with such eloquence, how once upon a time, before he'd got sober, he'd go to the Glastonbury festival, put on his 'I'm invincible' guise (hmm, I'm the fuckin' Badman)...and,

indulge in a monstrous drug fuelled celebration of debauchery…
"I'm thinking and acting like I'm with the bands or some shit, when in all reality, I'm a hopeless wreckhead crippled with insecurity." He described word perfect the unquenchable thirst of craving, the desire for more and more with no off button and no self respect. Oblivion at its finest. Total excess and insanity guaranteed.

"At the very end of the festival, when all the punters were going home, I'd blag my way backstage and stay on with the crews for the endless after party."

BOOM!! That was it, sold. I knew from that moment I was qualified to be there. Straight after the meeting, Warlock approached me and asked for my number. He reassured me I was in the right place, and to keep coming back. I went home that night inspired and completely hooked on this new way of being. "Fuck, if only I'd known sooner!" That desire to stop using drugs (the drugs were using me), the boozing, the partying and the chaos it ensued…deep down it had been there for a longtime, I just didn't know what to do with it. THERE IS ANOTHER WAY, Tony and Warlock were right.

The next day I received a text message from Warlock…"Feels good to be sober, right?…Have a beautiful day brother." Fuck me, I wasn't used to such pleasantries. I'd been long accustomed to the usual…"Where's my fuckin' money?"…or…"Where did you snide off to last night?" Warlock was right, it did feel good to be sober, and for the first time in as long as I could remember, I could tell it was definitely gonna be a beautiful day.

SKATE OR DIE

The very first weekend of my abstaining drugs, I had a major wobble. It was on the Sunday, just a couple days since I'd attended the rooms. I was feeling positive…recovering from the hellraising was my absolute goal now, but I wasn't out of the woods just yet, far from it.

"I was still learning the absolute importance of association to sobriety, not booze and chemicals in early recovery."

If I'd realised that at the time, I'd of saved myself the bother. Looking back, I'd certainly done the right thing remaining secret about my attending support groups, yet I was still working out how to hold myself in social situations. Putting it simply, sobriety isn't everyone's cup of tea…and in 2009…it certainly wasn't like it is now, where it's widely accepted (kinda). The way I see it, you've got three options when stepping in or out of the 'recovery bubble'…

1 - Don't tell anyone. Your personal aspirations are sacred and therefore not to be scoffed at. Keep it zipped and awkwardly make your excuses.

2 - Tell everyone and their dog. You're a reformed wreckhead who's 'seen the light'. Bulletproof, but be warned...it can potentially serve as a social hand-grenade. As soon as that pin's pulled out and thrown...BOOOM!! Pisshead repellant. Not necessarily a bad thing if you wanna safeguard your sanity in an emergency.

3 - Sidestep the issue. Similar to option 1...however, requires conviction, as you confidently explain with a rather nifty (and creative) reason for your lifestyle choices - "I'm a professional athlete, don't ya know?"

You're always gonna get 'that someone' (usually wasted) who's gonna try and fuck with your shit..."You tellin' me you're never gonna touch a drop ever again? But whyyyy??...surely you can have just one drink?...don't be such a pussy!" Of course the answer to the 'why are they fuckin' with my shit?'...is simple...cos they don't understand, nor do they care to...and I'd dare to go as far as saying they certainly don't want what you're seeking (not yet anyway). That's not to say they don't need it, or can't have it. Deep down they may have that lingering sense of..."Help me, please I'm drowning in sorrow!" I sure as hell know that one!

"It's really easy to flatline into oblivion waiting for something to happen, so it's business as usual."

Anyway, I'd attended an event where alcohol was flowing. I could feel the cravings getting increasingly stronger as I watched punters slowly getting more drunk. I was still precariously navigating the pangs of withdrawal, which at times were a mindfuck and damn right gnar. Just days sober, that time had granted me the sense of clarity to get on my toes…(cue option 1). A truly remarkable improvement to my old default…"Fuck it!" Without saying a word, I got the hell outta there.

"Back-door-Dave to the rescue, for all the right reasons."

For as long as I could remember, there hadn't been a single Sunday where I hadn't got bent out of shape. "What the fuck am I meant to do with myself?" In hindsight…go find a frickin' support group, or call Tony or Warlock…but I was still wrestling pride, ego and control. "Don't bother anyone with your problems…you can do this alone"…but I couldn't, that'd been the problem all along.

Feeling spun out and unsure what to do, I went and sat in my car. As I'm sitting there, I suddenly thought to myself…"Hang on a minute, there's a skateboard in the boot." Rewind to when me and Tasha were still together...I'd had an overwhelming urge to skate. She thought I was bonkers, but I bought a board anyway. It didn't really surmount to much...I was too self conscious and lacked confidence, so it was a non starter, but the board remained in the boot of my car ever since.

I have no doubt that initial desire to skate, was my 'inner child' desperately seeking the innocence and pure essence of what skating had given me all those years ago. It was incredibly empowering to be a skater. It gave me a sense of connection when I needed it most. My saviour, my friend, my escape. When drugs came along I lost my way, I simply gave up on skating, yet it had never given up on me, ever...and when I'd switched out rolling concrete for rolling big arse doobies, something changed. Popping pills became more appealing than popping ollies, and the only lines I carved were white. "Damn, how the fuck did it all go so wrong?"

"I took the time to reflect on how two whole decades had passed me by, yet somehow I'd come out of all that chaos unscathed."

With a burst of adrenaline (and immense gratitude), I started my car and found myself on a mission to go skate. That sense of freedom and adventure had always been such a fundamental part of skating.

As soon as those wheels hit concrete, it was like I'd come back home. I guess you could say I'd switched the ritualistic rush of chemical enhancement, for the ritualistic rush of adrenaline fuelled skating…an instant relief, losing myself once more from how I was feeling. With my focus switched to skating, the anxiety seemed to disappear and with it the cravings.

Funny how life can go full circle…skating saved me back in the day, and it certainly hadn't failed me now. With a very real realisation that I needed to stay vigilant, I decided from that moment I needed to get fit. I was a tad beer bloated, out of shape and unenergised. The rooms could take care of my mind, but what about my body? Each morning from that day, I made a decision to run 2 miles before work, and skate or go to the gym after.

"In the evenings, I could sit in a room full of recovering wreckheads and remain connected and stable."

It all became part of the vital support I needed, at a crucial time where I'd tried to do it on my own, but wasn't strong enough. If you're anything like me, those insatiable cravings will fuck you every time, unless you have the 'We'…I, Me, My got me nowhere fast. I needed help from others, and I certainly gained that 'We' from the people in those rooms. People of like-minds, totally abstinent (or at least trying) and most importantly, people with experience who knew how.

I still valued my old familiar friends as much as these new faces in 'recovery', so I continued to try and establish a healthy balance, but it didn't quite seem to help my cause. That'd been the issue all along - surrounding myself by the problem, a tribe of fellow caners. If I'm gonna be in the solution, it's imperative I be with those not caning it. Those poison thorns of temptation had to be removed somehow.

"With hindsight, I can see I still wanted to have my cake and eat it."

Music festivals were always a staple go-to each summer. Usually we'd bundle into someone's car and do a mass exodus to oblivion, Warlock style. So when the time came, I was extremely optimistic (naive) to think it was ok to even contemplate it. Perhaps my greedy gremlin was secretly plotting to have some playtime? With a quiet underlying sense of trepidation, I stupidly agreed to go with Itch, who drove us there. I spent the entire day trying my best to avoid drug fucked punters, which to be fair was near on impossible. I'd made the right decision just days ago to do a 'back-door-Dave' and go skate...but a festival? "Fuck what was I thinking?" I secretly endured tidal waves of cravings whilst pretending to be absolutely fine. "You alright Dave?"...."Yeah, everything's cool mate." Itch was very respectful of my sobriety, so he wasn't the issue...it was my resistance to accept I just wasn't ready to be in certain situations yet.

"If you don't wanna be surrounded by clowns, don't go to the circus...as they say."

The day turned into night, and thankfully Itch agreed it was time to leave. I'd somehow made it out in one piece, sober. What I realised from that day on..."Never put yourself in a situation you can't get out of." I'd done that all my life, but now things were changing...I was actually beginning to understand. Lesson learnt.

A rather extraordinary thing came out of my being at that festival, which at the time didn't really seem to be anything at all. I remember clear as day walking across the fields soon after arriving. I was carrying a bag of energy drinks (still learning), chatting to some random dude who was carrying a crate of beer. The dude was quizzing me..."Mate, why are you not gettin' fucked up?" I replied in the only way possible..(option 2, the grenade) "Cos I'm in recovery from being a wreckhead. I'm sober and don't drink... given it up mate." It blew his mind, just like it had mine when I first knew Tony the DJ was abstinent.

"I hadn't realised it at that time, but he was also trying to figure out how to get help. Unbeknown to me (and him), a seed had been planted."

Fast forward a couple years. I was sitting in a support group waiting for it to begin, when I catch the eye of some dude who seemed to be staring at me. "You don't remember me, do ya?"...he says, as I'm trying to think where I know him from. As I do, he goes on to say... "V festival...remember?" Blimey...as soon as he mentioned it the penny dropped. "Holy shit!" He then went on to tell me..."You showed me it was possible to get clean, to be sober. Well, here I am." I couldn't quite believe it...how something so trivial to me, could be so profoundly significant to him.

I guess you could say that 'option 2' doesn't just safeguard your sanity, it can also serve as a potent message of hope, for those who deep down need it most...and being at that festival sober, surrounded by tens of thousands of annihilated partyheads...well, if you can do that, you can do absolutely anything.

"Fuck man, this shit is truly powerful!"

BYE NOW, SEE YOU

Giving up your former self, the old you, the person you thought you were, is hard, bloody hard. It won't happen over night, so don't expect it to. That was my experience anyway. It takes balls, and it's something that once you commit to, will become the best choice you ever made.

If you're anything like me, you've probably often wondered what life would, or could of been. I wondered so frequently… "What would I be doing at this precise moment in time, if it wasn't for the fact that I'm flatlining my way through life?" A dedicated master of the art of being reckless…I had no real direction or motivation to even try and change the status quo. Through fear, I could not bring myself to make the vital changes. Instead, I'd become accustomed to, and settling for…"This is my lot"…or so I thought.

The relief of finally surrendering and admitting your powerlessness is indescribable. That insurmountable burden I'd carried around for all those years, was finally lifted the minute I said out loud…

"Hi, my name is Dave, and I am an addict."

I'd previously done a trial run, in front of that judge in the courtroom, to perhaps a couple of debt collectors and even a few drug dealers along the way to get out of punishment...but never did I sincerely feel it in my heart and soul. This was different. The decision had been made, and it was mine to own. Without that, it was never gonna stick.

In the height of the madness, I'd often had the thought... "Why am I doing this to myself?"...and it was very obvious how it was making me feel, yet I was so debilitated by the delusion of denial, that I just could not break free from it. The more I sat in support groups, the more unquestionable it became that addiction had played an integral role in my decline all along.

"Had I been the sort of dude who could stay stopped whenever I wanted? Nope. That's the clear cut deal breaker for me right there."

The rooms of recovery and the people in it, well, put it this way... when you've got countless people all sharing the same 'truth' about how fucked up denial, addiction and the chaos it ensues...I was able to sit there and quietly calculate in my own mind, and for me, eradicate any reservations, reinforcing my self realisation that I had indeed been an addict and needed to be there. All I experienced...

the lowest of lows, the 'romanticised' suicidal thoughts, the constant savage slaying of self and ultimately the demise of my mental health, it inadvertently brought me to a place of reflection. I had countless realisations that it wasn't meant to be like this, that I'd lost my way and just needed some help and guidance to steer me back to my truth.

After those early warning signs that cravings are very real...I started to realise that I was a 34 year old man-boy, having to learn basic life skills once more. The rooms, and the fellowship it brought, enabled me to see clearly that I needed to change my attitude a fair bit, in order to recover. I now know this as 'emotional sobriety'.

"It's one thing remaining abstinent from mindfuck chemicals, but actually getting well is another. I was told it takes time, and that's difficult for someone like me who's accustomed to instant gratification."

Tony had not only become my trusted confident, he would also act as a mentor. We had a chat about my work situation, which seemed to reveal I might want to consider changing my livelihood. Being a slippery salesman on the road to redemption ain't gonna cut it...and in the words of Tony..."It ain't good Karma man"...so I decided to say goodbye to that straight away. No more skullduggery. I pulled that thorn, which was one poisonous muddafudda, right out.

I resigned to the prospect of taking some time out to figure out what it was I wanted to do. In the meantime, I was gonna focus on my wellbeing. I decided to apply for some counselling sessions at a local treatment centre. Those sessions really helped me explore my emotional world. In the support groups I was still very anxious and too self conscious to talk openly and honestly, so having that counsellor enabled me to build my confidence. With their help, I applied for financial support. It felt shit getting handouts, but I just knew it wouldn't be forever. I had plans.

Work wasn't the only thing to get the chop. I just knew in my heart I needed to do the right thing and say farewell to Amba, and the other 'partners' I'd been entangled with. With redemption comes a conscience, and mine was now dialled in to at least try and be a better person, period.

"This would prove harder to abstain than I first thought...with every best intention, I was nowhere near getting it right."

Having said goodbye to Amba, I decided to go visit a 'mate' called Tamsin who'd moved to the coast. She was amazed and happy for me to be sober. We spent the weekend walking in the sprawling countryside and tending to her beloved horses. It was whilst there, that I had a moment of 'serendipity'…or maybe it was 'synchronicity', something I'd been learning from Tony. If you'd asked me what synchronicity meant only a few weeks back, I'd of said it was something to do with Swiss watchmaking. As for serendipity…"Isn't that some trippy character from a mad cartoon?"

Being present in life, connected, was to me a brand new experience. I'd been disconnected for so long, it came with heightened exhilaration that I was now able to notice things I hadn't even acknowledged before. How on earth could I pay attention when I'm off my crackers all the time? It was as though I'd changed the lens of my camera to which I viewed the world, giving it more clarity, more bang for the buck…sharper. Trees seemed to pop out as though to be three dimensional, I could hear birds tweeting with such vibrancy, where as before I'd wanna shoot 'em down for disrupting my paranoid existence, in those early dawn lockdowns behind closed doors.

"Everything took on a whole new meaning."

I'd found myself in Tamsin's study room, confronted by a bookcase covering the entire length of the wall. There were row upon row of books, and as I held my attention to them, my eyes seemed to lock in on one particular book just staring back at me. It had an orange coloured sleeve with the title 'The Teachings of Buddha' running along the spine. As I picked it out to hold, Tamsin came in and said…"Would you like to have it?…I studied it at college and no longer need it." I didn't really give it much thought, so I said… "Yeah, thanks"…and carried on flicking through the pages.

"For those coming weeks that ensued, I'd often dive into that book…and the one thing that kept jumping off the page was meditation, meditation, meditation."

Unbeknown to me…'meditation, meditation, mediation', was in fact the much needed 'stillness, stillness, stillness' that I was so in need of, yet had never acquired. The chill, the calm, the god damn peace of mind. Finding recovery was my introduction to that becoming a reality, and with a little help from some bald headed dude called Buddha, the art of 'stillness' would become the inner sanctuary taking it to a whole new level.

It was clear the teachings, philosophy and the general tone of Buddhism was very anarchic, compared to the more traditional and conventional ways to live. It seemed to me those bald headed dudes were a posse of outlaw rebels living outside the mainstream ideal. "Fuck yeah, my kinda guys!" I could see many similarities to the ethos of sobriety…after all, attaining and practicing total abstinence from all mind altering substances seems to be full on impossible for mainstream society…it's frickin' damn hard to do, which is why it's bad-arse-punk and a radical act of unparalleled strength. There aren't many who achieve it, and even if they do, some can't stomach it and quit. Far easier to follow the crowd and be a sheep, no? I know that's how it was for me anyway.

"Those blissed out monks refrain from all intoxicants and seem pretty chill to me."

The teachings encourage you to be curious, to not blindly obey, to turn against the mainstream and always, ALWAYS question the status quo…"Don't believe what you're told until further investigation…go find out for yourself through direct experience!" Nice. I'd kinda held this ideology anyway…"Fuck the system and all that"…Danger Axe the punk and skating was my introduction to that attitude, however, I just needed a wiser response to life. That book came at precisely the right time.

"Hmm…so maybe serendipity isn't just a trippy cartoon character after all."

On that same day, I decided to stop smoking cigarettes and roll-ups. Since being sober, I'd upped my coffee intake to get through the withdrawals…"Strong, dash of milk with two heaped sugars please." I'd also been skulling energy drinks throughout the day, and was still chuffing away on nicotine. I must admit, I remember thinking to myself..."Christ, I'm just as wired now as I was on the gear!"...I mean, it's not exactly comparable, but I just knew that if I'm gonna be sober, I wanna at least feel like it. I made a conscious decision to stop right there, disposing the energy drinks stashed in Tamsin's fridge, and I got rid of the fags in a random bin on a beach whilst out walking her dog. I haven't had a puff since.

"Something had clearly shifted in my thinking."

Like the layers of an onion, I was beginning to peel away any unwanted habits that I'd clung onto like my life depended on it. Each time, the hardest layer being denial. With hindsight, having found safety in recovery, I automatically assumed that if I can remove the poisonous thorns of chemical intoxicants, then surely the seductive thorns of female 'company' would be a breeze. Saying goodbye to those potent pleasures for an ex-thrill seeker is a tough one. That's been my experience anyway. I'd managed to cease certain things, namely killing myself on substances such as alcohol, cocaine and other narcs...however, the prospect of endeavouring to navigate romantic interactions was a whole new playing field.

"You telling me I gotta be a Saint?"

Hmm....well, I can only say, for me...that shit didn't come easy, far from it.

SHOULD'A, WOULD'A, COULD'A

Having to start over in my 30's was a minefield. It wasn't until I sat my arse down in those rooms that I seriously heard some truths. Hearing other peoples shite unearthed a ton of realisations about my own life. That's the beauty of recovery and support groups, you've got a shit load of like-minded people getting real, so naturally it encourages you to do the same, if you're ready.

Tony entering my life at the right time was the catalyst, instilling the belief and igniting a burning desire to do better. My life up until that point had been riddled with regret, so I felt I couldn't afford to waste another second. I kept hearing people in the groups say..."Get a sponsor" (think sober sensei)..."Work the steps" (a wreckheads guide to self improvement)...and I also heard..."You need to go to any lengths." Well fuck me, I'd go to any lengths to get what I wanted pre recovery, so turning that finely-tuned skill to good use made total sense...especially if it meant getting well. I decided to treat recovery no different to the getting and using of drugs. Get a sponsor?...well, like a drug dealer, I wanna go to the best. As for working the steps?...I'm gonna tear the fuckin' arse out of it, just like the drugs.

"So I embarked on a quest to find the Tony Montana of sponsors."

No different to the world of narcs, the same name kept cropping up as the 'go-to'…a guy called Donny Scot, a renowned Scotsman. Having got his number, I called him to ask if we could meet. A few days later we met at a cafe in town. To be honest, I was shitting myself. I could tell he was a no-messing kinda guy, but I just knew it's what I wanted, and more importantly, what I needed. I was well accustomed to gnarly, fuck-you-meatheads, so surely this dude who helps people recover would be a doddle, right? He spent the entire time trying to talk me out of sobriety. In hindsight, he was seeing how dedicated I was to the cause. Was I willing to 'go to any lengths' to get my recovery? "Yes I fookin' am." He told me to stay sober for 30 days, to call him each day at an arranged time, and...if I could do that, he'd help.

I knew straight away I could do it. I was ready. I'd managed to scrape through previously more than once. Those sketchy 'detox' January's. Granted I'd always somehow remain sober the entire month (through gritted teeth), safe in the knowledge that come 1st February, I'd more than make up for it. With hindsight, that obsession to get mash-up had never left me…but this was different, and I knew it.

"There was no question…I was committed 100%"

I got my 30 days…and I just knew I'd keep going. Attending groups regularly, hanging out with Tony and continuing to keep fit all helped. Through the groups I was meeting a variety of ex-hellraisers…all these really fuckin' cool people, fellow creatives and lost souls on a mission to heal, striving for a better life. I couldn't of felt more inspired and alive.

Donny Scot helped me traipse through the wreckage of my destructive behaviour. To begin with it was alien. A complete new challenge, but one I was keen to engage with. I don't think I could of undertaken this task on my own. That'd been the problem all along…not allowing anyone in, not trusting or asking for help. That blasted pride and ego man. Always stuck in fear.

"He helped me bulldoze my way through that fear and learn to deal with life head on."

One of the first things he encouraged me to do, was to…"Take ya god doon cotton wool oot ya ears n steck it in ya god doon moof." In other words…"Shut the fuck up and listen!" He was right. I never could acknowledge what was being said…always interrupting with selective hearing. Totally self-absorbed, either I didn't wanna hear it, or my head was too damn noisy and cluttered, racing at 1000 mph. As for being annihilated…you may as well of been talking to a brick wall.

A common theme that began to reappear throughout this early stage of self discovery, was there were a hell of a lot of things I hadn't been taking responsibility for. I'd simply checked out, avoiding any kind of accountability. I guess that's escapism right there, and what better way to do it than getting drug fucked. Through open and honest discussion with Donny Scot and fellow participants at the support groups, I began to unravel the carnage laid out before me. In those very early days of quite literally waking up to the truth, there was no more side stepping around the issues that came to light.

"My avoidant nature had been well and truly rumbled."

You may wonder why having to regress back to your past behaviour has any relevance to all this redemption malarkey. Well, I did too to begin with…and to be honest, it annoyed me a tad to say the least, because there was an immense feeling of inadequacy, shame, guilt and regret attached to it…and this in turn made me 'quietly' angry. I soon came to learn, however, that 'self introspection' would help me understand my thinking, my actions, and more importantly, how I could change them, for the better.

"I needed to be challenged, to get real and process the mess I'd dodged for way too long."

It was clear I hadn't been turning up for myself in life. Or to put it another way, I'd been misrepresenting myself. I kinda knew this on an intellectual level, yet I'd ignored it. I'd been anaesthetised long ago, and had remained in that uncomfortably numb state for so long, that it'd become the norm. Every day a monotonous bore of mostly suppressive emotion. Every little aspect of my life had become amplified into an astronomically sized ball ache of a problem. "Why won't it all just fuck off?" It wasn't until I started talking about my shit that I realised I wasn't alone. In fact, there were people like me with the same outlook in life dotted all over the place. "Ahh, well I'll be blown, so it ain't just me!" That was a true revelation in itself...and extremely reassuring, as it was empowering.

There's a saying that goes something like..."Without a reflection, how can one see their self?" Bloody brilliant, and bloody true. That was my problem. I was so absorbed in my own bullshit, I couldn't possibly see what I was doing and how it had an adverse effect, not only on myself, but to others. Perhaps that incident in the basement toilet where I saw my reflection of death, maybe that was indeed the most prolific reflection I ever needed? That initial jolt of acceptance it brought, would go on to serve me, so I could continue to focus on self reflection, introspection and a new life of freedom.

"To be out of that self-centred world was not only a relief, it was truly liberating."

I could see I'd stacked up so much regret. Those venomous thorns are killer. I lived my life by that blasted code…"Fuck it, it'll be alright"…accumulating a whole bunch of consequences along the way. I'd witness other people, close friends, progressing in life. New partners, jobs, homes, kids and so on, and I'd suffer in silence, crippled with envy, self-pity and confusion…"How the fuck?… Why such luck?" I'd see someone succeed, and secretly say to myself…"I could do that"…but I never did. Instead, I'd make a clusterfuck of a situation and my first thought would be…"Fuck it"…followed by…"I should'a done this"…or…"If only I could'a done that"…or…"I would'a, but…" It was the same old story for pretty much everything.

I learnt about procrastination. Honestly, I'd never even acknowledged the word before. "Procrastination, is that some kinda weird shit? The removal of swollen anal glands or something?" Nope - apparently not. Fear of taking action. Stalling. Throw into the mix not paying attention, and it's a deadly cocktail which did me over every time. Ditching this self defeating 'Should'a-Would'a-Could'a' mindset was hard to do, because it was so ingrained in me. It had been a life long habit which was hard to quit, but like all bad habits, replacing the old with the new was precisely what I set out to do.

"I needed to lose the mindset 'TRY'...and instead apply a new one...'DO."

Donny Scot helped me retrain my attitude from..."I will TRY and do something special for myself"...to a much more positive intention of..."I will DO something special for myself." As simple as that may sound, it took a shit ton of practice and a lot of failures (patience being a virtue I was still acquiring). Slowly but surely I began to make progress. With help, I was now squeezing out the poison thorns one by one, and beginning to replace them with the seeds of goodness.

That book Tamsin had given me was proving to reinforce this new ideology. With very basic instructions from that bald headed dude Buddha, I started to study the teachings on meditation (stillness), enough to understand it can really help the untrained (anxious) mind gain perspective and discipline. Previously, I'd had a serious lack of both, with zero capacity for 'mental stamina'...

which I now know to be essential for maintaining a positive mindset. "No wonder I never stood a chance against that pesky little fecker…that bloody gremlin ego/addict thinking!"

"I had fuck all mental defence."

I was still learning, but through continued practice and experimentation, I was beginning to uncover a whole new method of thinking. This proved to be a real game changer at a time when I needed it most, and one that has improved my life dramatically ever since.

RED FLAGS

Everyone knows the universal meaning of a red flag. In Formula One it indicates a crash has incurred and a possible premature end to the race. If you're on a beach anywhere in the world and you see a lifeguards red flag, it would usually signify to stay the fuck out of the water, it's dangerous...shark or a floater!…and we all know what a red flag does to a feisty big arse Bull. When looking back at my life in its entirety, I began to see something I'd never really acknowledged properly.

"It had been littered with 'red flag' situations...sketchy people, sketchy places and sketchy things."

One example to encapsulate this in its totality, is my experience on that god forsaken island, when I somehow made it home unscathed. All the signs were there. Big, almighty red flags swaying right before my eyes, but I was too blind to see them. Undeniable danger, however, those people, the place and the things that put me in so much risk and at harm never registered. Why?

When you're drug fucked, disconnected from all reality, delusional thinking appears to be rational. You no longer pay attention or take heed to 'red flag' scenarios. "NEVER, EVER get in a taxi and ask the driver to take you to find drugs or women." Remember? These very real, extremely volatile acts of insanity continue to play out, and it's like the body is there, but you're separate from it...kinda just participating in the mayhem as it unfolds...a slave to your own downfall, with absolute zero accountability. Now, of course when you're slap bang in the middle of a psychotic episode, I'd say it's near on impossible to separate what's actually real, and what's created in the confines of your twisted little noodle...but, the outcome is the same...chaos.

"For me, getting real, self-introspection and the desire to change my ways, brought a hell of a lot of insight...

...a much as it did self-respect, confidence and some much needed peace of mind."

It didn't just empower me, it installed a self belief that I could do anything, and I mean anything. Cocaine had always instilled a false sense of grandiose...a narcissistic, inflated ego adept to any worthy James Bond villain. This was a different kind of empowerment, on a whole new level...and it didn't cost a thing. All I had to do was share my truth with those who knew best, listen...and remain open and willing.

It was time to start working through the wreckheads guide to self improvement with my sober Sensei, Donny Scot. Step 1 - 'Admit your utterly powerless. Addiction has you by the kahoonas and your life has turned to shit'..."Hmm, let me see...er, yep...I believe I can safely say my life had been a complete clusterfuck." The evidence was clear to me now. Of course it wasn't all bad. When you start out experimenting in life there's always a sense of curiosity, invincibility and excitement that comes with that, but it definitely didn't end that way. Twenty years of undeniable evidence had left me with absolutely no doubt in my mind. Next!

"If I'd had any reservations about how bad it was, my wall of denial would not have broken."

As the weeks turned into months, I started to realise I couldn't do certain things anymore. These red flags were now really obvious to me. Tony had mentioned bad karma. "If you do the right thing, the right thing happens." It's kinda obvious, a very simple premise, however...like a lot of things, I hadn't been paying attention, and I'd somehow missed the point because I was too damn busy getting wrecked. Showing up for yourself and being present, reconnects a sense of conscience, and with that comes a healthy dollop of pride, integrity, dignity and authenticity...perhaps the moral compass for the map of life...and this means it's harder to get away with old behaviours without really noticing the consequences to them. "Bugger!" Ignorance is bliss.

"Oh well, I had to accept that if you wanna have a better life, doing the right thing counts, big time."

Attending regular support groups really helped me stay focused on the prize - remaining sober and living a healthier lifestyle. My wellbeing depended on it. Outside of that recovery bubble, it became evident I had to adjust my environment. I was still seeing my homies, who were still very much there for me...but it became apparent these dudes, my beloved old partners in mischief, were in fact major red flags...triggers, which if pulled, could well derail my recovery train. I was faced with the inevitable...

"I had to safeguard my wellbeing over everything, including my friendships."

We'd meet up in pubs around town...they'd sink pint after pint of beer, and I'd be matching every slurp with a tonic water and lime. In hindsight, I didn't know any better and neither did they. I was still new to all this. I didn't wanna be in pubs and around drunk people, yet I still had trouble communicating that to my mates. It's not just about being around booze and drugs, it's the crazy arse shit that potentially spews onto you from mashed up punters...in some cases quite literally! "Fuck, I was now on the receiving end!" The irony.

Jimmy knew it was a problem, he actually did me a favour by declaring..."I'm a red flag aren't I?"...I responded by saying..."For now, yeah." I just knew that if I'm gonna stay on this path, I gotta be around sober people...and I can't expect everyone to not drink just because I don't. I now know this to be a very wise decision indeed. That instilled the confidence for me to make a phone call to another dude, who was getting married. He was incredibly supportive when I declared..."Mate, I can't come, it's just too soon." I was a mere fledgling in recovery, who'd of been seriously outnumbered in a situation I wasn't yet ready to be in. I'd survived the festival, but this was too close to home, with too many homies gettin' on it…

"Imagine standing amongst the Arsenal fans at their home game, wearing a Tottenham Hotspur shirt…that's a newly sober person at a mash up wedding."

Me and Tony had been going to a music producer's studio to make music. He was a prolific space cadet, lovely guy, but fuck me could he smoke ganja. Wake and bake…I swear this maniac chonged in his sleep. We'd played out at clubs around London a handful of times. DJing was exhilarating, but being in a nightclub until 4 in the morning surrounded by drug fucked punters wasn't my idea of recovery, and neither was leaving matey's studio feeling half baked from inhaling the green. I was beginning to question my dedication to the cause. Could I stay safe and well whilst living a double life DJing at nightclubs?...For me, it was a big fat no, so I decided to stop. I called Tony and was straight up honest. Fuck me, this honesty malarkey was proving to be a good thing.

"It felt great to be able to speak my truth, to have a voice and use it. Perks of getting real - empowerment."

Navigating a pathway to redemption is like the board game snakes and ladders. For every high point, comes a low. Anyone who thinks it's easy all the time is hugely mistaken. For me, it was learning to accept that early on, and continue to walk the path regardless. There was so much power in the 'We' aspect of recovery, and the camaraderie it provided. Pre-recovery I could not do it alone, and now I didn't have to.

There seemed to still be consequences to my old behaviour that were coming back to haunt me. Some were unavoidable, however…where as before I'd deny all accountability, I was learning to accept 'what is'…and take responsibility for whatever came my way. I had immense apprehension when negotiating multiple old drug debts. My usual, old response to these, would be to either sidestep the issue, run and hide…or, blag my way out of it until I was forced to face the inevitable - pay with the pound or my blood. With hindsight, I think it was a bit naive to think the likes of Meathead Max the bone slayer was simply gonna say…"Ok Dave, sure, course you don't have to pay…oh, and whilst you're there, congrats on ya new lifestyle! Why don't you go treat yourself, have a spa break on me." Whether I liked it or not, I had to pay. As a stark reminder of what I'd left behind - there was one drug debt that'd been 'sold' to a rather notorious lunatic. I managed to settle it, only to later hear he'd taken his own life.

"Jeez, it made me realise just how lucky I was, not just to be alive, but to be free from that chaotic world of misery and insanity."

A true appreciation for what I now had was clearly evident…and to this day, imperative to maintaining a positive attitude. Celebrating 90 days of total abstinence, which for me was unthinkable, only amplified that feeling of achievement. Life was good, and just when I thought it couldn't get any better, a rather unexpected opportunity elevates my gratitude to new heights.

I'd recently bumped into an old friend. Eddy was a hairstylist, a larger than life creative who ran a prestigious franchise of high street salons. She gave me heads up her team were styling hair for a charity fashion show and Gala dinner, hosted by an extremely well known fashion designer, and did I wanna pop by and say hello whilst they're doing the casting for the runway models.

"Er…are you asking me if I wanna come and watch a bunch of beautiful women audition?…is that a trick question?"

Like a moth to a flame, I went straight to the hotel where the casting was being held. Now, my 'old thinking' was still reaping havoc at this point, as I'd automatically assumed it'd be a scene from a Miss

World contest. I mean don't get me wrong, there were certainly beautiful women there, but it was also a casting for guys. I decided to hang around for a bit, but just as I was making my exit, Eddy grabs a hold of me and says…"The host has asked if you'd like to be in the show." My initial thought was…"Shut the fuck up!"…and then it registered…"Holy shit!…Errr…Ok, sure, fuck it…I'll do it."

"Before I knew it, a Polaroid camera's thrust in my face and I'm being introduced to a frickin' fashion icon!"

Now, I've had many unexpected, fucked up, crazy arse things happen to me over the years, yet none of them truly made any sense. Come to think of it, neither did this, but I was so high on life, a life of freedom, that I felt I could do anything…including, what turned out to be me, walking down a runway in nothing but a pair of flippin' boxers in six weeks time! "Shiiizer!"

I left that hotel buzzing from the mere thought of being given such an extraordinary opportunity. I was also ecstatic to be contributing to a good cause (kids with Cancer). It wasn't that long ago I was taking advantage of charities for my own selfish needs, so now I was beginning to make things right and balance the scales.

A few days later I began to panic…"Fuck, what have I signed up for?"…and a ton of self doubt hit me like a freight train. Negative thoughts of…"You're a nobody"…and…"You can't do it, you'll be a laughing stock!"...were popping into my head. Proper imposter syndrome at its finest. So I did my damn hardest to focus on the positive, like how I could follow it through and actually 'DO' what I've set out to achieve. I'd discovered sharing my fears and insecurities with those who understood could empower me...

"That support from the recovery community helped massively, encouraging me to act instead of freeze in fear."

I needed to get in shape, sharpish...so I decided to ask a personal trainer I knew if he could get me runway ready, to help dissolve my physical insecurities. His response was..."You'll hate me, probably throw ya guts up...and it'll hurt like hell, but yeah, sure, I can get you in shape no probs." Those following weeks he was not wrong. He punished me, coming close to actually passing out on more than one occasion from one too many chin-ups, or another round of savage squats. I give him his dues, I was in shape.

A few days before the big night, on the absolute down-low, I decided to go and see a mate who ran a tanning shop. I'd always received immense banter from the homies for being so tanned all the time (perks of not doing a 9 to 5)...'Solarium Dave' and 'Dagenham Dave' were common names given by the likes of Bumble and Itch, hinting I was a user of such fake remedies, when in fact I wasn't. My head was telling me…"If I'm gonna be pretty much naked for all to see, I'm flippin' well wearing some kind of armour, so a spray tan would have to do!" I gave my friend strict instructions…"Pleeease don't transform me into a human Oompa Loompa!"

"The prospect of walking down a runway, dressed in sweet FA with luminous orange skin, didn't exactly appeal to the understated look I was going for. Luckily she got it spot on."

On the night of the gala, I was fluctuating between nervous pangs of adrenaline fuelled anxiety, and calm, self assured acceptance of 'what is'. I'd been studying more and more from the bald headed one. Meditative stillness had become a daily practice. It was early days, but it'd already given me a new perspective (and the ability to pause), helping combat those precarious moments where I'd completely lose my shit all together.

Backstage, male models were doing press-ups, laughing and joking whilst slurping on the complimentary drinks. I was just focusing on my breath, which I was learning to calm and regulate, bringing it to a sense of ease. What a marvellous revelation. I'd previously tried to do that with weed, booze and cocaine, and wondered why I'd had a heart irregularity and a nervous disposition.

I can honestly say that walking down a runway, whilst being heckled by an entire audience made up of mostly ecstatic women, turned out to be a very liberating experience indeed.

"In approximately 30 secs, I'd not only stepped up and faced my fears head on...but I'd also done it completely sober, in my panties, and I was present for every last second of it."

My brief encounter with the world of fashion, music and skating again, had ignited a desire to be creative once more. A seed had been planted and I just knew I needed to water it. I felt reunited with an old familiar friend, and I wanted to explore that relationship more than anything. Unbeknown to me at that time, the world of hair and fashion was about to become a huge reality in my life. It's like these synchronicities, were aligning me to my path...and now I was present, I could seize the moment without sabotaging it. Beautiful.

LONE WOLF

Coming home

COMING HOME

Getting help was the best god damn thing I'd ever done for myself. I now sat upon a pink fluffy cloud for the most part, with the occasional gust of wind knocking me off course a little, but I wasn't gonna fall off anytime soon. Nope, I was staying put.

Initially, I thought I'd hang around long enough to sort my shit out…"I'll be 'fixed' and able to do things moderately like 'normal' people." Hmmm, I soon realised I needed to stick around for the long haul. I hadn't been able to do it on my own up until this point, and with what was being unravelled, staying connected to a posse of 'truth seekers' was imperative.

With help from the likes of Tony and Donny Scot, I was beginning to find my way back to who I was always meant to be. Breaking down the walls of…"Fuck you, fuck this and fuck that"…a fresh outlook on life was proving to grant me a real sense of coming home. A belonging. It was from this place, that a quest to step into my true purpose was made.

"No more bullshit, no more skullduggery. Just the good stuff, with a few unexpected curveballs to keep me on my toes."

BLOOD LINES

A lot starts to unfold around this time. Life was revealing more and more to me, and it just seemed to keep getting better and better. I now know, with hindsight, that for me, it's only in the safe space of abstinence…that the true authentic process of self discovery could take place. Pre-recovery, I'd been searching, hopelessly trying to find that 'thing', but to no avail. It was clear real change was now happening, although some things were still deeply embedded in my behaviour. My Achilles heel had always been relationships, and I was about to find out that sobriety would prove challenging, especially when a beautiful lady enters.

"It was always suggested that you abstain from relationships in your first year of recovery. Bugger and bollocks."

I didn't quite warm to that idea, so I kinda just assumed rather arrogantly that it didn't apply to me. Some things are more difficult to change than others, right? Ignoring the advice of those who knew best, I started to see a femme fatale called Crystal Meth. Jokes aside, she may as well of been called that, because that's precisely how dangerously potent and addictive she was to me. I'd met Crystal at a support group…"What could possibly go wrong?"

Hmm. I was blissfully riding the crest of the recovery wave without a care in the world. Nothing was gonna get in the way of that, right?

I'd been spending more and more time with a guy called Rocco, a tattooist. We'd initially met in the rooms. I had the utmost respect for him, not just for the skill of his craft, but for the fact he'd been abstinent for many years. That blew my mind and inspired me. Spending time with Rocco made me realise I wanted to pursue a career in the arts more than anything…"No more piss artist!…this here dude has been resurrected!"

"All those years I'd suppressed my love of art…it all came flooding back uncontrollably like a tsunami."

With a cultural clitoris in need of some stimulation, the question was…"What exactly was I gonna do with it? I began toying with the idea of learning the art of tattooing, so I brought the subject up with Rocco. He was about to go away on a 3 month sabbatical, but said if I put together a portfolio of artwork ready to show him on his return, then he'd consider teaching me. Before leaving, he gave me a very clear initiation test. He'd set up a tattoo machine in his studio. What I wasn't expecting was for him to pass it to me. "What, you want me, to tattoo you?"…to which he replied…"Nah, it's for you"….I was like.. "What da? I gotta turn the needle on my own flesh?" I wasn't sure if it was some kind of sadistic, rights of passage ritual, or perhaps a band of brother, get you in the club type of vibe. "Fuck!" So I just went with it.

Before I know it, I'm dropping my trousers..."If you're gonna slice people up with ink, you gotta know how it feels to work with flesh."..."Errr, ok mate, whatever you say." Under his instruction, I proceeded to land the needle deep into my right thigh, slicing a not so straight line about two inches long, before pulling back out again. I only managed two more lines.

"Rocco thought it was hilarious, my hand shaking uncontrollably as I'm etching another 'blood line' down my thigh."

I never did produce that portfolio. Rocco stated the obvious - "If you really wanted to do it, you would'a done." I knew he was right. It was whilst Rocco was tattooing me, that he suggested hairdressing. He thought it was more me. I gave it some thought, but wasn't sure. Later that week I went to a nearby college and enquired about enrolling as a mature student. It was either do a music and sound engineering course, or consider doing hair. I'd missed the deadline for the music by days and couldn't get on the course. It wasn't to be.

A few days later I rang Eddy. We had a chat, and before I knew it I'm sitting in her salon having a cuppa and chatting about the possibility of working as a trainee hairstylist. She was up for it, on the condition I go to college and do a part-time course. I didn't hang about, and no sooner had I enquired, I'd secured a place.

"Never in a million years would I of even thought I'd be back at college in my 30s."

I have no shred of doubt that if I hadn't got sober, there's no way I'd of had the humility, confidence and self belief to follow through. As long as I was sober, I was present, and as long as I was present, I could think and behave with more clarity and conviction. I believe opportunity is always there, slap bang in front of us staring you in the face. However, when you're full of fear, drug-fucked or otherwise distracted like I was, you're never gonna seize the moment...and even if you try, you may not follow through. I know I never could. "Why am I so unlucky? Why doesn't anything good ever happen to me?"...Simple...cos I'm not paying attention and I'm too damn scared.

A fundamental part of the redemption process, and life in general, is to do the right thing, always. Sober Sensei Donny Scot and the wreckheads guide for self improvement had enabled me to see my part in things. I'd finally become accountable to myself. Learning to make amends for my 'not so skilful conduct', to put it mildly, was a significant game changer. Something was beginning to shift in me…

"I was starting to like myself for the first time."

With the advice presented to me, it was clear it did indeed make perfect sense to apologise for my part in any wrong doings. That concept was previously counter intuitive and alien to me. "What? Me? What do you mean I've upset you? Stop being so sensitive!" I could of written an entire library's archive on the people I'd harmed. As for me, jeez…I could'a dedicated a whole bunch of warehouses to store all my self harm in.

"There were some very obvious things I wanted to put right. Ghosts of the past."

Apart from my estranged Dad, one such ghost, was Red, who I'd not seen or heard from since that gnarly 'holiday' on the Island. I tracked her down and was comforted by her response, having told her I'd finally gotten help for my clusterfuckedness. She really understood how it all played out and was truly forgiving. I'd done the ultimate 'back-door-Dave' leaving that Island. Red knew all along I'd had serious issues. She'd confronted me to face my demons and get help, but of course I wasn't ready. As we continued to chat, it became really obvious that merely talking about that time in my life, sent an eerie, ice cold chill reverberating down my spine and through my entire being. It unsettled me somewhat, to the extent that I knew I still had a shit load of post-traumatic-stress lingering. Bit of an understatement. A psychosomatic jolt of terror to be precise, and with it a stark reminder of just how fucked things had got.

Once again, I'm reminded how truly grateful and blessed I am to be alive and well. I can totally see why those who go through adversity and overcome it, say it's like being reborn. Deep down though, I sensed I may need to get some professional help at some point. A lot of what I'd learnt so far, was to let go and trust no matter what. Fuck me, easier said than done. The more I processed, the more I became aware. It was like these giant, unavoidable, stinking turds buried deep in the ocean of my psyche, were now surfacing and revealing their putrid stench…every single one was a humungous floating whopper!

"So many unresolved issues…PLOP! PLOP! PLOP!"

There's a saying in the world of addiction treatment…"The good thing is you get your feelings back. The not so good thing is you get your feelings back." No shit. Those emotional turds from my past were seeping through what now appeared to be the mesh nappy of my consciousness...and my usual coping strategy...GET FUCKED!...was not an option. So what the hell am I meant to do? Well, easy to say now - "Embrace. Allow all things to arise without judgement and accept 'what is'..." Hmmm...so, naturally, being a rookie in early recovery, I turned to other 'things' to help cope with the feelings that arose. Crystal Meth came right on cue at a time when I 'needed' it most.

"For me, getting high on sex and 'love' was the obvious choice. I now know why they say do not have a relationship in the first year."

Going against everything I was told, I insisted (and convinced myself) all was well (including Crystal Meth), when the truth be told (with hindsight)...in the words of Donny Scot - "You may as well go speed dating at the local mental asylum." I was far from being emotionally equipped. Was my heart strong enough yet to withstand relationships? Hell no!

Anyway, crazy arse relationships and fallibility aside...I recall a defining moment which came around this time, that served as a reality check to just how lucky I was to be relatively stable. I'd been friends with a dude from the rooms. He was an ex coke fiend and music producer, and although striving to be abstinent, was literally hanging on by the whites of his knuckles. One Saturday afternoon I was having a pre group cuppa at a nearby restaurant, when I had an urge to call him. He didn't answer. Now, initially I may of just assumed he were busy and leave it at that, but I had this overwhelming sense to call again. I was just about to hang up, when all of a sudden he answered. It took a few moments for him to speak. I could tell instantly something wasn't right...as he quietly murmured into the phone..."I don't feel I can go on anymore, I just can't do it."

"He was in fact sitting in the bathtub, to put it mildly... 'contemplating' death."

If it wasn't for my own experience with desperation, hopelessness and the suicidal ideations of the past, well, I'm not sure how I could of found the words to persuade him to go on. How do you reason with such despair? That's the therapeutic value of empathy...and who better than one recovering wreckhead helping another. Just by sharing my experience, allowing myself to get vulnerable at a time when someone in need is at their lowest, BOOM!...shit happens and connections are made.

"He came and met me...'WE' hugged, he cried...and together 'WE' went to that support group, and 'WE' both lived to see another day."

That's the pure, unconditional POWER of support in numbers. People living in the solution, not the problem. Like-minded peeps on a mission to help each other no matter what, because they've not only been there, they've come through it. That hadn't been his first suicide fixation, but it was his last. That incident reminded me (and matey) of the importance of connection (the 'WE'), the dedication to the cause and the gift of life we can take for granted so easily.

After a lot of contemplation, I decided to contact my Dad. We hadn't spoken for years, so the thought of seeing him terrified me. He'd been right up there on my list of amends…but I still had that emotional block from the past. Another god damn situation where I can't escape unwanted feelings by numbing them. Seeing Dad after all that time and being able to face him as the person I now was, not the former, lesser version of myself, felt incredible. Once again, it felt as though I was being elevated to a higher place, empowering me and instilling a real sense of pride and self worth.

"Fuck man, it felt good to do the right thing."

Not only had I reconnected with my estranged Dad, it was his Mother, my dear old Nan, who I was able to see one last time before she sadly passed. We sat by her bedside at the hospital, as she announced - "I prayed every day for 20 years for you to come back to the fold." Well, your prayers were answered Nan, and I'm so relieved you were able to see your beloved grandchild (with your son) back where he belonged, before making your grand exit. Perfect.

May I just add - with hindsight, although seeing Dad after all those years initially felt extremely gratifying…and of course there was an undeniable sense of relief and happiness for us both…but the deep, fragmented wound of my poor little ticker was far from being healed. It's a nice thought to think forgiveness and making peace with the past is an instant fix…maybe for some it is, however, for me, mending my broken heart was gonna take more than a pub lunch and a hug. I now know patience and effort is key.

On a positive, I could see the effect my new found wellbeing was having on others. A real sense of calmness came with that. The instant relief Mum gained was very obvious, the moment I stepped off that hellraiser rollercoaster. Blimey, I sure did traumatise the bejesus outta poor Madre. This making amends malarkey was certainly not just about saying sorry…"Oh, I'm really, truly sorry… it wont happen again, promise." How many times have our beloved friends, families and whoever's heard that one? Nope…

"Actions really do speak louder than words."

Another gift of sorting my shit out, was the day I finally moved into my own place. It'd been a very long time since I'd felt safe and secure anywhere. I dedicated a lot of effort into making that place feel like my castle. I may of been a couple decades late, but I was finally learning to cope with life, and with it an indescribable sense of esteem for who I was becoming.

Everything was going so well. I had a home, I was safe, sane (ish), I was about to embark on a new career in hairdressing, and a real sense of appreciation and dare I say it, true happiness had now replaced the old debilitating emotions of despair, anxiety and all the misery bollocks. I now had real, tangible evidence that showed me that when you change your attitude, and with it your environment...dependent on those elements, positive or negative... will determine the outcome. With the help of those who'd walked the path before me, I'd found the courage to make those changes and create new possibilities.

"Although I still had lots to learn, fuck man, it felt damn right incredible how far I'd come."

HONEY AND MONEY

On the day I was due to enrol at college, I received a rather unexpected early morning visit. I was lying in bed with Crystal Meth (uh-oh). We both looked at each other as if to say…"Who the fuck is that?"…having heard three rather loud and intrusive knocks at the front door. Gone were the irrational paranoid episodes of seeing 'No Caller ID' pop up on ya phone, or a menacing thumping at the door. I jumped out of bed and went to investigate. As I opened the door, I was alarmed to see two Police officers standing there. My immediate thought was…"They must be looking for someone, but surely not me." I was wrong…and once again, I was issued a warrant for my arrest and taken away in the back of a patrol car.

"Fucks sake! Surely not in front of my new neighbours, sober, in recovery…wtf?"

As we drove off, all I kept thinking about was the enrolment later that day. It felt so unjust (again), as I sat with mixed feelings of humiliation, mild pangs of harassment and that ever so familiar voice of…"Fuck this horse shit!"…but overriding all of that came a stronger, wiser response, as a voice whispered softly in my mind… "Everything's gonna be just fine." Hmmm…"Will it?"…and as I'm staring out the window a thought pops into my head - "What would that bald headed dude the Buddha say?"…"Tell the cops to go fuck it?…or perhaps jump outta the car at the next red light?" Nope…it would be a definite - "Accept 'what is' with non-judgment."

"So I take a breath, and with it a vague (reluctant) sense of acceptance fills my lungs."

It was revealed to me that I'd been suspected of committing credit card fraud. "What da?" I mean, fuck...where do I begin? I'd lost track of the amount of credit cards I'd obtained, rinsed and erased from my memory. It soon came to light I'd been accused of stealing an 'ex-girlfriend's' card...and unlawfully using it without her consent. "Fuck...erm..." As soon as they disclosed her name, I knew the charges would be dropped. I specifically new exactly what card it was, when it was, and that I had not unlawfully stolen it, I simply hadn't paid her back yet (oops). She was royally pissed, quite rightly so, and to be fair she'd certainly got my attention. Like I said, I was still learning.

Whilst all this played out in the background, held in a cell to await my fate, one very obvious thing occurred to me. Where as before, pre-redemption, I'm pretty sure I'd of contested each and every accusation, proclaiming to be the victim and plotting my revenge...this time, I calmly sat, listening with an unfamiliar content feeling of trust.

The bald headed one had planted a useful seed, as I slowly breathed, and with each breath I took, a stronger sense of acceptance was reinforced. The focus of my breath anchoring me in the present moment, removing any association with the drama. I was no longer trapped in a cell, nor a prisoner of my mind, body or circumstance.

"Fuck, I could observe the situation indirectly, instead of taking it so god damn personally…and with that came an immense sense of power in the calm I was experiencing."

To put it another way - I was learning to let go of control, gaining more awareness of how my mind works and how it reacted to certain situations. I was becoming more conscious, and with it more skilful, learning non-attachment and the art of healthy dissociation. It was still early days, but the more I practiced this Zen-Jedi shit, the more I wanted to know.

A few days after my release, I enrolled at college. My former self would of swerved it. Consumed by anger, I would of got drug fucked and made a neurotic mess of it all. Another non-starter. Not this time. It didn't even enter my mind…if anything, it instilled the desire to want it even more. Progress indeed.

These latest consequences of my past, made me reconsider my financial status. Historically, I was a complete car-crash where money was concerned, so like every other aspect in my life at this time, self introspection was proving I needed to get my affairs in order. I still had over 30 grand of debt hanging over my head, so naturally I wanted to resolve it somehow. I couldn't afford to just pay it back in one hit. It'd been suggested to me by a very stern Donny Scot to repay it back in full, as a kind of amends process.

"I had created the debt, therefore I must do the right thing and repay in full."

"Hmm, not sure about this ya know." Having given it some thought, I wasn't convinced it was the right thing to do. I mean morally, yes…but it would'a taken me until I was about 158 years old with the money I was receiving in government handouts. On my moral compass, bankruptcy was perfectly ok. I knew I'd fucked up. I'd been irresponsible and naive, with no clue how to manage finance. It's not like you're taught it at school. Mum tried to teach me, but I didn't listen. Thinking about it, if the school had provided financial guidance, would I of listened? "Fuck no!"

"I've heard it said romance and finance are two things that can cause the most suffering in life."

The Achilles' heel? Honey and money? Hmm. Yep, certainly been my experience.

Taking responsibility for myself was now key. If I haven't got my own affairs in order, then I'm screwed if I'm gonna have any hope of looking after anything outwardly. I had extensive evidence to prove this to be true. Regardless of the advice given to pay back the money, I chose to take responsibility and clear the debt, fast... "Bankruptcy please squire, where do I sign?"

"It's extremely empowering to have a clean slate and a fresh new start."

The day it happened, an astronomical sized weight was lifted. Like I said, I knew I'd fucked up, my moral amends was to not fuck up like that again. Through that experience, I learned to manage my finances, to take responsibility and trust my own judgement. Dear old Donny Scot had my best intentions at heart I'm sure, however, he worked in a drug treatment centre, not an equity firm. It made me question whether I needed to find a new 'Sensei'.

Since the fashion show, I'd continued to stay trim and work out. So it came as a shock when I tore the muscle in my groin, causing a ruptured hernia. That intense training I'd undergone for my runway pants extravaganza (those wretched squats!), had inadvertently fucked me. I was admitted to hospital, and before I knew it, I was on an operating table. When I came round it felt like I'd been comatose. I guess I had. I hadn't been piss drunk, stoned or otherwise bent out of shape for sometime now, so it really hit me hard. I lay in bed absolutely flying, and I gotta admit it kinda unnerved me a little. I was offered morphine to recover, but I chose to decline. I could already feel that old familiar thirst rearing its ugly head.

"The craving monster was awake and wanted to play."

Pre-op, I was told I'd be having key-hole surgery, when in fact they'd opened me up, putting me back together with a nice selection of metal staples, pinning my flesh along a 6 inch gash on my groin, just above and to the side of my pride and joy. Anyone who's been opened up will understand the pain, then remove any painkillers you may of had...times that pain by a million and you're not even close. Fuck me, would I knowingly do that again? Hmmm...not sure...

"In my minds eye, I was on a quest to remain completely abstinent and grounded in doing so."

Crystal Meth stayed for the first few days of my recovery. I didn't quite join the dots at the time, but having rumpy pumpy on day 4 of a post-hernia-op, well...perhaps a clear indication there may be some unresolved issues I wasn't yet aware of. More will be revealed, as they say.

FEED ON YOU

Changing ones lifestyle from a former hellraiser to a saint was a massive learning curve for me. Granted the circumstances were slightly in my favour now, these latest endeavours hadn't quite made me feel too great. I was learning it was indeed progress, not perfection, as I hadn't quite expected the setback of ending up on an all too familiar hospital bed, nor did I intend to be back in a police cell anytime soon.

"I guess you could say I was beginning to understand the teaching in that book by the Buddha - "All things are impermanent"...including sober highs."

Learning a craft, a new skill, going to college and reconnecting to my artistic roots...something happened in me. It was like a chemical reaction had exploded into an electric current of super-charged power. I was unstoppable, with an insatiable thirst for self belief. I was channelling all of this unused energy and it just came pouring out of me. My artistic hosepipe had been blocked. An endless stream of creativity waiting to gush right down the tube, but a decline in my mental health had twisted and kinked the damn pipe, strangulating any hope…so for me, being sober, a clean pure vessel to unblock and channel such energy was key…and I truly believe, or should I say 'know', that I was beginning to tap into something far greater.

Halle-frickin-lujah. I used to feel so powerless. Like spitting in the wind…the phlegm always coming back and hitting you slap bang in the face. "SPLAT!!" A victim of my own doing. That's how it is when you're caught in a seemingly never ending cycle of suffering and dysfunctional behaviour, with an uncontrollable diminishing spirit as a result.

"Taking my power back, stepping into the shoes of the person I was always meant to be and reconnecting to life…well, it was like I'd flicked the switch and the lights came on."

The day had arrived and I finally started my training to become a hairdresser. I'd made a full recovery from the hernia op, and was feeling solid in my mind, as I celebrated a whole year of sobriety. I was now like a man possessed to be the best I could. Positive action and outcomes was sky rocketing my self esteem. I became confident, focused and self-assured in a good way. I now had direction and purpose for the first time in years, and I felt an immense sense of gratitude because of it.

Becoming a hairdresser was pretty damn scary. It was unchartered waters, plus I was a dude in my 30s having to eat humble pie and start from the ground up. Open mindedness and the willingness to learn certainly helps. Tony and Donny Scot instilled this in me early on, and it'd stuck. Things started to take traction real quick. Flatlining through life seemed to take forever, but when you're in flow and reaping the rewards of good behaviour, everything seems to go in the right direction rather effortlessly.

"I can see now that when you're aligned to a greater sense of purpose and intention, things become seamless. It's like the more I stepped into this way of being, the more it flowed naturally."

I'd been reading books and listening to lectures from the likes of Alan Watts, Ram Dass and Eckhart Tolle. These dudes were on the lineage of great thinkers tracing right back to the bald headed dude himself, Buddha. Same teachings, just embodied and taught in a different way. With their help, I could identify wholeheartedly to the 'truth' that I was being fed, which in this modern world is damn hard to come by. It certainly helped me remain focused on 'the path', and reassured me immensely that I was heading in the right direction.

College was the place I'd encounter fellow student Moon Child. She was drop dead gorgeous (uh-oh) and wild as hell, which seemed to excite me somewhat. When we first met she was a right little space cadet, which soon became something of an issue. I'd recently parted ways with Crystal Meth. It hadn't finished great. In fact, it'd got a tad toxic…to the point where I'd (quietly) lost my shizzle. Having confessed to having been with her 'ex'…who turned out to be her 'not so ex' throughout our entire 'relationship'…this revelation sent me spiralling. "Muddafuck!"

"Hmm…perhaps I was being dealt a huge slice of 'Karma Love'…?"

With every best intention, this 'Karma Love' didn't feel too great. All my insecurities came punching through to the surface - Rejection, betrayal, abandonment. BAM! BAM! BAM! If I hadn't thrown myself headfirst into my support network I'd of been screwed. I was desperately seeking a 'Calmer Love'…yet I couldn't quite seem to attain it. As soon as a femme fatale enters I'm cast powerless under their spell. With hindsight, it is of course very obvious to me now that I was looking in all the wrong places.

Firstly - When it came to romance, did I know the difference between love and obsession? Did I fuck. Desire, love, obsession, lust…it was all the same clusterfuck to me.

Secondly - I was still damaged goods. Yeah I was sober, improving with self development, but in all reality I was far from maintaining a healthy relationship.

Lastly - I still seemed to be attracted to drama. 'Kooky, wild and adventurous'…was in fact 'Unstable, unhinged and unpredictable'…"Speed dating at the asylum anyone?"

"I guess there were plenty more lessons to be learnt and much work to do."

One such lesson, was to acknowledge for the first time that a 'healthy boundary' was indeed needed. The whole Crystal Meth meltdown instigated the need to change my phone number, and with it a desire to come off social media all together. I never liked it anyway, but this was a good enough reason to do it. With the help of Rocco, I was (reluctantly) starting to realise, and appreciate, that relationships are in fact a complete mindfuck in early recovery. In my mind, I had already promoted myself to being well and truly recovered, having been on a high in this new life of mine. However, when it came to relationships, it was becoming clearer that I wasn't as well as I thought.

"That 'addict' behaviour of wanting instant gratification, well…it doesn't just change overnight. Not for me anyway."

The intrigue I experienced with Moon Child was fittingly astronomical. You'd of thought having nearly lost my sanity to the Crystal Meth drama, I'd of at least taken a 'relationship sabbatical'…but I guess that's the prickly thorns of desire. No different to drugs, each and every time I got pricked…"FUCK!!"… yet I'd always forget just how painful it was, and I'd go do it all over again in an instant.

"I guess that's the definition of insanity right there."

So no sooner had I 'cut off' from one clusterfuck, I found myself getting into yet another dysfunctional 'relationship'. I didn't really know it at the time (or did I? Fuck, denial man) but I'd literally stopped using drugs to change the way I felt, and had simply continued to use 'romance'…or rather sex, lust and desire, to get a fix. I'd been seeing Moon Child more and more, blindly leading myself down another garden path of destruction, and once again I'm not only entangled in those deadly brambles, but I'm speeding towards an all too familiar brick wall with the wheels buckling...WHAACK!!

Drugs are like lovers. I had a different lover for every occasion, be it ecstasy, cocaine, opiates, booze or weed...each one an irrational, unhealthy attachment. Seduced and helpless, I'd crave the unattainable sense of comfort, connection and fulfilment, as if I were a vampire. This blood thirst rampage led to anything I could get my thangs into...money, sex, 'love', status, material things...all in a desperate bid to fulfil the need for validation.

"Unbeknown to me, I hadn't yet grasped the essence of the situation...that, until I learn to get from myself what I'm hopelessly trying to suck from these tirelessly empty carcasses, then I will always continue to be a vampire with an unquenchable thirst for more. Damn."

When you're engaged in a process of self introspection or redemption, you're always looking to attain the good stuff, never the bad...isn't that the same for all of us? We strive only to be happy..."You can leave the shite mate, I don't want none of that, but thanks anyway!" So when shit happens, my immediate response is always to avoid. Yet recovery (and life) has taught me well. No matter how hard it is...I must now turn and face the shit, and own it.

"As vulnerable as I may feel, I must remember it's true courage, strength and empowerment…to be ok, with not being ok."

It was on a bleak Winter's morning when I made the phone call to Rocco. I knew I could rely on him and trust him. My pride had taken a massive hit. I was broken. It was well into my second year of abstinence from drugs, the alcohol, all that madness from my former life, yet here I am again, in this all too familiar place of despair and pain. That **black-hole-void-impending-doom-solar-plexus-fucked-up-I-don't-wanna-go-there-fuck-you-fuck-this-and-fuck-that** feeling was still right there. In fact, it was even more apparent than I'd ever felt before, due to the inability to numb it with chemicals…and now, even getting a momentary 'love buzz' from yankin' ya doodle or meeting femme fatales, could no longer mask what lay beneath.

It was hopeless. I'd come so far with this new life, the wonderful journey of self discovery in recovery had granted me so many new found joys, but I just could not shake off that underlying sensation that resided deep in my soul. I had to get honest with myself…it was my doing. What did I expect? Moon Child was wild, a fun time girl. In my mind she was perfect…but in Rocco's words…"Play now, pay later." Fuck man, he was right and I knew it. Once again I'm reluctantly having to do the right thing, removing myself from the situation. I had to cut it off, to not allow it to breathe. I now know that's what I gotta do in order to not allow something to manifest.

"The allure of intrigue strikes again!"

This scenario had played out before, but this time it really hit home...leading me to the conclusion that I really did need to get some help. It was evident - I could not maintain any kind of healthy or sustainable relationship. Since the age of 16 I'd always had a 'significant other'. Be it an official girlfriend, a lover, or whatever the hell you wanna dress it up as. I had not been on my own, just me. I couldn't. I was too damn scared.

So, I learnt a lot (again) from this relationship. Heightened awareness has a habit of granting you two options...

1 - Ignore. However, that underlying sense of ignorance will never leave you alone. That's what chemicals are for right?...numb it!

or 2 - Take positive action. Courageously (and skilfully) changing the outcome for a better one.

I was still bouncing between those two options, but I was becoming more honest with myself about who I wanted to be morally. I started to speak to people going through similar situations. "Trauma therapy...childhood trauma therapy." Those blasted words were repeated to me constantly. Having heard it before in support groups, it'd always been the dreaded 'T' word...and I certainly wasn't ready to go there yet.

Instead, I secretly started to attend support groups for sex and love addiction. If I'm honest, they freaked the fuck outta me. What I did relate to, was the amount of energy I was putting into focusing on female validation. Maybe around 99.9 percent. One of the suggestions I was taught at the groups to combat these 'fixations', was to develop and use the 3 second rule. What that entailed, was limiting your 'playtime' window to 3 seconds (aka flirting), then you're to abstain from engagement (look away). Based on my track record, I was seriously lagging..."3 seconds? Fuck me, more like a free for all!" I couldn't go up or down an escalator without doing a 'check' process in my head..."Look at all those prospective partners passing me by." Seriously, it's all I thought about. "Yep!..she was definitely looking, for sure I'm in." As for only engaging for 3 seconds, hmmm...

"Does a fixed stare without blinking for as long as it takes to get an acknowledgement count?"

I'd only ever have interest in the ladies in any given situation, everyone else just faded into the background and held less significance really. That was my attitude at that time. Anyway, I proceeded to stick with it and 'work the program'…but after a few of those support groups, I decided to seek outside professional help to truly make sense of it all, and unravel this twisted knot deep in my core.

Now, I'm not saying that those support groups aren't of value. They are, and I learnt a lot…like the prospect of wearing boxing gloves to maintain the 'no hands-down-pants rule'…jokes aside, I achieved an almighty 60 days and counting, but alas it got the better of me and I cracked under the pressure (excuse the pun)…oh, and… top tip to combat 'uncontrollable sexual energy' - dropping to the floor and doing 20 press-ups. Hmm, seems to actually work, however…what the fuck am I supposed to do on a packed London Underground? Imagine you're getting the eyeball from a sexy stranger on the tube and it's causing you havoc. Do I make a grab for the overhead handrail and smash out 20 chin-ups if the 3 second rule fails me? Nice and discreet. Nope, for me, I felt I wanted to do it another way.

"I knew in my heart I needed therapy."

I now understand that when drugs, sex, food or whatever obsessive behaviour is active, that's simply a symptom of a more insidious and far greater driving force which lies beneath. For me, support groups, counselling etc were all amazing for the initial first stages of support, gaining vital awareness and laying foundations for the path ahead. It's the only way I could stop the active addiction and 'short circuit' the obsession to get fucked up…but I found that progressively, the underlying beast of that **black-hole-void-impending-doom-solar-plexus-fucked-up-I-don't-wanna-go-there-fuck-you-fuck-this-and-fuck-that** feeling would always, always reappear at some point.

In a short space of time, I had literally been through the addictive spectrum, stop using chemicals (it's still there), stop eating sugar (it's still there) stop jerkin' off (it's still there) stop rumpy-pumpy (it's still fuckin' there)…oh, and stop absolutely all social media and guess what…? (Yep, IT'S STILL THERE!) 'It's still' equals 'it's still an issue'.

Through investigation and direct experience, it was evidential and undeniable. I concluded that ALL distractions (take your pick - there's a limitless choice) simply allowed me to escape from reality…the essence of simply being. AVOID. AVOID. AVOID. It's like a carousel. The fantasy realm had once been my go to (still can)…then drugs became top of the stack. Then I got sober. I'd been on a pink fluffy recovery cloud with unicorns and rainbows and all the good stuff, then BOOM!...My Achilles' heel revealed itself...sexual desire, women, the love drug.

"It was like I was still getting fucked up on those highs and lows...and my reality was fluctuating somewhere between clean and serene and desperately dire."

This was a familiar crossroad. I'd been here before when I started to realise I needed to somehow get sober. This was no different. "Fuck, total abstinence from the ladies?...and Trauma therapy? Ok ok, I get it...I know I gotta commit. For now, as hard as it may be, I must establish a firm relationship with who I am, focusing solely on me without the emotional crutch of another...but the dreaded T? Ahhh maaan"...I still wasn't ready, because deep down I was terrified. Therapy meant revisiting my childhood, and that meant pain, sorrow and heartbreak. It was an eventuality though, and the day would soon approach for me to take the next step and invest some time, energy and money in getting some much needed professional help...but first, further realisations of self discovery were coming my way.

THE ART OF LIFE

I'd passed my hairdressing qualifications with flying colours and was now building a solid foundation as a competent hair 'artist'. I remained at Eddy's salon, but I was already getting the overwhelming urge to branch out and try my hand at hairstyling in the fashion world. In true Lone Wolf style, I wanted to do it my way, and break away from the confines of any conventional structures.

Without the complications of any unnecessary 'romantic interludes' to sabotage my efforts, I was now finding myself proactive rather than reactive. When you face your inner demons and overcome adversity, and you're driven by an unleashed force of creative energy…it instills a firm belief in you. That was my experience anyway. Procrastination became a thing of the past, and I was beginning to gain a distinct sense of faith, a knowing…that anything is possible.

"Meditative awareness was without doubt an attribute to my focus. I was still studying and learning how to do it, but something seemed to be working."

That being said, I was having a little spot of self-doubt creeping in about doing hairstyling. On one hand, I felt unstoppable, the other…I'm second guessing my efforts. Why was that? In hindsight, I think it's fair to say it's perfectly natural to have some doubts, maybe even some last minute nerves…however, this was most definitely more than just a passing thought.

It was a Saturday morning. I was doing my usual walk en route to Eddy's salon. As I strolled along, I had an increasingly overwhelming sense of reluctance to go. Fear had crept in, and I could feel dis-ease in my physical body. I was aware that the narrative voice in my incessant stream of thought was getting louder and more critical, the tone becoming somewhat darker and more negative - "That god damn tyrant wants me to suffer!" Sure as hell I couldn't help but notice, as it continued to rattle on…"There's no way you can be a Stylist?"…"You ain't cut out for this mate, why don't you just admit you're a failure?"…"You're wasting your time, get out whilst you can!" Classic imposter syndrome.

"Fuck. That voice had been blissfully absent in my noodle for quite some time (or so I thought) and now it was back in residence."

With the presence of awareness, came a bolt of realisation that punched its way through the unconscious part of my being, knocking it to one side for just long enough for me to observe what was going on. As it did, a softer, kinder voice reappeared again, and whispered gently - "No, you're precisely where you're meant to be…it's ok, everything is cool." I'd been aware of that calmer voice in the back of that police car not so long ago. It was the voice of reason.

I think for the first time in my life, I truly understood the duality of dialogue that plays out in my mind. Conscious versus unconscious, sanity versus insanity, truth versus delusion, good cop versus bad cop, authenticity versus arsehole, whatever…if you're anything like me, that 'split-personality' thought process we identify with is undoubtedly there, always waiting to pounce.

"I've heard it said the neurotic-ego is doing push-ups waiting to strike, abso-frickin-lutely…so how the fuck am I gonna defend myself from it?"

Well for me, the answer to that question was to master my mind. The teachings on meditative awareness had done me proud. Stillness had created a more conscious experience, so I was beginning to see it. That god damn committee meeting in my mind…all those characters sitting around having a debate, talking out loud, hurling abuse and arguing - that's always been the workings of my mind. They create and feed me endless lies, to which I had always believed. In time, with dedication and practice, I developed enough ability to not only observe this inner dialogue (and not fall for it), I could now begin to counterbalance and replace some of the characters, mostly worn out tyrant dictators, with more skilful, genuine and kinder ones, resulting in a more harmonious experience.

"For me, positive affirmations, reassuring me in times of need…always resulted in peace of mind."

I thought getting sober meant all that nasty stuff magically disappeared. I mean, don't get me wrong, I was fully aware I once had strong voices of cravings, that addict gremlin wanting to feed… but they were a distant memory (or so I thought). The obsession to use chemicals had gone, but I still had the voices of desire rampantly pecking away at me, and those cravings were no different…

"Eat more cake, buy another pair of trainers…go on, have a cheeky tug, you know you want to!"

The gift of paying attention, this here rookie was beginning to catch those fuckers out…"Oi, no mate, shut the fuck up and settle down!" That morning, I could'a bought into that lie, as I usually would'a done… "Oh hi, morning Eddy…won't be in today, got the squits and it's causing me havoc!"…but I didn't. It may not sound that significant, but when you're a slave to those voices in your head, living out your life to their every command, I'm sure you'll agree that unless they're instructing you to do good shit, you're fucked.

I'd previously read one of the teachings by Buddha…'As we think, so we become'. This latest incident led me to truly realise just how profound that statement is. I started to meditate on it…"As I think, so I become"…When you really sit and seriously consider the truth in that. It's such a simple premise. Some might say elementary, but like most things, it's so simple we miss it…and simple doesn't mean easy. A powerful antidote to an otherwise untreated state of mind. What that realisation did, was quite literally shine a whopping great big light on the self-sabotaging ability of the mind. Be aware, pay attention…do not listen to the lies and do not attach. This is what I've learnt.

"Those voices are not our authentic self. Certainly weren't mine, and they were trying to derail me…as they'd always done in the past."

The knock on effect of this self realisation, was later that week, I decided to take one hell of a leap of faith, and I left Eddy's salon. I just knew that for me, if I was to expand my growth, not just as a human, but as a hairstylist, then I needed to take myself out of the fishbowl and put myself in the ocean. London was where it was at, and I set my focus on becoming a top hairstylist to the stars.

"As we think, so we become…right?"

Audacity had always come naturally to me. I guess you need a shit ton of tenacity to be an outlaw hellraiser or a slippery salesman. Comes with the territory. I'd always been well attuned to taking risks, and saying yes to opportunities was now becoming the norm, especially with a new found belief that I could actually now do things, rather than saying no because of fear of failure.

One day whilst on the train home, I saw an article in a London newspaper about a unique and 'hip' studio run by a famous international hairstylist, which seemed to jump right off the page at me. I immediately imagined myself being there. That 'knowing' sensation was very prominent. I just knew something good would come from it. At the time, I had no idea that sense I'd got, was what I'd now consider to be the presence of being in alignment, in 'flow'…the power of creation, manifestation. I know that sounds all cosmic and deep, but fuck me is it true (for me anyway).

"I decided to take a risk. I gave it a call."

I was greeted by a friendly young woman. I was upfront and honest and told her I'd heard about the studio and wanted to work there. I went on to boldly say I was prepared to give my time freely to be part of their team. I could tell in her voice she was impressed by that gesture. She took my details and went on to explain that the creative force behind the brand, was currently working in New York and would get back to me on his return in a few days. We said our goodbyes and that was that.

"Something inside of me just knew I'd get the gig."

Just two days later, he called asking me if I'd like to go see him. By the end of the week I found myself sitting right there in the very studio I'd seen in that picture. Like the cat that'd most certainly got the cream, I sat amongst the eclectic mash up of worldly artefacts, ranging from old Victorian dressers to slightly odd taxidermy. Apart from the weird, wild-eyed fox, which fixed its glare from across the room, I felt a distinct sense of belonging in that place…the coolest studio in East London. Audacity and a spot of self belief goes a long way. Simply thinking - "I CAN!"...and acting on it…

"I had literally manifested my vision of where I wanted to work."

I was becoming seriously tuned in to this new concept..."As I think, so I become." The more I practiced it, the more it worked. 'If' became 'when'. It was like some kind of unseen magic, providing an enormous sense of wellbeing, and further instilling a belief that I could achieve absolutely anything I put my mind to. Like a skilled archer, I could set my eye on the bullseye, pull back and unleash my arrow, knowing with complete conviction that not only would I hit the target area, but I'd hit dead centre. May I just add -

"Rome wasn't built in a day, and they certainly didn't achieve it simply by thinking it could be done...there was work to do!"

It was once on board with that crew, that I ended up hustling an assisting position on a well known brand, which led to TV commercials, fashion shows, editorial shoots and film work. Shortly after, I landed jobs working completely freelance as a session stylist doing red carpets, music videos and celebrity. I literally did all this within the space of a year, and with no social media. I had realised my goal of becoming a hairstylist to the stars. As we think, so we become.

"I was doing it strictly old skool, with the added benefit of this secret belief system working for me each and every time."

There was one incident which was a stark reminder why I don't use social media…and for me, compromised my sanity at a time when nothing else seemed to…

I was booked to do the hair for a Hollywood actress. It was a cover shoot for a magazine and we spent the day in a posh hotel in Mayfair. As per usual everyone's buzzing around doing what needs to be done. I'm in the zone doing hair and chatting away to the 'talent'…in my mind, I've already married her and named our first daughter Leia. (Red flag no.1)

It was in the lift with the photographer and my new wife heading down to the ballroom for our next shot, when she declared…"Let's do a post of us all and I'll tag us in." As I'm sure you'll agree, this is frickin' gold dust…but for me, I just could not have a healthy relationship with this kind of thing yet. It's why I came off it. As soon as she mentioned it, and may I just add she was obsessed with using the word 'obsessed' (she wasn't the only one), I became very aware of the sensation within my body. (Red flag no.2)

"Ignorance is bliss, however, awareness smashes that ignorance to pieces."

Intrigue. Adrenaline. Dopamine...pop pop popping. "Hello ego, how are you?" Yep...my ego suddenly raised its head like a meerkat on speed. A strong feeling of..."I'm seriously missing out!" followed, as did that all too familiar energy of compulsion, that always arose when I'd used social media. "Fuck man, it's on me...potent little fucker." Suddenly I was faced with an opportunity to dive back in to that other world, the vortex of online oblivion. I know it sounds a little crazy, but that's how it was for me, and I really did not wanna go back there.

I had enough awareness to observe the thought process, but that pranged out meerkat wanted to play...and I found myself ducking into the men's room, where I secretly downloaded the sticky-icky app. I then proceeded to try and remember the correct password. "Fuck!...It's like I'm locked outta the god damn cookie jar!" After a bunch of failed attempts I gave up and deleted it.

"Back-door-Dave...Whoosh!...off for a crafty fix, hoping no one would notice. All too familiar behaviour."

After failing to get my 'fix', I felt like I was missing a trick. "Feckin' FOMO!" She did the post and I wasn't tagged. "An outcast. A social frickin' outcast." Hah..oh well. Didn't stop me from being in that hotel in the first place, nor did it stop me from styling her for red carpet the following week...and it certainly didn't hinder me going on to do bigger and better things. The only thing that missed out, was my ego.

"In all my experience, I have never needed a social media platform to exceed my aspirations."

I have always, always succeeded regardless...so it is possible. Good old trusty word of mouth I believe is unparalleled, works for me anyway. Oh, and whilst we're on the subject, I had a very prestigious and well known brand director say to me, very specifically...that I could in no way whatsoever, be capable of achieving my goals in the way I intended. We'd been discussing how to be successful. I'd disclosed my thoughts to her, outlining my belief that I could achieve anything I set my mind to, in a way that I deemed possible. I learnt a very important lesson here...

Said person categorically dismissed the...'As we think, so we become' ethos...based purely on what I can only presume as their lack of 'knowing'. I couldn't help but want to prove them wrong... which I did, by continuing to say a big fat YES to opportunities, without irrational fear (or non believers) hindering my progress. This newly developed skill (and belief) was serving me well. By nurturing (trusting) this strong sense of inner knowing, intuition as I now know it...I was unstoppable, going from zero to hero at such a rapid pace, smashing ALL limitations thrown at me within the world of creativity.

"What I took away from that incident, was to be more careful with who I share my ideologies and aspirations with, because not everyone shares our vision, nor do they perhaps wish to."

Without a shadow of doubt, abstaining from all mind altering substances and a growing development in meditative awareness, was allowing me to tap into a completely different frequency. It didn't make me better or more special, it just empowered me to be more present, focused and connected to all I was doing…resulting in fuckin' cool shit.

CHANGING LANES

The same week I was due to celebrate my second anniversary of total abstinence, Amy Winehouse tragically passed away. Having seen her progressive downfall in the public eye, I kinda felt more affected by it, because I just knew the outcome was inevitable if she didn't stop…and then she was gone.

When you're living proof that recovery is possible, you kinda just wanna reach out and grab those in need, who like you, are caught in the perpetual cycle of madness, and help them. I was embodying the solution to that insanity, and I wanted to pass it on.

"There's a saying - 'You keep what you've got by giving it away'. It's so true."

My life had already surpassed what I'd previously deemed possible. I had a home, a career and I was beginning to earn good honest money, but more importantly...I had developed integrity, a true sense of appreciation and was becoming more and more authentic. I still had unresolved issues internally, and I knew they weren't going away anytime soon, but Amy's death kinda put things into perspective...a stark reminder of how lucky I'd been.

I was approached one day by a friend of mine, a fellow recovering wreckhead, to see if I'd be interested in volunteering for the charity set up by Amy's family, in honour of her legacy. They needed a guy in recovery to go into schools and do talks on addiction. I didn't have to think about it...I'd never met Amy, but I felt a strong affiliation to the cause. Different stories, but I definitely knew the struggle, sorrow and pain. Soon after, I met her family and the rest of the team at their London office. It was a great honour and a huge privilege to be part of an organisation, which effectively was turning the ultimate tragic consequence of addiction into a positive outcome.

"From that day, I gave my time freely to the Amy Winehouse Foundation whenever I could. That in itself was extremely humbling."

For me, charity held a lot of significance (and shame), based purely on the fact that I used to be a selfish swine. Those dodgy daylight robbery days of extracting financial gain and profiteering from innocent victims, had left me with a gut full of guilt to last a lifetime. One of the biggest amends I could possibly make, was to correct my plundering salesmanship of the past...and to give back, big time.

The Amy Winehouse Foundation allowed me to make that amends on an epic scale. They'd developed a 'skills for change program' for the educational system, backed by the government and funded by the Big Lottery. Years later, it still continues to reach and impact the lives of thousands upon thousands of young students throughout the UK.

The more I represented the Amy Winehouse Foundation (and those still suffering), the more I started to get a taste for it. I also started to delve deeper into my past than I'd ever done before. Doing talks on addiction and drug awareness in schools, I soon learnt you had to get on their level, so I'd share my experience of going to school. I mean fuck me, those students, when I talked about my alienation…the torment of bullying, body image and trying to fit in…I could tell they identified with every word I spoke. That in itself was incredibly profound.

"It was as if I was giving them permission to be real too."

Something started to shift in me, and I felt the urge to follow my now familiar and trusted intuition. For me, if it feels right, it usually is right. There was a strong desire to do these talks more than style hair. I'd achieved above and beyond what I'd originally set out to do, and was beginning to lose the mojo for it. I started to question my path for the future.

I felt like a double-agent. Conflicted, because on one hand I was getting real, perhaps finding my true purpose and meaning by going into schools, sharing my life experience of strength and giving hope to unsuspecting students. It felt incredible to teach skills for change, to point them in the right direction…"It's an 'inside-job'…it's not about money, prestige or body image, it's how you feel from within, not how you look on the outside." Yet on the other hand, I'd leave and go to some ridiculously lavish hotel to do the hair for a celebrity who had no clue to what I'd just done. For me, it was a complete contradiction to be part of the machine that makes people look glamorous, before they step out to be idolised by waiting fans and papped by photographers. That machine isn't necessarily a bad thing, nor is the end product - the art. For me, the art of hair and the creativity that comes with that was amazing, as was working with like-minded creatives…fellow artists, musicians, singers etc…however, it wasn't all like that and I was becoming notably uninspired.

"I knew things were really shifting when I turned down a major A-list celebrity to do a talk in a school for free."

The more involved I became with the Amy Winehouse Foundation, the more I drifted away from wanting to be in the world of celebrity and glamour. There was a time when I craved the buzz of being backstage at London fashion week, watching half-naked models brawl as I fix hair to the sound of some mardy, narcissist fashion designer screaming demands at whimpering assistants. I once lived for 12 hour photo shoots, 18 hour video shoots…and I had some incredible times for sure, but in my mind, I stopped seeing the 'glam' and started seeing 'sham'. Becoming more self aware, it's hard to ignore sleep deprived models 'nodding out' on set…"Wake up!…more coffee please…seriously, if you're only gonna eat one boiled egg today, then I'm not surprised love." Of course I'm not saying this is standard behaviour or the entirety, merely stating what

I observed on occasion, from my own direct experience in that world at the time.

I continued to keep that duality of contrasting life paths, but I just knew I had a greater purpose to fulfil. It was an eventuality… this here pirate was about to set sail on a mission.

LONE WOLF

Hard wired

HARD WIRED

Some things just will not budge. Total abstinence from all mind altering substances? - check...Flourishing prosperity and abundance? - check...A greater sense of moral conduct? - check... Complete peace of mind and a feeling of utter bliss? - err...

Now, don't get me wrong...this redemption transformation from demon hellraiser to a saint caper ain't too shabby. In fact, I would not trade my new life for the old one if you paid me a billion in cash. "No fuckin' way pal." I'd been granted the opportunity to give it another shot, a rebirth you could say, but that realisation I'd only been standing on the tip of the iceberg forced the inevitable.

That **black-hole-void-impending-doom-solar-plexus-fucked-up-I-don't-wanna-go-there-fuck-you-fuck-this-and-fuck-that** feeling was undoubtably there. Having had what I'd considered to be a 'spiritual awakening', I automatically assumed I'd be truly enlightened...bugger and bollocks, that bloody saying 'more will be revealed'...well, for me, that meant finally dealing with that familiar Gremlin residing deep in my soul.

"It was time to do the dreaded 'T'....childhood trauma therapy."

JOYPAIN

Where does one find the Tony Montana of therapy? There's a shit ton of stigma attached to psychiatrists and therapists. I had some major preconceptions of my own…"Fuck those bow-tied bozos, they're just a bunch of glorified pill pushers." I for one made sure I had a discerning sniff around first, to get a vibe…(and it certainly helped having a good friend recommend someone). There's no way I'd go and share my entire life's suffering with some random Herbert I'd only just met. I made 1000% sure that whoever's gonna delve into my shit, was right for the job. I also had the luxury (and awareness) of understanding that for me, 'spiritual sickness' requires a 'spiritual solution'…"So no 'magic' pills for me please doc." Tried that one, didn't work.

"Legal or illicit narcs for me equals more of the same."

Whilst we're here, let me be absolutely clear. My understanding of 'spiritual sickness', is that deep sense of disconnection to my authentic true nature, to others and the world around me. That feeling of imminent doom, delusion and that lingering depressive, repressive and utterly bewildering inability to function in a pure, natural way. Or to put it another way…"Mind, body and soul -

fucked!" Abstinence based recovery and meditative practice was my introduction to the solution…a spiritual journey of self discovery, free from the confines (and dependency) of conventional methods of coping (i.e drugs - illicit or otherwise). To the best of my ability, it enabled me to reconnect and function in a purer, healthier and more stable way. A place where I could learn to express myself with authenticity and begin to heal. I strongly encourage anyone to find out what works for you. It's subjective…and if you can learn to trust your intuition, you too will embody a natural ability to feel what's right. Maybe you already have, and if you haven't…perhaps go find out.

"For what I needed, it was meditation not medication."

I was now finally ready to engage in professional help with the post traumatic stress I clearly still had. In my experience, childhood trauma, or any other trauma for that matter, doesn't just disappear. It's there, deep in your being, and it takes action to work through.

All these 'irrelevant little things' we file away, which are in fact almighty mountains of a 'BIG monstrous thing'…where do they go? I heard someone say it's like the 'Trash' or 'Bin' folder on a computer…you dump a load of unwanted shite in there, and just assume it's disappeared, without giving it any thought. Yet, where does it go? It's still there on your hard drive, right?…you just don't see it.

Those wildlife documentaries where Wildebeest get hunted down by Lions…if they're lucky enough to escape being eaten for lunch, they flee to safety and immediately 'shake off' the attack. If only we knew how to 'shake off' the traumas we undergo in life, perhaps we may not feel the need to escape or medicate. That gnarly trauma energy, be it Wildebeest or human, remains trapped on our cellular hard drives, not just psychologically and emotionally…so it makes complete sense to find a way to reduce the power it has on the physical form…our bodies.

"I've heard it said you cannot heal a dead leaf on a tree simply by stroking it better. You gotta get deep down inside the roots and provide nutrients."

When I first set out to do trauma therapy, I knew the most fundamental 'thing' I needed to process was my parents divorce. That was at the very root of this tree of mine. I was asked by the therapist on the consultation session what I wanted from the treatment, my first response was simply…"I wanna be able to cry properly and do intimacy." Therapy would go on to teach me why I couldn't. I mean, I kinda figured it out anyway…"I'm the Badman, Joker, fuckin' Tankman"…and…"Fuck it, it'll be alright"…but I'd never given it any real validation, until now.

Apparently, the day Mum sat us down to declare the end of her marriage, I broke the tension by laughing out loud…"Boys, your Father and I have decided to separate"…"HAHAHAHAHA!!" I have absolutely no recollection of this. Oh well, guess ya gotta do what ya gotta do. In all seriousness, that reaction, and lack of memory of it, kinda tells you a lot about the art of deflecting pain and masking it…and was certainly a strategic coping mechanism I'd used from that day forth.

Laughs and memory blackouts aside, this coping strategy to navigate your sorry arse through the minefields of life, kinda just becomes hard wired. It's a blueprint for survival, and one that's so ingrained, it takes a double hard bastard to crack it.

"In fact, it took a team of trained-special-task-force-therapists to blow the fuckin' doors off, and even then I wasn't surrendering without a fight."

Coming to know the psychology behind childhood trauma, or any other traumatic experience I've had, has been unparalleled in my recovering from these events. I could not 'think' my way better, tried that, didn't work. "As we think, so we become"…if only I could apply this to my healing? (In time I would know how)…I could not 'read' my way out of it…same goes for talking. I had to take action, and that action meant seeking counsel in specialist therapy.

"I can honestly say it was the single most challenging, heart wrenching, gut churning, rewarding, inspiring and magnificently beautiful experience I have ever encountered."

It's hard to translate in human words what I encountered throughout that process. To use having been possessed by a demon as an example - it was like having a professional exorcist literally vacuum the fucker right outta my soul. That pain from my past, that deep wound which caused me so much despair was finally being treated. "Halle-fuckin-lujah!"

It was in that incredibly safe and nurturing environment, surrounded by skilled professionals, I was guided safely back down the winding pathway to my childhood and the events that caused those wounds. Confronting and exploring our sometimes difficult past is a challenging process, which most of us attempt to avoid, me included. It was of course a very painful process, to regress back to a time, the darkest most terrifying of times, but I can honestly say that on the final day, I walked outta there for the very first time as mere mortal David, finally putting the Badman mask down to rest, along with all the tears of freedom I shed.

"Finally crying for myself. It was pure self acceptance and the ultimate in redemption. I cried and cried and cried in that place."

To put it simply - childhood trauma therapy allowed me to reconnect with my inner child, a 7 year old David. An innocent, frightened little pup who'd got caught in the crossfire. It enabled me to literally scoop that wee lad up in my adult arms, and begin to 'reparent' him back to a place of safety, love and acceptance. In floods of much needed tears, I apologised for abandoning him for all those years, lost in the haze of oblivion.

"Forgiveness for oneself is priceless. It's the key that unlocks the door to our freedom."

So much emotion I could not previously release was purged. I literally spewed my toxic guts up with years upon years of unwanted, contaminated 'energy'. I was always convinced that if I connected to that 'energy', or emotion, I'd drown in my own pool of sorrow. I'd feel the physical sensation reach my chest and throat, but I'd block it every time, not allowing it to go any further. So that's what the **black-hole-void-impending-doom-solar-plexus-fucked-up-I-don't-wanna-go-there-fuck-you-fuck-this-and-**

fuck-that feeling was all about. That's what drugs were for. As soon as that sensation became too amped...BANG! I'd hit the bottle, or reach out for something, anything not to endure that horrendous feeling. Makes perfect sense why I homed in on Mum's sweet tasting sherry to begin with.

Allowing myself to be 100% vulnerable with NO distractions, finally enabled me to release that full to the brim pool of tears. That purge instantly freed me from the tension within my body that I'd held onto for so many years. It was like someone had pulled a giant plug out. Ahhh...the relief. My emotionally constipated, bellyache of trauma finally took a rather big dump! I could now begin to nurture that part of me, to dare myself to be 100% vulnerable more often, in my own time and in my own space, without the fear of drowning. At first, it didn't come easy, but I was slowly acknowledging it was ok to let go and release. I could see the strength in that process, not the weakness. On an intellectual level, I'd realised it takes immense bravery to show your vulnerability, to speak your truth and share what's really going on...however, now, I was truly embodying it.

"More than ever, I could see my pain was now my power."

I was encouraged to be angry in that process…and I mean to unleash real, full on fuckin' fury. Fuck me, to finally express myself and direct that anger towards something and someone that wasn't me, in a way that wasn't destructive was worth the expense alone. To give back all those unwanted emotions and 'belief systems' I'd harboured for all those years (none of which were mine)…to remove and dispel the poison thorns of fear, anxiety, shame, guilt, remorse, the resentment, the sense of betrayal…to have a voice that counted…to let go of the 'story' I'd repeatedly told myself and continued to blindly believe and torture myself with…to validate the events of the past to those Tony Montanas of therapy…it was all truly incredible.

I discovered 'JoyPain'…to know that embracing pain will always be met with reward, resulting in growth…and that you will experience joy in doing so. Who'd of thought? I certainly didn't… I'd always associated pain with hatred and self harm…I'd either run from it, or revel in it in a warped, self defeating kinda way. Gettin' real and owning your shit is empowering, which means it's frickin' liberating. We are taught the opposite…to suppress it. Boys don't cry and all that bullshit. "Stop being so sensitive and man the fuck up!"…NO NO FUCKIN' NO!! There is absolute powerhouse muddafunkin' strength in vulnerability. We have just got to trust it, and that's the difficult part, in a society where it's normalised to create Avatars of ourselves, pretending to be something we're not and presenting a false narrative…that everything's ok (I'm the fuckin' Badman), when in reality (behind closed doors) is it possible we feel disconnected, inadequate, lost, overwhelmed and alone perhaps?…well, only you know the answer to that.

"Feelings will not kill us? What a revelation."

It takes courage to trust, that although feelings are indeed sometimes challenging, causing discomfort, they will not kill us, and we certainly do not need to act on them. They are impermanent, they come and go…and always pass. When I first got sober, my feelings were raw...but what did I expect? I had not allowed myself to acknowledge them, let alone feel them. Over time, I learnt to embrace them. I began to realise that unwanted emotions are not necessarily a terrible thing. An uncomfortable feeling can indeed be a positive, I just needed to change the way I perceive it and grow to trust that. Of course it's a lot easier said than done. Turning to face these emotions is challenging, but we owe it to ourselves. Better to conquer ourselves than to win a battle or a war…as they say.

Patience and tolerance were never my strong points. Learning to meet discomfort and suffering with love and acceptance, not hatred, is a daily reprieve…and takes a shit load of effort and repetition, but it does get easier with time.

"Undergoing childhood trauma therapy had created a huge shift in my response to this."

That wound is deep. It's still ingrained, hard wired...but I'd taken the power back, finally obtaining a bigger slice of the emotional sobriety cake. I still knew I had work to do, but I could now associate pain with joy. JOYPAIN. Result.

THE SHAME GAME

The word and emotion SHAME kept cropping up a lot whilst in therapy. For me this fucker was the elephant in the room. In fact, the entire elephant population of Botswana had decided to join me. I never truly understood just how powerful the feeling of shame was, until now. I learnt I'd been dowsed in that shit all my life, like a thick layered skin of petrol...and it'd been set wildly ablaze, uncontrollably burning me with hot scolding flames of debilitation ever since.

Once I'd gained emotional intelligence and understanding, I took that knowledge into the school system, and witnessed first hand the mass shaming that went on every single day. I knew on an intellectual level just how humiliated I'd been at school, but I'd never quite joined the dots to just how damaging it'd been to my wellbeing, until now.

"I clearly hadn't been the only poor mortal subjected to the tyranny of such ravenous ridicule."

Ever been privy to a bit of banter? You know the kinda bashful slating you get from your buddies, ya chums, your beloved besties. If you're a guy, you will definitely know about this one..."Saw your Mum last night John"...Really?..."Yeah mate, she loved it!"...Classic British banter at its finest.

This oh so 'wonderful' banter is commonly accepted as simply 'just what you do'. In fact, here in the UK we see it as an act of endearment. I'm the first one to admit I undoubtedly gave as much slating love as I got. To slate, or be slated is something I try to avoid now, unless it's coming from a good place and does not cause offence. There's a fine line between..."Your Mum was round my house last night"...and something perfectly innocent which doesn't cause a shame attack.

"We all love a chuckle and a grin...but I guess it's the spirit in which we do it that counts, no?"

Growing up and being a reluctant participant of the schooling system, and especially attending an all boys school, jeez...this kind of tortuous ridicule was rampant throughout. You are literally subjected to a tirade of mental, emotional and verbal abuse, oh, and if you're lucky, you'll have some physical terrorism thrown in for good measure, fabulous. If you're unfortunate enough to receive all this unwanted attention, you've got limited options for your line of defence, especially if you're anything like I was, vulnerable and passive. It took me a while to work out that to avoid the humiliation of being a target, you gotta buck up and bash some skulls, metaphorically speaking.

"Survival of the fittest...time to don the Badman alter ego and reluctantly go kick arse.."

Having gone back into schools to do talks was not just rewarding, it was proving to be a bit of a trigger. I found myself having psychosomatic pangs...nothing I couldn't handle, but it unsettled me somewhat. We were teaching resilience, and I too was having to up my game and stand guard, not just over myself, but at times the wellbeing of students.

I was now more self aware to those 'pangs' of PTSD and the power it holds. It was clear bullying and shaming had created a nervous disposition caused by these 'attacks'. A sudden noise, an unexpected movement, or an overwhelming dose of unwanted embarrassment had rendered me on high alert.

Shaming seems to be enmeshed in modern culture it's sad to say. You only have to look at the gossip columns of certain publications or online social media to bare witness to the onslaught...

"Look at what's er face from that reality show who's got the duckbill platypus beak and the melon lips."

I have a very dear friend of mine who was publicly shamed, their addiction made readily available for all to see when published on the front page of a national 'news' paper. How delightful indeed, so much so, they had to escape the UK and go into hiding in order to not only flee the parasite hound dog reporters, but to quite literally safeguard their sanity and life. Having fled geographically, it didn't stop the social media barrage of haters. Reading hashtag..."You dirty sick cunt!...Your Mum should die!"...on your social feed, ain't exactly gonna make you feel better now is it? If people really new the full extent of what someone goes through in crisis...would they still behave this way? Who's the sick cunt really?

To me it makes perfect sense why it seems the norm to batter your 'opponent' or ya pals with your finest cut down banter. Using that learnt behaviour, me and my mates used to do it all the time.

We didn't know any better, it's just what we did to entertain ourselves from the otherwise monotony of life at that time. Admittedly it was bloody funny, yet there was no harm done, right?

Let me give you an example of such antics...

We need to go back to the hellraising days, a time when I was living away from the hometown I'd been ransacking. There was this one time two chums came to stay, which kinda left a lasting impression shall we say. Now when these two jokers got together, it would always be me on the receiving end of the banter bullets. It was just one of those power dynamics that seemed to always formulate.

"Me and matey one on one, no probs, no banter. Me and the other matey one on one, no probs, no banter. Me and the two amigos together, I'm gettin' it, big time."

I'm sure anyone who knows what I'm talking about, will know that when you get that trio-combo, one of you is always gonna get the short straw. Back then I had no power or boundaries, nor the balls to simply say..."Oi, NO!...shut the fuck up...I am not prepared to be spoken to like that chaps, so please stop." So it simply played out and I let it happen. I'd tried my best to ignore it, or laugh and make out I wasn't bothered, but the truth was I was reeling from low self-worth, disempowered and crippled by the shame of not feeling good enough.

Getting some shut eye was never gonna happen when sharing a room with these dudes…and when the hair of my armpit was set ablaze, I decided it was time to retreat for my safety and peace of mind (yeah right!), crashing out on the floor in the living room, directly next to a room rented by some university student girl.

In the dead of the night, I was awoken by footsteps going past my head and through into the laundry room, which led to the downstairs toilet. Pretending to be asleep, I could sense the light had been switched on, followed by a startled gasp coming from the young student girl at seeing me spread out across the floor of the living room.

"When I awoke that morning, thankfully my eyebrows and the rest of my armpit hair were still intact."

As I gained perspective, to my horror, I saw I was not the only one laid spread out…right beside me, in all its glory, were the open pages (and legs) of a grot mag…and right next to it an almighty mountain of wankerchief. "Muddafuckers!" Oh boy…they had executed a rather fabulous stealth attack in the dead of the night. Unbeknown to me, they'd acquired that rather fine publication of filth-eroticism from the convenience store opposite. Waiting patiently until I was completely sparko, before carefully laying out the crime scene. Genius.

I have to say, I've got a cheeky little grin on my face recalling this episode, as I can imagine those fiends doing their utmost to contain their laughter as they carried out this dastardly feat. Gotta give it to them, they had stitched me up a treat.

"I can see the funny side now, but jeez man...seriously, I could not look that girl in the eye for the remainder of my stay."

That incident, like so many others, would spark the rampant flames of humiliation that always engulfed me, incapacitating me like a Witch burning at the stake. It would trigger layers upon layers of buried ridicule, taking me straight back to the traumatic experiences from my past.

This is just one example of countless escapades that just seemed to be the status quo throughout my former life. It takes a very strong (and determined) character to stand up to such behaviour. Easier said than done when you're outnumbered and outgunned, but once you find that inner courage and step into your strength, it will be backed up with an immense feeling of self-worth, empowerment and freedom.

"Integrity and a true authentic self is what I discovered from conquering my powerlessness."

The way I see it, until we find our mojo, the nature of shaming will continue to germinate like a disease. It's insidious, and will always most certainly overpower ones ability to defend against its viral toxicity. It's why I numbed it. To escape its relentless stronghold. Feel more shame? Get more fucked. Simple.

The art of bullying. A learnt behaviour we may witness, not just through television and the media perhaps, but through cracks in doors, at school or overhearing gossip coming from strangers talking on the phone…and maybe we learn such antics by studying our peers, parents and other family members bicker, attack and manipulate.

"A 'festive' Christmas Day extravaganza with the fam, anyone?"

It makes perfect sense that we unconsciously take these new found skills to the playground, classroom and eventually into adulthood. Or was that just me? From those very early childhood experiences we may encounter, to entering an 'education' system and being subjected to an array of abuse we did not sign up for, we are continually exposed to a tirade of shame bullets…dodging them and occasionally being struct by one at close range, or simply getting caught in the crossfire. Like a conductor to an orchestra, the shame leader will skilfully lead their band of merry shame members to a crescendo, leaving the poor receiver feeling utterly worthless. They will play in harmony, blindly following the actions of their master, abandoning any trace of autonomy or sense of moral conduct. If you have ever been subjected to this misfortune…I assure you, YOU ARE NOT ALONE.

Is it any wonder we have the attitude…"If you can't beat 'em, join 'em." I know I did.

DON'T BELIEVE THE HYPE

One of the most important aspects of my joining the Amy Winehouse Foundation was to educate, to share a positive message and to inspire. Helping in the quest to fulfil Amy's legacy was an incredible honour. I was truly grateful to be given the opportunity to be of service for Amy, her family and for the greater good.

"Helping prevent a similar tragedy was always their mission."

When I first started to share my lived experience in schools, I'd only talk about certain things. Things such as my school days, getting into drugs, the partying, and how it all progressed uncontrollably into an almighty clusterfuck. As I became more confident and skilled at talking, I soon realised I could do it with ease. Removing the stigma attached to addiction was always important to me, because I felt it never served me. I always held the viewpoint that an addict was the dude lying facedown in the gutter with a needle hanging out of his arm. That was the problem...I thought just because I'm not shooting up smack or sleeping homeless on the streets, then I wasn't that bad, so I couldn't be a real addict, because I'm not a junkie...but in all reality I had been.

"Stories were different, but the feelings, behaviour and consequences remain the same."

Sharing my life story didn't just provide insight, it granted more acceptance for just how fucked things had got...and I was starting to get further towards the truth. One such truth was a secret I'd buried so deep, that I'd convinced myself it wasn't real...sound familiar? Denial at its finest. I hadn't told a single soul, because the shame and fear of this secret was so insurmountable I'd become frozen by it, terrified of not knowing what to do. Once sober, I quietly went and sought help privately...finally daring to share it for the first time. It was only doing talks in schools, that I began to reveal the full impact of such a tale.

Rewind to the madness. I'd found myself at a private party hosted by some rather well to do types at a stately home…

"It was like walking into the Mad Hatters tea party on Acid."

It was wild…think pink flamingos and dwarves in tuxedos. That night I met this incredible girl, I thought she was stunning and I fell for her immediately. One thing leads to another, and before I know it we've sneaked off to be 'naughty'. No sooner had we started our 'cheeky interlude'…when an abrupt 'SMAAASSH!!' on the door fucks the ambience, and we're greeted by a rather terrifyingly big burly doorman, who proceeds to make his presence known by snarlin' down at us with a definitive…"I am about to kick the fuck off this bedpost and rip your head off"…kinda look. He demands we get out. "Maaan!"…I could not get my head around why? "It's a god damn party!"

"For whatever reason, that was that, my arse was out on the street. How's your feckin' luck?"

About a year or so later, I was out partying. It was a busy crowded night and I was standing there scanning the punters, when I suddenly clapped eyes on the girl from that party. I couldn't quite believe she was just yards away from me across the dance floor. As I stood there transfixed, a guy who I kinda knew as a friend of a friend approached. He came straight up beside me and whispered in my ear…"You know she's got HIV don't cha?"…and as quick as he was to sidle up and say it, he was gone. I just remember feeling a shudder of weight slam down upon me. It was like I'd just been told the date I'll die and how. BAM!!

Now, at that time, it's fair to say I had fuck all self awareness. Far from self assured, I was hanging on by the skin of my teeth. It's easy to see now, just how completely detached from reality I'd been. Gone was any rational thought to discern the legitimacy of what I'd just been told. "I mean come on, really?" With the emotional maturity of a 12 year old, crippled with a debilitating fear of trust and taking responsibility, a questionable bombshell had been bestowed on me, crushing me…and I literally did not know what to do with it.

"So, I did what I always did. I buried it. I buried it so deep that if I could not see it, it simply did not exist."

Standard procedure for absolutely everything I could not process on an emotional level. I kept that bombshell, along with a whole bunch of other stuff, buried deep within the 'hard drive' of my psyche.

Filing cabinets full of X File cases of secret squirrel information, which I could not disclose through fear of being judged or ridiculed. The most fucked up thing about that bombshell, other than not being able to share it, was the fact I carried on regardless to whether or not it was substantiated, with a complete disregard for myself or any other person. What the fuck was I thinking? That's delusion, denial and trauma for you. It is no excuse, simply a valid reason for such ignorance, selfishness and insanity.

"Keeping up the pretence of built up bullshit is tiring. I really had been as sick as my secrets."

Once sober, I quietly checked into a clinic at the hospital to get a bunch of tests done. As suspected, they all came back negative. I had another load done a year later to be absolutely certain. Again all clear. I often wondered about that liaison, and the night that guy snidely dropped the bombshell declaration. Of my incredible ability to bury it along with all the other inconvenient 'truths' that came my way. How my irrational 'zero to imminent death' mind completely failed to process any sense of order, therefore rendering me no other option than to live with uncertainty, fear and denial. To put it politely - from a now rational and wiser viewpoint, I can only presume the motive for that 'very happy to inform' guy, was in fact a rather jealous young man, who perhaps simply felt threatened and inferior, and by telling me such false information, may in some twisted way make him feel more superior and better about himself, whilst making me feel like shit. He was also spreading damaging misinformation about someone, without them having any means to defend theirselves against such a savage attack.

"Such slanderous bullshit 'hype', only comes from venomous cowards who hide in the shadows."

Anyway, who knows…but I can't help but feel it's the only logical motive for someone to spread such harmful accusations about another human being. No different to the shame game, this kinda dirtbag tyranny is commonly used to strike down our opponents, be it our peers at work, the playground or like me, perhaps in this scenario…a rival love interest. Envy is a real bitch man.

So, you see…the moral of this here tale is a powerful one. A very real representation of just how fucked things get when we bury our secrets and hide from reality. It's why I decided to go a little deeper and get brutally honest in schools and hit them with a sucker punch of truth. It held immense power, to talk so honestly from the heart, the impact it had…I could see it in their eyes, they too were connecting to that truth, their truth.

"You talk with honesty, it is more likely to be received with honesty. No bullshit."

Those needing that 'realness' most were found in pupil referral units, institutions for students kicked out of the educational system. Usually the last stop before the big boy prison system. These poor feckers were fully fledged gnar, highly traumatised and coming from severely dysfunctional environments. Proper frontline ghetto gangster shit from the streets of London. 'I'm the Badman' times a billion.

I remember one time I was sitting front of class, these two lads casually sat there, one drawing a rather fine hand gun, the other had created a masterpiece...a doodle, consisting of a heaped pile of dead bodies, with a towering building with bodies falling from the top. Gives you an idea of the torment hidden in those depraved little souls.

"The dude drawing the gun asked me - "Oi, you ever shot anyone?"...if firing an AK47 at a wooden torso counts, then yeah."

The way I see it - it does not matter whether you're from a state or private school, or ended up in a pupil referral unit...if you have been misunderstood, abandoned, neglected, starved of love, betrayed, shamed or abused in any way, the commonality was clear as day - we all suffered from some kind of unresolved trauma. This realisation brought me an immense sense of humility and gratitude. Not just for my own awareness and recovery process, but for being able to inform others and pass on insights and a little bit of wisdom where I could. It was becoming clearer to me what my purpose in life may be.

A splash of serendipity took place as if to insure I was pushed in the right direction. It came in the form of an invite to style the hair for an international 'superstar'. Although I kinda knew deep down my heart wasn't in it anymore, I accepted the job as a favour to a friend. Within the first hour of turning up, I was in a side room with the make-up artist asking her to talk me out of leaving. Putting it simply - when you're talking to troubled souls from broken homes with broken hearts about the nitty gritty of life, ones enthusiasm for, let's just say 'fragrant behaviour' disappears somewhat. So when you're met with the 'joys' of a newly famous 'princess-diva' and their band of merry yes men, you kinda think… "Fuck this for a game of soldiers"…and that's exactly what I did.

"It doesn't mean to say their craft, art or career is not relevant or important to them or anyone else, because it is…it just wasn't to me anymore. So that was the end of that."

Shortly after I took a full time position with the Amy Winehouse Foundation. I would go on to help develop training and facilitating for their flagship resilience program, becoming involved in multiple projects, including their music initiative for the underprivileged. Every single aspect of that role was an absolute privilege and an honour. It'd been a huge leap of faith, but one that had secured me on a path towards my true purpose.

DRAMARAMA

"Kill 'em with kindness"...hmm, something I've had to learn the hard way and certainly hadn't practiced. I'm not talking about killing someone with a smile on ya face, nope...I'm talking about being 'non reactive'...meeting ALL behaviour with decorum and compassion.

I'm a good natured guy at heart, aren't we all?...but back in the day, although that kindness was present, I wasn't. "Fuck you, fuck 'em and fuck the whole thing completely." Now that's more like it. It's not like I was going around snarling at everyone. I had many guises to mask what lay beneath. I'd be all charm and smiles, kinda like a blissed out zen-boho-psycho. You know the type? "Heyyy maaannn, how's it going duuuude?"...yet the wrath of my altered state would subliminally lay low in the shadows, festering like a volcano waiting to blow. It would usually surface in combat with loved ones, and most definitely authority figures…and once triggered, would erupt into an almighty shitstorm tirade of verbal abuse.

Being one hostile muddafunker got me nowhere fast. Self absorption kinda does that to you. Self examination illuminates the 'why?' to this underlying cesspit of insecurity. So, the billion dollar question is…"How the fuck do I sort it?" Well, to put it simply… there's work to do.

"Resentment is one toxic emotion."

If unprocessed, it will slowly eat away at your soul and have absolutely no remorse feeding on your sorry arse. When I started redeeming myself, I became aware for the first time the full extent of what resentment is, and the nature of its toxicity. If I'm honest, I hadn't even been familiar with the term. "What the fuck is a resentment?"

I remember an incident that took place within the first few days of finding recovery, that sums it up perfectly…

I'd been with Tamsin, the girl who'd given me that book by the bald headed dude Buddha. We were out on a busy Saturday trying to find a parking space. As we entered a car park I spotted one. Being so busy, I jumped out and stood in the vacant spot. As Tamsin drove around to it, some guy started reversing in to where I was standing. I exploded with a tirade of verbal abuse, slamming the poor guy with obscenities and cut downs. He in turn engaged and was more than happy to commence battle, and there we have it…

"A good ol traditional 'road-rage-slaggin-match' we've all become accustomed to."

Why such fury? Immense hatred spewing out uncontrollably over such a trivial thing - parking a friggin' car! I always seemed to have these outbursts when governed by the…"I'm fuckin' Tankman mate"…line of defence. Borderline narcissistic, egomaniac territory. It comes with a threat to my persona, and certainly signifies a grandiose sense of entitlement. "Don't fuckin' take what's mine, now fuck off!" What I came to learn, was it'd been a coping mechanism for as long as I could remember, symbolic of a barking dog, the growl to warn you I'm on high alert and ready to chomp ya feckin' feet off! "Leave my fuckin' bone alone!"

"This insecure response to life, had been created by the disconnect trauma causes."

Losing the ability to be present in my body, meant I'd lost the ability to navigate such situations. The end result? Gone was my authenticity and any sense of intuition…that gut feeling of what's right or wrong. So, I'm left wondering why on earth I'm recreating more and more of the same drama, regurgitating an uncontrollable, never ending cycle of suffering…blaming absolutely every single thing on anything or anyone but me. Sound familiar?

That parking episode really freaked me out, because I knew, even then, that something wasn't quite right in my demeanour. I realised a multitude of these reactive resentments had accumulated over the years. Some deeply entrenched, and no different to the shame I'd discovered, most, if not all were hidden, because like everything else, I'd buried it deep down in my 'hard drive' psyche. Therapy and a deeper introspection was unlocking the doors to these little feckers, and I was faced with the inevitable task of having to greet them with (reluctant) open arms.

"I used to pick up tiny doses of resentment, such as someone looking at me the wrong way, or saying the wrong thing…and I'd hoard those unwanted interpretations in the darkness of my subconscious."

Back then, the lens for which I viewed the world was completely distorted. Simple, rational interactions became totally misinterpreted. I'd twist and mould reality so it became my own dysfunctional truth. My mind could not relay simple narratives.

Instead, I'd take simple dialogue and it would become a completely different language all together.

A classic example of this would be an interaction with a partner. Now, if your state of mind was anything like mine had been, it would go something like this...

Them - "Dave, I'm going for a drink with a couple of mates tonight."

Me - "Oh, ok cool." (On face, I'm smiles and acting like I don't give a damn, however...deep down, I am 'discombobulating' and the paranoia is kicking me in the arse as I'm thinking - "Who are they really meeting?")

Them - "Thanks babe, you know I love you."

Me - "Yeah yeah, I know I know, love you too." (On face, I'm still hanging on to a barely there grin, but...I am completely consumed with an underlying force of - "I am fuckin' fuming...I am sure they're cheating on me and I can not handle the rejection or insecurity I feel." To top it off, I am too crippled in fear to do anything about it, so I direct it inwards).

"It would always end in an argument. I'd internalise my emotions, become sullen and not knowing what to do with my mood, I'd lose my shit."

I discovered this melodramatic-mindfuck-malarkey all blends rather seamlessly to codependency. Fuck me, I could right an entire book on it, as plenty have...however, putting it simply, codependency for me, is a total lack of autonomy and an absolute 'need' for another. This meant the inability to be ok on my own, and instead, have full reliance on 'something or someone'...oh, and while we're at it, allow it to completely floor me.

"Can't live with them, can't live without them."

That insecurity fuelled an obsessive craving to be liked, to be popular, to be right, be the best, be seen, be heard...yet none of it filled that emptiness and sorrow, nor could it cure the disconnection from self. It can cause us mad fuckin' humans to act out in such ridiculous and unskilful ways...and it makes perfect sense to wanna be engrossed by other people's shit, their misery, their demise, because momentarily, it made me feel better about myself. Vindictive, venomous vanity. It's all interlinked to a complete identification crisis with ego. "I'm the Badman"...who craved attention to be adored, even from people I did not care for. Perhaps they didn't like me much either, yet I'd still seek their validation...which is frickin' batshit crazy if you really think about it.

"I fuckin' despise you...please love me!"

Learning healthy boundaries was absolutely vital to my new found wellbeing. I'd learnt the basic 'baby boundaries' of saying 'NO' to certain people, places and things...those 'red flags'. People pleasing is common. A blatant disregard for our own needs, to instead meet someone else's...and when it's not reciprocated, we feel let down.

"We must absolutely put our own basic needs first in order to be safe and secure...protected."

Once we're in check, we are strong and reliable to serve others. We are no good to anyone unless we ourselves are dandy. I know it's cliche, but those classic safety drills the air stewards demonstrate on any flight are bang on. The ones where you switch off because we all know if it's going down we're fucked! (Or is that just me?) They demonstrate so merrily how the oxygen masks will drop down when the shit's hitting the fan, instructing the adults to do precisely what I'm saying...be selfish. "Whack them oxygen masks on ladies and gentleman, then fix up your whining kids."

Redemption and the bald headed dude Buddha taught me selflessness...now I'm rediscovering a need to be selfish again for all the right reasons. Once I learnt basic boundaries, I began to expand and start to have the confidence to try them out, gaining a greater sense of freedom from this new found skill. I also started to learn how to create 'invisible boundaries'.

"The power of creating an invisible boundary, is no one needs to know it's there."

So how do we create one? Let's use the example of a person you feel is draining your energy. You know the ones...emotional vampires. Take take take and all you feel is depleted. Why are we never taken into consideration? (I was a pro vamp fiend). Self absorption renders you completely oblivious to your need to feed.

The great thing about invisible boundaries, is we don't have to do the whole confrontational chat, unless you know it will be acknowledged, understood and respected. Or, maybe you've tried a million times, yet it's always got you nowhere. The one where you speak your truth but they do not hear it. Or, they say the classic... "Yeah I know I know"...but they don't know, cos if they did, they'd bloody do something about it. So, if this is the case, do it differently. Instead, say nothing.

"Simply remove yourself from these famished little vamps, thus making yourself invisible and safe."

If you get caught out and are subjected to an unexpected vamp, make your excuses…"Oh hi, err…apologies gotta dash, gotta go and detangle my cat from the barbed wire fence in the yard…see ya!" Then get lively. The bottom line is - remove yourself. Alternatively, apply another tactic - the invisible boundary of time management. Simply create a timeframe that works for you which you deem to be safe and manageable. I'd recommend no more than 2 hours with a vamp. You should still come away with your sanity intact, dependant on their need to feed.

"You wanna meet for a catch up…midday at Skully's ok? Cool…oh, and just so you know, I've got a colonic at 2."

I know this sounds really obvious and basic, but like anything else that's simple…it does not make it easy. The art of being Houdini is a skill to be cultivated and fine tuned over time. In doing so, not only will you empower and protect yourself beyond measure…but in turn, those hungry little vamps will go feed elsewhere. There's no shortage of people to feast on I assure you. If you're anything like me, you will get pangs of guilt when first practicing this skill, because you're undoing a lifetime of people pleasing…however, in time it becomes natural. I used to be 'back-door-Dave' to be sly and get drug fucked, to isolate. Now, I do it to be safe in a blissed out bubble of serenity. Ultimate freedom guaranteed.

INJECTION OF REJECTION

Ever found yourself standing in line waiting to be picked? I'm not talking about the identity line up at a Police Station (or maybe that's you ya little rascal?). I'm talking about those early life scenarios, such as waiting anxiously in the playing field amongst your pals, hoping to be chosen to be a valued member of their team, group or gang.

When it came to sports I was actually pretty good. I always got picked for football, I had a good left foot and was skilful enough. At secondary school I went on to play for the rugby team, cricket, basketball, swimming and most athletics including cross-country running, all early signs of my persistence and defiance not to be beaten.

"That unyielding resilience seemed to always pull me through any situation I found myself in."

The inevitable happened, and once I became more intent on the experimentation of self destruction, all motivation and performance simply fell away. Smoking cigarettes didn't exactly fit the criteria of an aspiring athlete, nor did droppin' acid or gettin' baked all day. I'd had a good run playing football for a local team, winning many trophies, scoring goals and accumulating lots of proud paper clippings for Mum...until one day I got dropped from the team, because some new kid who was the shizzle rocked up and took my spot. That for me was a fatal blow...a lethal injection of rejection, which sent me spiralling into an already out of control oblivion of self loathing.

"Fuck the jocks, outlaw skaters were always my posse anyway."

That fatal blow to my non existent esteem, was a continuous feeling I encountered on a multitude of occasions throughout my life. It was evident its retched misdemeanour still continued to play out, even in the self discovery process of redemption. Therapy had shown me more than ever, that these deep rooted wounds could and would flare up in any given situation where the sense of rejection was involved. It is no wonder, considering the biggest rejection of all (childhood alienation and a diminishing family unit)...was right there at the core of it.

Whenever I've done talks in schools, I would always outline this simple fact of life..."We are a by-product of our environment." It really is that simple. Whether we like it or not, those strange adult creatures we're influenced by in early life, really do shape us, along with all the exterior social elements. Hang out with good honest people, guess what? However…if we're rollin' with wreckheads?… yep, you got it. You wanna meet articulate and curious people, go hang out in a library.

"Want a girlfriend who loves piercings, tattoos and adores Black Sabbath, head for Camden Market."

Being back in schools reminded me of how puberty had tranced me big time, adding to an already heightened sense of inadequacy and dissociation. Body image is a curse for some, it certainly was for me, serving as a fundamental reason to dislike myself even more. Adolescence is such a crucial time, when all we're striving for is acceptance, connection and feeling part of. This early life conditioning really does mould the shape of things to come.

Students would always ask me about my tattoos, of which I have a lot. Each one tells a story. I'm a walking tattoo tapestry, the 'illustrated scars' of my life. To begin with, I used to say…"I'm not here to talk about tats"…but then the penny dropped.

"I realised it was all part of the compulsion to fit in… give me that injection for my unfaltering rejection!"

For me, having a tattoo is a ceremonious ritual, serving as a rite of passage to manhood. Adrenaline is pumping. Intrigue and the desire to experience danger had already done its job in getting me there. The pain is, by its very nature penetrating your skin to the core, and in that moment, you do not feel any other emotion underlying the pain of the needle piercing your flesh. Or is that just me?

Back in the day, I could recall most, if not all my tattoos were times when drugs (or a lover) were not available...or the chemicals (or whatever else) was not working, and I needed to fix that underlying **black-hole-void-impending-doom-solar-plexus-fucked-up-I-don't-wanna-go-there-fuck-you-fuck-this-and-fuck-that** feeling...so I'd be creative - "Let's get inked up instead, that'll do it."

Now, I'm not saying everyone who's got a tattoo is doing it for the same reason, that's just how I saw it. Covering myself with ink wasn't just about 'artistic-self-gratification', it was a commitment to the life of an outlaw, a Lone Wolf..."Fuck the system!"...it was rebellion and identity. Reconnecting to my true nature, embodying compassion and acceptance for myself, not hatred, I still have tattoos, but as a much healthier form of expression, and dare I say it...spiritual experience.

"It's certainly not a self-defamation ritual or a coping mechanism."

Processing and beginning to heal past trauma transformed my relationship to most if not all things. Take skateboarding…I was master-of-mash-yourself-up. Team pain was certainly my mantra. To any rational human being, it does not make sense to relentlessly slay yourself, attempting the same insanity over and over until you make it…pushing yourself to unimaginable extremes, breaking yourself and any boundaries along the way, smashing right through those conventional barriers of what is deemed possible. There's a certain addictive/obsessive 'genius' to that process, diminishing fear and reason at every obstacle. It requires an 'autopilot' perspective, enabling you to 'tune out' the pain and risk associated…it becomes 'normalised'. There's a fine line between channeling this 'genius' for irrefutable greatness, and the unskilful detriment to the human spirit.

"I guess it all comes down to perspective. I still get high on adrenaline, but I guess you could say I do not have a death wish anymore."

Anyway, that feeling of rejection you may get…whether it's not being picked for the school sports team, the dream job, a lover, or not being invited on a so called friends holiday perhaps…these 'minor' incidences can be fairly monumental. I've witnessed mature grown adults (myself included), who given one spike of that fatal injection of rejection...and WALLOP!...they are straight back to that kids party at the age of 8, when their best mate failed to give 'em a party bag full of sweets, which every other kid seemed to get.

If you've suffered an early life of insecurity, felt neglected in any way or are traumatised to fuck, you are probably carrying a whole bunch of unresolved issues around...and, perhaps you may do what I've done...self-medicate. These triggers that come our way, mean we can either go through our entire life playing the victim, recreating old patterns of behaviour, continually being floored by our past wounds, or...we can take the power back and do our damned hardest to process and change it. It does not come easy. It is far easier to remain (in denial) a victim of our ignorance, and continue to medicate.

Relationships, especially intimate ones, are a classic arena to be constantly tested. Those past insecurities can, and always will flare up if I allow them to hold power over me. It's about having the awareness, and to begin to take positive action, changing the outcome...so they do not have to take centre stage all the time.

Once again, easier said than done.

LONE WOLF

Tune in

TUNE IN

What frequency am I on? Who or what am I tuned into? At what point do I determine whether or not I'm happy to settle for who I am, or what I have? Do I push on and continue to evolve, or do I simply freeze in time like a prehistoric Mammoth in a block of ice, frozen forever? It appears I have now developed a more natural, kinder response to life…where I want to remain open and curious to the myriad of ways to explore this wonderful thing called self discovery.

Our life experience can be a beautiful journey, if only we allow ourselves to have it. Sometimes however, it can be tediously monotonous and inexplicably uninspiring. This, will usually happen for me, if I take life, or myself too seriously. I also come unstuck if I close off from the infinite abundance of potentiality that life offers. Equanimity, humility and presence…as always is key. To know and trust I am ok with the good times as much as throughout the bad. If you're anything like me, we can sometimes anticipate 'being on a roll' as too good to be true…self sabotaging, inadvertently causing our own wheels to buckle.

"One thing is now certain, I must continue to take action in order to grow...and sometimes that can be difficult as it is painful."

MYSTICS, MAGIC AND MUD

Change is scary. Period. It takes a whole lot of courage and a considerable amount of strength to even consider taking those steps into the unknown...but, it has been my experience that if you dare to take the leap and dive into the abyss, then it always seems to work out just fine. Sounds like blind faith, right?

Personally, I needed help, I could not do it on my own. Tried that, didn't work. I'd always procrastinate in a truly monumental fashion, swerving any resemblance of taking responsibility, because the unfamiliar territory was too damn terrifying.

"Putting it simply - I didn't dare to trust, and fuck blind faith."

Some seek religion, others a guide of sorts, or professional help... depending on the options presented to you. I would say it all comes down to who you are, the circumstances you're in and what resonates at that time. There is no right or wrong, simply what works for you. The one common denominator though, to help guide us out from the gutter, in addition to the willingness to do so, is some kind of faith. Faith it'll be ok. I used to say…"Fuck it, it'll be alright"…when the truth be told, I had absolutely no frickin' clue it would.

There's a lot of unfortunate stigma attached to 'faith'. It can debunk any efforts to have it. I stayed well clear of any inclination towards it, and all aspects associated, based purely on the bias it wasn't exactly punk rock.

"Not getting into all that weird cult shit, no way matey."

On top of that, I'd had my own entrenched ideology, due to my perception that if there were some God-like Invisible Force, why the fuck is he, she or it punishing me this way? I had no reason to believe in that 'Supreme Power'…yet every time the shit hit the fan, I'd send the Bat signal out in a desperate bid to be saved. Have I simply been a jammy dodger, sidestepping the clutches of the Grim Reaper, each and every time it went tits? Or…is there something far greater at play, that has intervened in my being here to tell this tale?

I started to question this 'Is it luck I'm alive, or the will of some Higher Power?' on a deeper level. What I came to understand, was this faith malarkey doesn't have to be so black and white. Religion doesn't even have to come into the mix, not if you don't want it to, and even if it does, it's how you relate to it. If your religious (or non religious) experience embodies love, kindness and compassion...why would you not dive in? Of course if we cannot understand the language of love (as I didn't)...then how the fuck are we expected to speak it? Just because someone speaks Japanese, doesn't mean they're indifferent, they just speak words we are yet to comprehend. If we took the time to study it, we may just find we can relate.

How many times have you heard - "All ya gotta do is love yourself"...back in the day, my response was pure and simple - "Yeah I know I know"...but the truth be told, secretly I'm seething in bewilderment...

"*Yeah fuckin' nice one mate, thanks for the advice, but how the fuck do I do it!?*"

So, why is 'faith' such a brain bender? For some it's an extremely personal thing. I believe when the human limitation of our linear ego thinking gets in the way, it serves as a hindrance to the true nature of our experience. The difficulty (and problem) will always be in defining it with conventional human language.

"Whether you think you have 'faith' or not, if you embody all the 'good stuff', then surely you bestow the best universal qualities of life."

It's been my experience this 'true nature' of being, only came when I let go of my ego (control/fear), and came to know a more expansive, boundless existence, tuning in to a higher level of consciousness…and if that's my 'faith', then bring it on. For me, faith started out as something far removed from the conventional sense. Instead, it came in the form of slight glimpses of hope (and self belief). Moments in time that seemed to puncture the stalemate of my reality with tiny sparks of light. It was enough for me to take note, and through a series of synchronistic events, lead to a final realisation.

Those flames of hope, became an enormous sense of comfort and reassurance, illuminating my entire being and enabling me to see clearly for the first time in ages. With time, slowly but surely, this all led to a growing relationship of trust with that newfound thing called faith. Early recovery had proven to reinforce my trust of the unknown…to allow myself to remain open, willing and honest to the best of my ability. Those principles enabled me to study different teachings, some from thousands of years ago, that still held a relative purpose to this day. The bald headed dude Buddha insisted…"Do not believe what I tell you, go find out for yourself."

Fuck yeah...that was the complete opposite of dogmatic dictatorship. So that's precisely what I did, I went and found out for myself and had my own experience.

"All that was left to do, was cultivate and nurture what I found, as it guided me along the path to freedom."

When that book on the teachings of Buddha first fell into my hands, it revealed a practical solution inline with what I was already doing...learning about the mind, attachment, insanity, delusion. The philosophy jumped right off the page. My mind had become open...like a parachute, I now had a chance of landing safely. Before, my closed ignorant mind would not allow such information in...so it is no surprise I'd crash land every single time, breaking myself with each fall.

"Meditation. Meditation. Meditation...it's all I kept hearing. So I applied it."

Getting to a place where I'm comfortable within my own skin, to not have to tune out to escape that feeling of dis-ease is a real blessing. It can feel good to be here, present, in this moment, right here, right now...but it can be extremely hard to experience these fleeting moments that come and go.

"To remain tuned in, to be hitting a desired frequency of consciousness takes discipline and practice. Constant, daily effort. No different to the gym, you wanna get fit..."

It's like tuning an old car radio. You lock in to a channel you like, yet as you drive along the signal drops out...so you gotta keep dialling back in to remain tuned in to the same channel you enjoy. This seemed to be my experience of maintaining equanimity and peace of mind. I realised if I'm gonna reap the gifts of a higher level of consciousness, I have to tune in, over and over and over. For me, attaining 'nirvana' and 'self-abandonment' are two sides of a coin. Addiction and mental illness was all about the perpetuating wheel of madness, a constant need of repetition and dedication. Embodying wellbeing and 'the good stuff' was no different, except you're flippin' the coin over from insanity to serenity.

I began to explore more avenues of spirituality. Where can I find the Tony Montana of enlightenment? Where do I get the next dose of serenity? Synchronicity, or chance if you like, had already lead me to Buddha, so what and who was next? To reinforce this dedication to the cause, I switched out my television for a meditation 'shrine'...which consisted of placing a traditional zen cushion and mat in the corner of my living room where the TV once stood, decorating the surrounding area with candles, incense and all that kinda jazz.

"The only thing missing was beads, bells and a bald head!"

I guess starting to untangle that twisted knot of trauma, had really helped me reduce the 'dis' in the 'ease'...so I could focus far easier on being present, and the quest for pure bliss. Along with a new meditative focus, I began to learn yoga and delve more into mysticism. With an insatiable thirst for knowledge, I was on a mission to get as high as I could, without the dirty comedown of drugs. Silent meditation retreats, monasteries, and eating and chanting with monks all became part of my exploration.

"I once saw a calendar on the wall of a Buddhist monastery, and instead of Monday, Tuesday, Wednesday...every single day was called 'NOWDAY'. Genius."

A friend of mine told me about a ceremony taking place...the ancient Native American ritual called Inipi. They'd read a book about this incredible man called Silva, raised by the Native American Lakota people, who for hundreds of years have lived in the Midwest. The Lakota term Inipi, more commonly known as 'Sweat Lodge', means 'to live again'. Symbolic of the universe, its spiritual experience reconnects them to their oneness with it. Redemption had shown me a 're-connect'…and the sublime experience of meditative practice had granted me a taste of what was on offer here - a divine connection with the true nature of all life force. My friend lent me the book. As soon as I started reading, my immediate thought was…"Where do I sign?"

"I had no idea who this man was literally days before I found myself sitting by his side, receiving incredible wisdom and guidance in ritual."

The ceremony was held on a cold November day, in a remote spot completely off grid, amongst sprawling acres of farmland. We arrived about midday and joined a group of approximately 20 fellow 'truth seekers'. Prior to arriving, we were instructed to apply nil by mouth, bring water and swimwear. My initial thought had been…"Fuck me, what am I getting myself into?"

The Inipi was a structure made from willow poles, covered in thick layers of blanket and cowhide. In the centre, a pit had been dug out where red hot stones would be placed, brought in on a pitchfork through the opening, carefully stacked once everyone's inside. About 10 metres across from the Inipi, a sizeable fire had been roaring from the moment we'd arrived. It was there the searingly hot stones lay.

Whilst waiting for the preparations to finish, I learnt why everyone had decided to attend. The common theme being either intrigue of the unknown, with an eager lure to the wonder of this ancient ceremony, feelings of disconnection or discontent within ones life, or simply a desire to cleanse and purify ones mind, body and spirit. I was definitely in the curiosity camp, and most certainly felt a nice deep cleanse was needed.

One thing I was nervously anticipating, was the smoking of the infamous 'peace pipe'. "Do those Indigenous dudes get baked on mystical marijuana?"..."Am I gonna be trippin' out losing my shizzle?" So I was happy to know this wasn't on the menu. Back in the day I would'a been all over it...absolutely one trillion percent down with anything I could get my dirty paws on. Smoke it first, ask what it is after. Standard. Having not smoked for some time, I wasn't too keen to fill my lungs back up, even if it was a guaranteed deal breaker to attain ultimate bliss.

"I was just popping by for some purification chief."

Apparently, certain types of tobacco can be very sacred, holding great power to those who understand how to use it in ceremony...'it is not to be abused or overused'. Hmmm...these wise dudes certainly know how to maintain some decorum. Was it just me, or do us numpties in civilisation have a tendency to tear the fuckin' arse out of absolutely anything and everything?

Silva lead us in a pre-ceremony discussion on the teachings of the Lakota elders. We then in turn shared with our fellow space cadets, setting intentions for ritual, followed by a prayer and meditation. It was then into a changing area and into our swimwear, ready to commence battle.

"Why is there always one dude who insists on wearing a cheese-wire thong?"

Although bitterly cold, standing there in nothing but swimmers felt rather liberating. Maybe the dude in the cheese-wire had it dialled after all? There was a beautiful lingering in the air of majestic stillness…somehow the pouring pissing rain under the dusk sky, only added to the ambience - a trance like glow coming from the flames, illuminating a silhouette of the Inipi and the surrounding landscape. One by one we're cleansed with a sage 'smudge', before saying a prayer to the sacred Gods, blessing us for our dance with the divine. It kinda reminded me of those pill-popping-acid-gobbling days, where I'd set an intention secretly within the darkness of my paranoid mind…"Please don't let this be the end!"

We entered the Inipi crawling through a tiny 'hobbit doorway'. Ladies seated around one side of the pit, men on the other, forming a circle. I found myself facing directly opposite the doorway, across from the pit. I remember Silva saying this was the most intense place to be, slap bang in the centre of this tomb inferno.

"I felt slightly unhinged by this prospect, quietly contemplating whether to make a fuss, or remain there and endure the full intensity of the unknown. I decided to stay put."

There was literally enough room to sit cross legged, barely able to sit straight without your head touching the roof. As I'm 'processing' a heightened sense of claustrophobia from being crammed into such a confined space, the hot stones were loaded into the pit and stacked, and the opening of the Inipi sealed shut. It was go time.

I don't think I was alone, when I say I felt an increased sense of angst wash over me as soon as that door was sealed off. Visibility was minimal, just the glow of those searingly hot stones, which had a fuzzy hypnotic haze. I soon realised that centrepiece would be our altar. It was where I'd fix my gaze, and with every intention, try to maintain my focus (and sanity) throughout the entire ceremony.

Silva had given us a heads-up. In a nutshell, it was…"be in your heart, not your head." Wise words indeed. Stillness (and trauma therapy) had taught me how to be in my heart, so it was a familiar instruction and one I knew I could follow. Meditative practice had shown me it is possible to not judge reality. Whatever arises, let it be. A moment to moment acceptance of 'what is'.

"Although far from mastering this technique, I sure as hell was glad I had the awareness."

One incredible lesson you learn from facing and overcoming adversity, is acceptance. Addiction and mental illness taught me the art of powerlessness, recovery from it granted me the gift of accepting it. Of course there's always resistance, however, you learn to meet it with kindness. Everyone has this ability, yet realising it and actually putting it into practice is a whole different ballgame.

Just as we're about to start, a woman sitting to my left is hit with a full blown panic attack. "Holy-fuckin'-moly!" I sure as hell know how that feels. This had the potential for us all to fall like dominoes. In the dark fuzzy glow, a silhouette scrambles over bodies as Silva helps her make an exit. Her anxiety sent ripples throughout…"Am I the only one who's quietly thinking - fuck, should I follow?"

Drums and chanting are the way of the Lakota, adding to the mystique of this ancient ceremony. As we began to follow their rhythm, the first drops of water hit the scolding hot stones. As you can imagine, if you've ever sat in a sauna, they reacted with a piercing hissing noise, followed by a rush of steam that shot up my nostrils with an insanely sharp burning sensation, instantly filling my gullet with such ferocity.

"An almighty surge of adrenaline smacked me around the chops, with a sudden jolt of...'Fuck, what have I done?'...Too late now!"

Silva had instructed - if anyone became overwhelmed by the intensity...bow down low where the air is more refined. "Fuck!... you can't swing a cat in here, and I for one ain't no hobbit." From that first 'hit' of mega-vape, it was one almighty tug of war between sanity and insanity. An unrelenting battle to let go of controlling the experience and being in my heart, and being dragged back into the madness of my mind.

So, I found myself facing my demons again. The inner workings of my noodle with no means to distract, in what I'd consider to be acutely challenging circumstances. Or, to put it another way - I was freakin' the fuck out with no exit plan. Now, if you're anything like me, you are your own judge, jury and executioner. That catastrophic tyrant-ego-mind will pulverise you every time, unless you learn a mental defence against it. In theory, that's what meditation's for...

"Master the mind, and it will no longer master you."

The intensity of the situation brought a whole new level of understanding. I had to literally barter with myself (the rational part), to reaffirm I had indeed chosen to endure this onslaught, and it was indeed I, who had placed myself within those conditions...so, shut the fuck up, relax, accept 'what is' and deal with it. Easy right?

I recalled a story I'd read about in early recovery, of a wise man on his deathbed. Surrounded by his disciples, a young man asked the dying elder..."Master, tell me one thing to help me live a skilful life?"...the Master simply replied..."Wherever you find yourself, want to be there."

"Fuck me, the impact of that statement somehow found its way back to me just when I needed it most!"

The heat grew ridiculously intense, with the searing glow of that volcanic pit emitting face melting temperatures. Any bodily fluids I may of once owned were now seeping out of every pore, adding to the mass moisture from the plumes of vapour. It was like some kinda fucked up flashback to Lord 'E'…sitting in a 'chill-out' tent in some random field sweating ya bollocks off, clutching the seat of ya pants as waves of unadulterated euphoria sweep over you uncontrollably. "Hmm…not yet acquired that glorious sense of gratification…maybe that'll come later?"

The beat of the drum and the 'trance-vibration' coming from the chanting, served as a reminder I was not alone in this peculiar situation…and as soon as I'd drift away back into the ego mind, I'd forcefully will myself back to the rhythm of my heart and begin to chant again. In doing so, I found myself rockin' back and forth like a crazed lunatic. This letting go, the swaying, rockin' back and forth, the chanting…not knowing the words but saying them anyway…it was precisely what Silva meant…"Be in your heart, not your head." Allow it to happen.

"Completely surrender and immerse yourself in the unknown. Let go of control and trust the process."

Trusting the unknown is hard to do, counter-intuitive even…but experience and evidence shows you it always works out if you allow it to, you just gotta get the neurotic mind out the way. That's where faith comes in. Leap and the net will always appear. With every effort, I kept reaffirming…"Want to be here…want to be here." Each time the ego-mind diminished, my senses accelerated…as I began to hallucinate. "What da fuck!…I can hear a roaring grizzly bear coming from behind…is that one of the guys trippin' out losing it…or am I?" On and on it went…the repetition of the chanting, the drum, the hallucinations, the sizzling of water on fire and the fierceness of the steam cutting the air of each strained breath. It was endless and exasperated me to the point of near on breaking.

When Silva finally announced the ceremony was coming to an end and the final blessings were chanted, if I could, I would'a leaped over and kissed him in victorious joy. "Oh boy, the relief!" An incredible feeling of gratitude and pride washed over me, and with it an almighty sense of achievement…I'd made it!

"I had endured a slice of Lakota magic and it felt frickin' incredible."

When that doorway to the outside world opened, a jet stream of ice cold air shot in. You could feel the vacuum swirling around infusing you from within. It was so calmingly refreshing, and it felt so pure. One by one we slowly began to leave the Inipi. As I crawled out I will never forget the sense of euphoria (ahhh there it is!) as my hands and knees first touched that wet, sodden mud on the ground beneath me. The sky was pitch black, yet the stars were brighter than I'd ever known. Through the pouring rain I could see the fire still blazing just yards away, which added an extra comfort to our grand exit.

As I edged further out, I was suddenly struck with an enormous sense of newness. Everything just seemed so amplified. As I continued to crawl I had the maddest realisation - it was as though I'd regressed back to the very first moments in life, to a baby coming out of a mother's womb. I know that sounds crackers, but it's how it felt. It was so incredibly profound…I was awestruck, spellbound by the purity of it all. Just me, practically in my birthday suit, crawling in the mud. My body completely drenched in fluid as I leave a small confined 'womb'. The only thing that was missing was the midwife and an umbilical cord.

As I slowly got to my feet, it was like I was walking for the very first time, each step a milestone. I remember looking around and everyone seemed to be in the same blissed out state. A bunch of adult babies stumbling around buzzin' on pure ecstasy!

"Fuck, man, those Lakota homies were bang on…Fire, Air, Water and Earth…the ultimate life force, reconnecting you to that oneness of creation. It was breathtaking."

I dared to ask if anyone'd heard the roar of a grizzly bear. It was met with looks of bewilderment, which may suggest I was a tad loco…and there was me thinking it might of been the dude in the cheese-wire thong.

According to Silva and the Lakota elders, if you're lucky enough, you may experience an encounter with a spirit guide of sorts. So, who knows, maybe a grizzly decided to pay me a visit, I'll never know, that or I lost my shizzle, or someone else had and decided to impersonate a bear...whatever, it didn't matter, I felt humbled, honoured and truly grateful to be part of such an incredible experience.

HUMANOID

The modern world is changing, and with it how we live our lives. We're being forced to adapt more than ever, seamlessly vying to fit in with this relentless way of being. Or is that just me? Grand scale FOMO times a billion…with an endless abundance at a blink of an eye, is it any wonder we may struggle to avoid being engrossed by some, if not all the enticing, glittery 'things' on offer?

"Smartphone technology is incredible. You're one click away from Larry at 'speed-demons' dropping off ya nice new toilet brush, before you've even had a chance to take a dump."

We now essentially carry a personal computer and entertainment device at all times. I can communicate with whoever, wherever, whenever. Marvellous. So, is this technological advancement anything to worry about? For all its pros, for me there does come a price. Having spent multiple years in active clusterfuckedness, I can't help but feel those tentacles of entanglement wrap around my being like an octopus on crack. Smartphones for me are seriously 'sticky', and I'm not talking about what goes on behind closed doors when no-one's looking.

The way I see it - through technology we have never been more connected. Through technology we have never been more disconnected. It's a paradox, and one that's undeniably true, no? Tech reliance seemed to come out of nowhere, and now it's as normal as taking a dump before you clean your teeth (thanks for the brush Larry). If used in a healthy and moderate way, then in theory there are many pros.

"If you feel inspired, motivated or it simply brings you joy, laughter and wellness then great, crack on."

For me, I think the trick is to know when and how to detach from technology, to peel myself away from those tentacles and be autonomous, not governed by it. To enhance my life with it, but do not define myself or existence within it. I'm talking about non attachment. To be ok with or without, and to know you always have a choice. Do we truly realise this?...and more importantly, do we apply it?

Let's face it, we've all been seeking connection since the day we popped outta the womb to say hello. We've come a long way since then. Pubs, clubs, no different to churches and temples, or following (worshipping) celebrity or sport. It makes perfect sense we're still searching for that inherent primal connection online. I know I can...and you don't even have to leave your sofa, let alone the front door.

"Gone are the days of going out to check in and make an appearance, we got it right here in our hand in an instant."

I've always been a tad hesitant of tech. Not cos I'm some old codger who doesn't get it...it's just not something I feel I need in my life all the time...yet I still use it. I came off social media because it just didn't work for me at that time. The Crystal Meth femme fatale shenanigans didn't help my cause. I was using it for all the wrong reasons. "Where can I get my next feed?"…(literally) Besides, it did me a favour, I'd rather hang out with my chums than zone out on a screen. "Why the fuck am I always looking down at my screen anyway, instead of up, out and around at the world passing me by?"…and…"Why am I allowing this to consume me? In fact, I'm being violated!" Am I the only one who finds it intrusive?…or notices the obsessiveness arising from a constant barrage of intrigue, the hit of adrenaline which always kicks in…that rush of dopamine every time I'd receive a notification, be it a msg, comment, like or follower.

For me, it's 100% addiction that always surfaced. A potent drug, chasing the unquenchable thirst for validation from others…and because I'd discovered previously I had to achieve total abstinence from narcs to be free from their grip, I decided to apply the same principles to other areas of my life, including specific platforms of tech.

"It's extreme I know, but it works for me and I can truly say I feel frickin' liberated without compromise."

When I started practicing meditative awareness, I was learning a lot, especially about the nature of the mind, our thoughts, sensations and ultimately who I was…and more importantly who I wasn't. I began to differentiate between this false sense of identity, the ego and the myriad of masks I'd create. I just could not find a way to have a profile on social media, without feeling like I was living my life as an avatar.

Is it possible to be in the online realm and still exist in the real world? It's undeniably brilliant for business, the arts, marketing etc…however, I fail to see how the online space 'is the real world'…because from where I'm sitting, I can't taste, touch or hold that virtual reality. Maybe I'm missing a trick?

"I guess you could say it all comes down to perspective and personal experience."

I've never been one to be a sheep. I'm a Lone Wolf, simply going against the stream of convention. I found a way to operate, with absolutely no limitation whatsoever to hinder the aspirations I choose to achieve…"As we think, so we become." So it is possible, and I'm not the only one. It doesn't mean I'm better, and it certainly doesn't mean I'm right…only it works for me and I'm blissfully present in life more than I'm not. Do I miss that shitty comparing lives bullshit I used to do? No fuckin' way Jose! That in itself is a blessing. It is a gift to be comfortable within your own skin, without the need for validation. Now, I'm not saying everyone who uses socials is a sheep, addicted or not comfortable in their own skin…

"Maybe ask yourself this though...am I?"

Do I have a screen attachment?...am I spaced out all the time?...is it the first and last thing I do each day, all day, every day?...living in the online realm, lost in the vortex of the amazonian matrix...have I fallen down a sticky-icky rabbit hole, with an inability to sit with myself without needing to scratch the itch? Or, do I always have to log on and zone out? Only you know the answer to that, or maybe you don't.

The social pressure of comparing lives can certainly make you feel inadequate if you allow it to (certainly fucked with my shit)... and as for a heightened sense of anxiety, I'd even go as far as saying it not only decreased my state of consciousness, but at times depleted my mental health to a big fat zero. With the awareness of denial getting in the way, and knowing the power it holds, I could really see the avatar (ego) was taking over my authentic self, so I quit, sharpish.

Was the cult of selfies the true introduction to this peculiar behaviour we now find ourselves deeply entrenched in within the tech realm? The obsession to be seen, heard and liked. It's so far gone it just seems 'normal'. Are we now in a world surrounded by spaced out humanoids? Self important, narcissistic clones, so numbed out by the hypnotic entanglement of tech, that we're inadvertently allowing any trace of individuality or authenticity to slowly ebb away into nothingness...

"Is this a potential clusterfuck waiting to happen?...or has it already begun?"

Let me give you an example of an observation, a social experiment even, that I was involved with whilst engaging in the educational system. It's based primarily on my own direct experience, with additional input from hundreds upon thousands of young people, between the ages of 11 and 18 across the UK, both state and private sectors.

I created this scenario for unsuspecting students to take part in, based on the teachings of a Buddhist Monk. He says quite simply..."You want to know if you're addicted to something? Simple, go without that something for 7 days. You will soon know if you're addicted." You could try that with absolutely anything.

"Sex. Drugs. Sugar. Shopping. Hands-down-pants. Caffeine. Vape..."

Now, with some students, you know they have issues, or family, even parents that do. You see the signs. When you've been in the madness you know it well, and you spot insanity in others. Some have no identification with drugs, addiction or mental illness. They're simply not affected, or so they think. So, to start, I'll say to them - "Ok, before I talk about how addiction affects me, I'm actually gonna make you feel how addiction can affect you, right now." The students will look confused. I'll then explain they need to imagine they've got their mobile phones and to switch them off (in theory they won't have these in sessions).

"At this point they're already displaying gasps of disapproval, petulant sighs and general angst."

Next up, the imaginary box. I now explain (teachers included) I'm gonna take their phones and place into this here box. At this point the noise level and energy has ramped up and it's getting kinda wobbly. This is a standard reaction. Once myself, with help from teachers, have just about managed to calm things down, I'll explain the box will be placed in the teachers staff room, to be kept safe for 7 days. Cue riot.

"Welcome to how addiction feels!"

Again, once we've just about calmed everyone down, I'll ask the students (and there's absolutely plenty of takers at this point) - "Who would like to share how they feel right now?" The following is just one example of a very typical answer, which I'd help them process by means of dissecting. Remember - this is an 'imaginary' exercise...it's not even real.

Student - "I'm really angry."

Me - "Why?"

Student - "I need my phone."

Me - "Why do you need your phone?"

Student - "I just do." (or/and) "What am I meant to do without my phone."

That's just one example, but the majority of students share the exact same reaction. To their credit, there's a minority that proclaim to do without quite happily. Most teachers admit they could not do it either. I'll explain it's ok to feel this way, it is not their fault. They've been brought up to know no different. Isn't the world we live in an incredibly addictive society, heavily dependent on distraction? You only have to speak to any parent, to know whether they too are at the mercy of those sticky-icky tentacles of entanglement. I've done enough parent talks at schools to know many parents (not all) allow kids to be preoccupied by using phones, tablets, TVs, gaming etc as a means to give the parent a 'breather'. So it's actually learnt behaviour, encouraged in some cases.

"These poor fuckers stand no chance of avoiding screen addiction."

So there we have it…what do you think? With countless observations made, does it appear technological advancement may of inadvertently created a breed of young humanoids? Could we now have a generation of genius gadget fiends, evolved way beyond their years? Do they behold incredible knowledge and with it undeniable ability? Or is it too much, too soon perhaps? Hmm… information overload times a trillion equals burnout, system failure, meltdown.

Could this lead to a pandemic of manic-hyper-madness from these crazed young spaced cadets? Has tech reliance created a posse of Tasmanian Devils on PCP…and with it (detri)mental disorders as a result? Is ADHD now a trend? Being a 'fuck up' seems to be rather cool these days, no?…"Please Mummy, can I see a psychiatrist for my 16th birthday? Kelly's just got her ABC-XYZ diagnosis and it's so unfair!..Please Mummy, please!"

Jokes aside, the way I see it…you can seek out all the other labels you wanna whack on it, take as many 'magic pills' as you can get your hands on…but in all seriousness, is there a link between rapid, machine-gun-fire screen attachment, and having the attention span of an erratic, amnesiac tadpole on acid? What do you think? Is it just these youngsters? Maybe ask yourself this…

"Can I sit in stillness and 'just be', without the need for agitation or distraction?...and...does my brain feel fried?"

Anyway, I'll go on to explain to the students, and they'll hear it in my story, that the relationship they have with their phone, may be similar to the relationship I had with narcs and all the other stuff... including 'sticky-icky-apps'. If you 'need' something, if you feel you 'can't' live without something, then it's likely you're very much dependant on it.

"Attached. Entangled. Addicted."

It's a very simple way to observe the nature of addiction. Go without for 7 days. Imagine life without that 'something' and try it. What does that look like?

Two questions I now use as standard to gage a behaviour.

1- Why am I doing it?
2- How does it make me feel?

I will say this to anyone, be it a student, teacher, parent, celebrity, the god damn Pope, it don't matter, there is no way around this one, it's really simple...when you're on your own, and I mean in the blackness of your own space, the nothingness of being left with yourself, just you...be it at home, or lying next to a beloved in bed at night...when you're there, in your thoughts, it is only in that stillness the absolute truth of your existence will reveal itself. Even if you are not being honest enough to see it whilst distracted, or through a mask to your pals...you will have to own it. It is unavoidable...when faced with yourself you have to acknowledge your truth and get real. What you do with that is up to you.

Before I learnt to disentangle from my thinking, it was in those moments of aloneness when everything came to a stop. My mind would be racing as I'm lying there in bed each night, on my own or next to someone, it didn't matter...and in my head I've got nowhere to run or hide. I'm stuck with it. My truth, whatever that may be.

"It was in those moments the truth seemed to eventually outdo the denial."

1- Why am I doing it? Cos I can't fuckin' stop, that's why.
2- How is it making me feel? How long you got?

For me, an attachment to 'something' is avoidance. Another form of escapism and an inability to be in reality, the here and now. I am not being present when I'm essentially glued to a screen. It's that simple. So why is that?…Well, the world we live in, is it really any surprise we may find ourselves craving escapism?…and if that escapism brings a sense of relief from the otherwise dull (or perhaps painful) existence of life, why would we not choose to jump right in? I'm not saying we shouldn't find joy and laughter in the 'theatre of life'…we sure as hell need that. I guess the question is - "Is my life so god damn miserable, that I need to look at this shit and change something?"…or…"Do I even give a fuck?" Well, only you know the answer to that.

Knowing total abstinence may be the only bullet proof way of being truly free from obsessive behaviour, is it possible to apply the same principle as I would with any other attachment, and completely 'starve it' ?…Hmm, easier said than done. I switched my smartphone for an oldskool 'dumbphone'…I lasted two weeks. Maybe one day I'll feel the need to give it another go, but for now, I strive to do what I can to maintain a healthy balance as best I can.

"I still struggle with screen intrusion…so abstaining from sticky-icky-apps certainly makes this easier."

Do we find the time to sit in silence and watch the clouds pass us by? Do we ever acknowledge the beauty in a birds song?…or dare to walk barefoot on grass and feel the ground beneath us? If the answer to that is…"Errrr???"…then perhaps it's time to unplug.

For me, meditative practice (yep that again), be it traditional or otherwise, (which for me includes regular engagements of stillness, creativity, (pro) activity and immersion in nature)…are the only methods that seem to assist in the ability to ever come close to dealing with such affairs…being present.

CRAZIES

Giving up a 'glamourous' career in hairstyling had been a huge leap of faith. It was one I can safely say fed my soul, granting me a greater sense of purpose. This was crucial in my quest for personal evolution.

Working with the Amy Winehouse Foundation opened many doors, providing the opportunity to enter places I never thought I'd be. I found myself participating in discussions, debates and conferences in London's Parliament, City Hall and the Home Office. The first time I attended such an event, was an evening full of Lords, MP's and the like. I thought it vital to wear the correct attire to such a gathering…blazer jacket, low cut DMs and a tee-shirt with a punk sticking his middle finger up with the slogan "PUNK IS NOT DEAD." Perfect.

"My subtle way of dropping a grenade into a social situation I wasn't yet comfortable with. Dynamite."

I stood up in front of an audience of scholars, mental health 'experts' and a bevy of fellow 'freedom fighters', speaking on addiction and behavioural disorders, providing insights into my own lived experience and the work the Foundation carried out in the educational system. I met some dude along the way, who'd also shared his experience, a gold toothed ex-gang member from the streets of London. His story was incredible. He'd been blasted in the chest with a shotgun by a rival drug gang. His buddy had been killed on the spot. The homies managed to carry him down a street into a neighbouring area, knocking on a front door of a house. They were let in by an elderly woman, which if you think about it is bloody remarkable. Fast forward a week and he's lying in hospital with said woman, just sitting there watching over him. She turns out to be the wife of an MP, insisting he leave his old life and go live with them. He declined...but on his return to the streets, had an epiphany the night his crew had planned a revenge attack. He walked away and ends up back at the couples house. Give them their dues, they took him in with open arms and showed him another life with unconditional love and kindness. Soon after he enrolled in college and studied politics. He now has a seat in

Parliament, working with MP's to combat knife crime on the streets. Legend.

"We went on to collaborate in some of the gnarlier schools in London, doing talks on problem behaviour, addiction and gang mentality."

Another incredible opportunity I had, was the absolute honour of visiting a psychiatric unit to sit with the patients and talk with them. From a teenager going into my 20s, I always considered myself to be a tad unhinged, having this distinct feeling something weren't right in my head, fearing I may end up institutionalised, either in prison or perhaps a secure mental unit. It became a reality, fortunately for me it was to engage with those 'clients' about my experience with overcoming mental illness.

"It was extremely humbling to be asked to sit and speak with such incredible individuals. They're my kind of people. Misunderstood, a little strange perhaps, but far from vanilla."

Just like the movies, it was over the top clinical and felt very sterile, enough to send you mad, even if you weren't. There were 12 'clients' attending the session, all accompanied by their individual nurse...all dressed in white as you'd expect. The eldest 'client' was 21 years of age. He believed he was the reincarnation of Jesus, intent on communicating telepathically to Portuguese superstar Ronaldo. Apparently, he could determine game tactics and outcomes. "Oi, Jesus, don't suppose you got this week's lottery numbers?" Gotta love him. The youngest being 14. Out of the 12, 9 were in for 'skunk psychosis', a very common occurrence indeed. I could really relate to this condition, having self-medicated..."It keeps me calm maaaan."...(micro-dose low strain hash/weed may of done)...and it most certainly led to a spot of nuttiness on more than one occasion. Having learnt to 'normalise', 'function' and 'contain' it for a length of time, I managed to switch skunk for alcohol. I believe for me that was damage limitation at a crucial time in my life. Did not mean I was fixed though, far from it...

"I'd just 'cross-addicted' to another drug and coping aid."

It was a morning session split into two sections, due to the 'clients' removal for a 20 minute interval to be assessed and given their meds. From what I could see, these complex individuals were experiencing episodes of varying mental conditions on the spectrum. Some extreme, others not so. Now, I'm no doctor, but I do understand human behaviour, the nature of the mind, and how it relates to unfavourable conditions, including extreme traumas....many of which often result in problem behaviour, addiction, delusion and ultimately institutions. From what I've experienced...by communicating to the 'person', not the 'illness', without a shadow of doubt real connections are made.

"We discussed my struggles with drug abuse, the underlying torment I held, and how I'd felt so misunderstood, alone and different to others."

The message I was conveying was one of hope. Out of the 12, I'd say at least half were with me. Jesus was fluctuating between the galactic airwaves and the seat of his chair. Those that connected related to what I was saying, asking questions and shifting their attention from vacant-zombie-space-cadet, to engaged human being. I know it provided a lifeline, because 3 hand written letters were passed to me via staff a few days later. They were letters of absolute hope. They outlined for the first time they finally felt understood... that it brought an immense sense of relief, clarity and reassurance over their 'condition', for someone to really listen properly, I mean really comprehend what they had to say.

It is so incredibly important to feel like you are being heard, being seen, valued, understood and acknowledged. For me (and many others including those 'clients'), one of the most damaging acts carried out to another human is neglect. Being neglected, not being allowed to have a voice, to communicate on any level, as a child right up to an adult, it is so detrimental. It causes fundamental problems.

"Disconnection causes breakdowns in relationships, creating isolation, confusion and instability."

The way I see it, people aren't just born crazy, we are by-products of our environment. Maybe some peeps really do pop out the womb with the DNA to be crackers, who knows...but if you're anything like me and it's been, shall we say 'a little nutty', then it's understandable you may experience some nuttiness. It makes perfect sense to me the world we live in is, let's face it, completely fuckin' mental. Always has been...a sick society riddled with dysfunction, so it's no surprise some of us might experience pangs of weirdness along the way, no? So if you're feeling overwhelmed with angst for the current state of affairs, join the club.

Insanity is an interesting label. It has a lot of stigma attached to it. The true definition of insanity is...according to the wise words of some grey haired dude...

"Insanity is doing the same thing over and over, again and again, expecting different results each time."

Hmm...to me that sounds very familiar. Definitely rings true in my life. Am I alone? Me thinks not...download-subscribe-rinse-delete-repeat...or maybe it's the classic...get completely walloped piss-blind-drunk, declare - "I swear I'm never doing that again"...and then, well...you can fill the blanks.

Coming to know oneself behind the myriad of masks (denial/ego/pride/fear/delusion etc) and truly understanding the nature of the beast is a blessing. It can also be a curse if taken too seriously. I often laugh at my own bullshit now...I still fuck up and I'm far from perfect...but putting it simply...

"Is the desire to tweak and refine these crank behaviours, greater than the desire to remain stuck in denial with your head up ya arse?"

Deep down I always had a distinct inherent knowing life could be better. That dream of the white horse, I never forgot. There was a wanderlust with an insatiable desire to experience it all, I just got side-tracked and lost...developing and honing the art of dysfunction to a T.

The more I've studied my own mind and insanity, the greater understanding I have for others, based on the premise that if you know yourself, you can't help but know others. I gain great comfort in knowing that. We are all incredible beings, trying to navigate our way through this clusterfuck of madness, and rather than separate and alienate because of someone's strangeness or indifference, endeavour to draw close and connect, to reach out and join the dots.

"There is a real therapeutic value in one human being helping another."

I also believe us 'crazies'…the square pegs, the aloof, the misunderstood, the cranks, nut-jobs, the loons and the weirdos… we're so tuned in we appear to be tuned out. We know there's more to life than the lies on offer, so we intuitively 'check out' and unsubscribe from the mainstream agenda.

That intuition is easily lost to the institution, whatever that may be, so we've just got to harness our 'shadow side'. Our enemy is lack of self worth, self belief and the courage to go forth and achieve…but once we realise our true potential and step into our power…BOOM!…We are magnificent, intelligent, creative beasts that can do anything. We are the masterminds, mavericks, the crème de la crème, the mustard, the bomb, the shizzle. We are the dudes, dudettes and the everything in-betweeners that can make change. We inspire, motivate and elevate to a whole new level. We believe anything is possible, because deep down we just know it is, and anyone who doesn't agree simply does not get it. They are not like me or you, because they're not dialled in yet. We operate on a completely different frequency. It doesn't make us right, it does not make us better, it just makes us different.

"Society fears different. The 'crazy' people. The misunderstood. The weird. The wonderful."

It's been my experience whatever we put our minds to, we will exceed beyond any self imposed limitation, if only we could just trust and believe this is so. That is our Achilles heel, where we come unstuck. With our excellence comes our fragility. We are hypersensitive. We feel pain, not just our own but the entire planet's population. We are empaths...we feel exasperated by the cruelty and injustice, crippling us into retreating and going into our shells, for safety, 'sanity' and solitude. For some, this exile of solitude becomes a dark baron existence. A place where dark shadows linger and for some, deprivation. It can be gnarly, and any hope of ever leaving this dark existential world can feel near on impossible. That is where the drugs and escapism enter, to seek comfort and sedation...and there on lies the start of our demise and decline in mental health furthermore.

There is living proof that IT IS possible to come out of this episode...that feeling of alienation, desperation, the despair and disconnection from reality as you perceive it. Change IS possible. I know so many people who like myself have experienced the darkest human conditions possible and have transcended. We crossed that bridge to a safer place of refuge. There is no right or wrong way to get there. One thing's for sure - connection and the right people who truly understood my condition was vital to set me on a path to freedom. A posse of lost souls, the wounded healers...finding a power greater than my lonesome arse was the biggest game-changer I could'a ever dreamed of.

"Community and connection is imperative...the WE."

Together WE are not alone. Supported (by those who knew), I discovered life is everything you could wish for...although challenging and baffling at times, and that's ok. I can sometimes still feel like an alien from another planet, wondering why the feck I'm here and what's the meaning to all this weird planet Earth stuff. These weird human things I coexist with, odd creatures like myself that can sometimes do weird shit when no one's looking...and that's ok too.

It wasn't until I stopped being drug fucked that I achieved this. Turning my focus to natural remedies, I slowly began to peel away the years of institutionalised conditioning, which ultimately led to a significant shift in my consciousness, and with it came my intuition and a heightened sense of self belief, power and worth. It was meditation, not medication…and all things wholesome that restored me to sanity and the purest form of human spirit. Everything I thought I was getting from mind altering substances…that 'comfort' or 'connection'…I immediately embodied through safely exploring and developing a true relationship to my internal and external worlds.

"Peace of mind comes effortlessly, once you learn to connect to the tranquility and natural rhythm of the breath and your body."

Now, if you're thinking… "Jeez Dave man, reel it in dude!"…or… "Fuck me bore off!"…I get it. It's not exactly sex, drugs and rock n roll…but ask yourself this - "Is my current way of doing things surmounting to a feeling of unbridled peace and tranquility?" If yes - BINGO!…do not change a thing. However, if deep down in your gut, you've got even a whiff of uncertainty about that answer, what the fuck you waiting for?

If nothing changes, nothing changes, right?

BE THE LOG

There are countless fellow disciples of truth, every single one has helped me along the way…and I have the best agent money cannot buy, faith. Without that guidance, unravelling that twisted knot in my psyche is hard at best. The hard-wiring of my past life conditioning had been soothed, and by doing so, I could finally function in a far healthier way.

"Empowered and free, life was truly magical."

I was well aware synchronicity would always point me in a direction, even if it looked uncertain or far from obvious. I'd become attuned to trusting intuition, that gut feeling...to know that if it feels right, it is...and do my best to let go of the outcome and realise everything will be ok, always.

A friend of mine, a film director, suggested I read a book called The Artist's Way. It's about attaining a higher level of creativity. I immediately purchased the book, and decided to dedicate my focus and immerse myself.

"Within the first week, I dusted the cobwebs off my estranged guitar, and couldn't stop journalising creative writing, reconnecting to my love of art."

The more submerged I became, the more I realised how important it was to be artistic. Since giving up the hair game, I'd channeled all my energy into being of service. I realised my true soul purpose was to do both, and that book lead me to that conclusion. Is it just me, or are we all programmed to believe we can only pick one purpose in life, to stick with it until end of days? Well for this here pirate, that was never gonna happen.

"I see life as chapters...and like any pirate, they don't just sail one ocean."

With absolutely no limitations, I was now living my life with full faith that whatever I focus on, I can make happen, as long as I do the work. For me, this journey of self discovery meant working out who and what I'm meant to be...and to fulfil it. If you'd asked me back in the day who I was, I'd of tried my usual mind-fuck-telepathy-trick, second guessing what I thought you wanted me to say, and what you wanted me to be. Craving validation, if it meant going on an expedition no questions asked, I'd of told you I was an experienced mountaineer. "I'm fuckin' Bear Grylls mate."

My fucked up school experience taught me many things, mostly about survival. Shapeshifting. I kinda had to do it. When you're young and the teachers ask…"What do you want to be when you grow up?" Good ruddy question. Hmmm. Let me think about this. Erm. Maybe I'm already aspiring to be a great artist. Nah. Maybe a spaceman (that became reality)...Maybe I'll grow up to be a spy, something really cool like that. If I knew then what I know

now, my answer would simply be…"When I grow up I want to be happy."

"If I am happy, everything else seems to take care of itself."

Apparently, it was John Lennon, who as a wee nipper had that exact question from a rather dismissive teacher. When John answered with…"I wanna be happy"…the teacher quipped…"I don't think you understand the question child", to which John brilliantly replied…"No Sir, I don't think you understand life."

Fuck yeah Lennon.

Happiness for me is being truly free. It's a really simple premise, yet so damn hard to grasp...attaining our freedom. Are you free? Do you feel a sense of absolute liberation in life? Have you found your true purpose yet? Your heart and soul's desire. If it's an honest yes…I frickin' well salute you. If it's a no, do not give up.

A true sense of freedom only came when I gained a strong sense of purpose…and with it authenticity, integrity and stepping into a power greater than my ego.

"Letting go of fear, pride, control and bullshit certainly helps."

I received the following teaching from a zen master, who outlined the importance of understanding the true nature of life, our minds, and the unskilful behaviour we're so mindfucked to act out on...

Imagine you're a log floating down a river. The river is a stream of pure, flowing consciousness...a life force, taking you (the log) onward down stream to the unknown. Sometimes the river is gentle, with a sense of stillness as you float merrily down stream, and sometimes the river becomes a swell of chomping rapids, throwing you around in a turbulent frenzy until you come to rest again.

"The flowing stream is a constant, unpredictable force of nature you have absolutely no power over."

Now, imagine the riverbanks...one side is 'happiness', the other 'unhappiness'. Inevitably, our log becomes embedded on the riverside of 'happiness'...it remains stuck for some time, before eventually slipping back into the flowing stream. Along its way, it becomes embedded and stuck on 'unhappiness', and so on. This is life. We fluctuate through the constant, unpredictable and ever changing stream of consciousness (or unconscious). Like the log, we drift between happiness and unhappiness. This is simply it. We are either happy, or unhappy...however, unlike the log, we attach to happiness, clinging, not wanting to let go of it, and when that state of being goes we're left with an overwhelming state of depletion (unhappiness), which we want to get away from as quickly as possible. Sound familiar? The wise response to this ever changing state of being would be to accept 'what is', happiness or unhappiness, chaos or order...and like the log, go with the flow and not judge the experience.

"If we are happy, great, embrace...but do not attach, as it is impermanent. If we are unhappy, (bollocks) embrace...but do not attach, as it is impermanent."

Buddhist philosophy calls this 'The Middle Way'. So, just like the log, a skilful approach for me floating along the river of my life, would be to not cling to the riverbanks, so I can get to that great ocean of infinite abundance...aka true happiness and freedom. Bloody easier said than done, and if you're anything like me, it can at times seem impossible to embrace these moods, good or bad. Similar to the weather, our temperament is changeable...however, we can in fact learn how to change our relationship to these pesky moods. I don't know about you, but I spent a lifetime completely addicted to my emotions, still can if I allow myself to indulge.

Training the mind to not attach, to see impermanence and be able to let go of the shite is a revelation. Connecting to stillness and your inner calm (I assure you it's there deep down)...you can allow things to dissolve, you've just got to make time to be present and learn how.

"There is nothing I know that is comparable…it's why I keep bangin' on about it."

I began to explore (and discover), that in each moment of presence, if there's no attachment, then surely there's no addict? If you truly observe the nature of what I'm saying, you too may bare witness to this non identification to a 'thing'. In pure consciousness of the present moment, is anyone who they think they are? Hell, I'm not even Dave, that's just a name I've been given, right? It's important for me to say - this wasn't a 'aha!' moment…more of a gradual realisation through many moments of contemplation. I'd encourage anyone to sit with that for a while and perhaps do the same.

The Buddhist term for this mindfuck is 'Anatta', meaning 'No self'. That Native American Inipi sure as hell reinforced that understanding. The way I see it, don't matter whether you're someone of authority, fame, prestige or wealth…or perhaps you identify as an addict, or have been labelled a convict, they're just linear labels to boost identification and a sense of self or status, no?

Now, of course I can only imagine for some, they'd want to cling onto that title as if their entire existence depended on it.

"Once you hit the 'fame game', those sticky-icky tentacles of seduction will have you chasing that shit all day long."

Then there's perhaps the unwanted attachments - is it wise for the ex-convict who's been out of prison for some time, to attach to the identity of a convict? Would they truly be free of their former life in prison, had they not shed this label?...or, would they still be shackled a 'free' person, unable to truly be empowered beyond measure? Same goes for the ex-celebrity, whose 15 minutes of fame has slowly ebbed away into a non existent state of irrelevance. If they were incapable of letting go of that 'old attachment' of the past, surely their freedom is yet to be discovered. In fact, quite the opposite.

I guess what I'm trying to say, is through my experience of meditative practice and mad shit like Inipi's, I was breaking the spell of that muddafunkin' ego to pieces, and with it the realisation of 'No self", free from the shackles of attachment, mind, or the confines of materialism, labels, systems or agendas. Ho'oponopono (get ya chops around that one!) is a traditional Hawaiian self healing technique I came across. Having decided to study and practice it, I found in essence, like all other shamanic-indigenous rituals, its sole intention is the same...to bring our focus back to a 'zero state' of being...to reset and replenish, and be one pure-arse-beast in spirit as nature intended.

"Once again, let's remove all these layers of 'who we think we are'...and be empowered."

Some say addiction is an illness, a disease. I do not discredit that opinion, it's just not how I relate to it. I see addiction as energy, and just like any other energy it comes and goes. It's transient, which for me means impermanent. The energy of addictive behaviour can still arise within my experience of being, but it does not define me. I no longer identify it as being who I am, only if I choose to allow myself to attach to its energy, I will of course become entangled until I choose to let go. Today I have a choice. Previously I did not realise this. Be the log.

"Remember - As we think, so we become."

That realisation in itself is incredibly empowering, and for me is a kinder response to my experience of life. "ADHD?...I'm a creative live-wire you numpty...autistic? Fabulously artistic!" I found the more I practiced this perspective, the more I transcended, letting go of many old attachments along the way. I began to feel better about myself, incredibly 'lighter', and more importantly I started to trust myself and be more in tune with my true nature. I now know the key to everything for me is that inner trust. If I can ask myself… "Do I trust me?"…and the answer is an unfaltering…"Yes"...(which it is) then I know I'm good.

"Do you truly trust yourself?"

To give you an example of the power in this mindset / methodology, I came across a brilliant story, referring to an observation carried out with a bunch of 'inmates' at a prison in Australia. Week in, week out, a Buddhist teacher would visit the prison to teach the 'inmates' (those who were open and willing) the core principles of Buddhist philosophy. He would insist (naturally) on only speaking to them on a level, from his heart, directly to theirs. No different to how I'd communicate to the students in school, those 'clients' in the psychiatric ward, or how I'd now view myself. In doing so, he gained valuable insight - over time, he was informed not one single 'inmate' reoffended having left the prison.

Through the process of non attachment and non judgment of 'labels', only seeing the person underneath, beyond, and outside of those limitations, he had cultivated a more loving response. Through regular practice and dedication, they too began to believe, reprogramming their entire 'belief system' (positive affirmation)… so no matter what circumstances lead them to prison, upon release, not only were they physically free from the confines of those walls, they had in fact been liberated in mind and spirit, embodied by the ultimate freedom in life…a reconnection to their true nature.

"Don't believe me or some random bald headed Buddhist dude…go find out for yourself. You never know, you may find your own slice of freedom."

Getting back to my hearts desire and true purpose in life, creativity and service…time to make this shit happen. I began facilitating music 'therapy' sessions at a school for performing arts in London. I'd previously done a talk at the school where Amy Winehouse studied. Those creative spaces always felt good to be in. When I spoke to those young artists about the perils of life, I swear Amy was standing right by my side throughout. What an honour and a privilege to rep her legacy.

The sessions were specifically held for a group of students considered to be the school's 'drop outs'. My kinda people, the 'crazies'. With the help of the school's Vice Principle (legend), the music teacher (epic) and a colleague who was once homeless on the streets of London (respect), we got those students (broken-homes-broken-hearts), who may I add were severely lacking in social skills, nor the self discipline, belief or motivation to engage, to slowly, but surely turn up. Not just for the group, but for themselves.

Over the course of a few weeks, those students went from 'social outcasts' to 'rockstar redeemers'. How the fuck? Yep you got it…by cultivating the key principles taught by that Buddhist monk. By believing in them, they in turn began to believe in themselves, becoming more empowered through having a purpose other than being labelled a 'Fuck up'.

"We cultivated a belief mindset of 'Yes you feckin' well can'…"

That ethos was a methodology I was now well attuned to, and from my own experience, I knew that.."Yes I frickin' can"…meant anything we put our mind to has the potential to manifest, as long as we believe and take action. So using that synergy within the group, we allowed those students the space to create. Those incredible 'crazies' wrote, rehearsed and performed their own original song live at the Christmas showcase, to an audience consisting of the entire school's population, including parents and staff. We insisted they headline, despite the school's reservations. They absolutely smashed it, were idolised by their peers and received a standing ovation for their efforts. WALLOP! FUCK YEAH!!

"Talk to the person, not the 'problem'…good shit happens. Simple."

Needless to say their non existent self-esteem sky rocketed, and those students left that stage with the evidence they too could believe in, that ANYTHING is possible. Shortly after that awe inspiring showcase, I bid farewell to the Amy Winehouse Foundation. I wasn't entirely sure what I was gonna do, but my hearts desire and purpose was already set in motion. All I had to do, was not focus on the fear of the unknown, and trust it wouldn't go tits up.

TIGERS AND ZEBRAS

For me, travel means adventure. At times a solo mission of self discovery, often leading to unexpected experiences to learn and grow from. The curiosity alone, instills me with an extreme sense of excitement, so when I found myself joining a rather unorthodox hiking expedition up a mountain range in the arse end of nowhere, you could say my adrenaline was jacked to the hilt.

"Initially, I couldn't wait to get going on this epic crusade, but in the back of my mind lingered a very real fear of heights...which unbeknown to me, would unearth an 'undertone of psychosomatic bones' I hadn't yet processed."

The night before setting off, a fellow thrill seeker I'd met whilst travelling, informed me of a young man dying, having fallen from the exact spot I was heading. Marvellous, how reassuring. Death by selfies in precarious places perhaps?...or unexperienced chumps like me gettin' outta their depth?

The day of the ascent I had a very distinct sense of dread, which I couldn't quite shake off. The ridiculously high ride in a cable car to the drop off point reinforced this. I remember thinking to myself..."How the fuck am I gonna hike my arse up this thing, if I can't even bare this feckin' ride?" To top it off, I was at the mercy of trusting the three amigos...'turbo-charged-adrenaline-junkies' I'd not long met, who appeared not only a tad unconventional, but utterly fearless.

As we set off, my best intentions were to fall into a groove, focus on my breath, and do my utmost to 'want to be here'...'be the log'...and embrace 'what is'. In the distance, way up above, lurking, was the forbidding reminder of what lay ahead.

"Oh boy, what have I signed up for?"

Now, in my mind, we're up Mount feckin' Everest. Reality…some highish range, no biggy, but for someone who's got fear of heights kickin' his arse, it's monstrous. The higher we got, the more refined the air, clearly an indicator to altitude. As we zig zagged further up along the trail, we came to a point with a large, red, triangular sign on a post with native context. Well I'll be fucked if I can read it, but it had warning sign written all over it. Perhaps it said - "DAVE, WHAT THE FUCK ARE YOU THINKING YOU MORON? TURN BACK, IT'S NOT TOO LATE YOU FOOL!"

"My immediate gut feeling was to stop right there and go no further."

It was one of those moments I related to so frequently in my former hellraising days. Risk taking and fuck the consequence. That old crusty code of conduct…"Fuck it, it'll be alright." I mean don't get me wrong, sometimes it's good to take risks and leap. This was not one of them. I could feel the adrenaline pumping, as I overrode that gut feeling and continued to put one foot in front of the other. Huge mistake. As the three amigos proceeded, I looked around to scope the level of seriousness. The way I saw it (catastrophic), the path ahead was no wider than your average ten-pin bowling lane. To the left was the mountain face, a vertical wall of endless gnar, to the right, a sheer drop of nothingness. About 20 yards in front, the pathway disappeared around the edge of the mountain. On the rock face to the left was a thick steel cable, bolted to the rock all the way along. Holy fuck, suddenly it dawned on me…"Belt clips, we don't have frickin' belt clips!"

"Clip on to the cable and you're good to go. Fuck. Well we ain't."

It was now obvious what that sign said. "Ahh man, was that death up here because some twat hadn't taken belt clips?" I was literally hanging on for dear life to the cable as my legs began to buckle, and for the first time in years I had a full blown terror attack. Fight, flight or freeze? Yep, I ain't going nowhere!

"Bollocks! How the fuck did I let this happen?"

Just as I'm reaffirming in my mind how fucked this was, the amigos disappeared around the corner out of sight. "Fuck, I'm hanging on to this here ledge, all on my own. What happens if they don't return?…Worse case scenario they bump the fatalities. Do I somehow edge forward, to see if they're anywhere to be seen? Do I stay stuck to this here cable? Or edge back to safety and leave them?" The thought alone spun me out with the fear of literally wobbling off the damn edge. "Be the fuckin' log Dave, be the fuckin' log!" Yeah right!!

As I was making every effort to compose myself, they reappeared. "Errr...are you ok?" In an instant I replied.."No I flippin' well ain't, I can't go on!"

"Game over. I felt awful, but I just knew I was doing the right thing and looking after myself."

Fast forward to a welcome return to ground zero (Hallefrigginlujah!), and a very stark realisation that my body (and mind) was perhaps triggered somewhat by the 'jolt of terror'. Fast forward a few months, I had another mountain to climb (metaphorically speaking), when I was unexpectedly hit with a resurgence of post traumatic stress. In hindsight, that climbing incident had most definitely left an underlying sense of dis-ease, enabling a chain of repercussions to play out.

A friend and colleague of mine, kindly put me forward for an assignment mentoring an incredibly successful man, who'd accumulated a fortune beyond measure. I was flown to his 'off grid' pad in the wilderness, where I'd assist in his ongoing 'recovery' for 'burnout'. Not long into the stay, I noticed he'd been swerving anonymous calls to his mobile phone. After one too many 'mystery calls' gone unanswered, I decided to question it. He responded by simply saying he didn't know who it could be.

"This was enough for me to have concern, not just for my own safety but for his also."

I started to go through a series of scenarios in my mind...things like - "Maybe it's an old business associate who's after money?"...or... "Perhaps he's seriously pissed someone off? Yep...Definitely the business associate"...and I even started to go down the rabbit hole of..."Someone's gonna hold him to ransom for a big fat payday." Rational/irrational fears started to escalate and swirl around my mind like a frickin' tornado. "Fuck me, I thought I'd sorted this shit!"

The next 'No Caller ID' that came in, I insisted he answer on speaker. We were greeted by just the sound of breathing. "Speak up Lord Vader, tell us who you are." In all seriousness, I was looking dead in the eyes of the fella, and sensed I wasn't the only one feeling unsettled. "Turn the feckin' phone off man." I couldn't quite shake the overwhelming sense of angst. "Dude, are we alright? Are you in trouble? Are we safe?" His response was not what I wanted to hear. "Yeah yeah, don't worry about it, it's all cool." Hmm, if only I shared that sentiment.

Fear of the unknown is a real bitch. For a while now I'd developed a strong sense of trusting the unknown…but, I wasn't entirely convinced (or sure) of what I was dealing with. "Fuck man, isolation once more." Again, my mind starts to reason…"Was he even being honest with me? They gave a fuck, right? Hmmm, maybe not…should I be concerned?"

"In fear of my immediate safety, that night I dragged a heavy filing cabinet against the door of my room as a precaution (wtf?)."

One thing I've learnt in life which is invaluable - ALWAYS ASK FOR HELP!…and sometimes it comes from the most unexpected places. Thanks to the gardener and the housekeeper (yep, that's right), a discerning decision was met, based on the evidence. Green fingers explained - "If someone was gonna kidnap for a ransom, they certainly wouldn't call beforehand"…Hmm…ok, that made total sense. "Oh hi there, just a quick courtesy call to arrange your abduction…tomorrow night ok?…we'll supply the duct tape." The housekeeper said it was just as likely to be an ex calling. Fuck, I hadn't taken that into consideration. A stalker psycho ex? That was plausible.

"The way my mind had calculated it, it was a high terror situation, sending me into the old familiar survival mode of fight/flight/freeze...Badman at the ready."

Having got my senses back to a calmer zen state, just... (BREATHE!)...I was able to see out the assignment without completely losing my shizzle. On my return home, I knew best to see a specialist. That debilitating fear of insecurity and terror had crept back in, and I wanted to understand why? So I called Kristoff, a psychological wizard. He's one of the good guys and has taught me many great things. It was his genius mind that helped me understand the nature of what was going on...Tigers and Zebras.

Tigers. Big, powerful deadly hunters. They strike with brute force and can tear you apart in seconds. Then there's Zebras. Not far off the size of a Tiger, yet seemingly far less harmful, docile even. More likely to munch grass than human flesh.

"Given the choice, I'd rather fancy my chances with a Zebra than a Tiger any day."

The hellraising years had 'inadvertently' placed me in many precarious situations. Some psychological, some physical...every drop of menace was a 'Tiger Attack'. Traumatised by these experiences, I'd been left with an underlying residual trauma energy, running through my veins like a fiery venom, waiting to poison me every time it released its potency.

The triggers, they're the Zebras. Harmless, yet in my mind a Zebra (in this case those anonymous calls) appear to be a badass muddafuckin' Tiger, so big and ferocious, my default setting was to scramble up the nearest tree as high as I could and hide (the filing cabinet). In the confusion of my warped-neurotic-perspective, impaired by previous trauma, I see the stripes, but cannot differentiate between the harmless docile grass munching Zebra, and the deadly brute force of a Tiger. The crank-calls, the isolation at the residence, entrapment of my 'situation' (all stripes)...but instead of rationally seeing it as safe (Zebra)...the killer-venom-trauma-energy kicks in and I'm like "FUUUCK!"...overcome by terror (ferocious Tiger) as a catastrophic scenario plays out in my mind - masked men dressed in black, abseiling down from the roof like a scene from a John Wick movie, crashing in through the windows to kidnap the homie and reek havoc.

"They see me, so they simply do what they gotta do to make their escape untraced...POP POP!"

What I came to understand, was PTSD (post traumatic stress disorder)...or 'residual trauma energy'...was still very much underpinning my nervous system, causing this reaction. Childhood trauma therapy enabled me to reduce significant amounts of 'old-scar-tissue' related to early childhood, yet my body still held 'scars' from the battlefield of life. These remnants clearly having control over my unprocessed thoughts, behaviours and actions when triggered. This is known as a 'somatic experience'. Until my body learns to relax and feel safe when exposed, my mind will always override it and fuck shit up.

"The awareness alone was incredibly empowering, as was the opportunity to process more extensively my past trauma, reduce it...and move forward from it."

This latest episode, once more revealed to me the multitude and complexities of the human existence. "Fuck me, layers of an onion?...How many more bloody layers before I get to the core?" That Native American Inipi, was undoubtedly the closet thing I'd experienced to stepping out from the limited, linear illusion of our 'worldly' conditioning. I was beginning to see my life's path was serving as a means to give me what I needed, in order to heal the wounds inflicted from my past.

In doing so, I was becoming better equipped and more empowered. With a large slice of humility, I could see the positive in what would otherwise be deemed a negative...and now (as long as I'm present) with heightened awareness and understanding, whenever I see those pesky stripes, I can reassure myself and determine whether it's a docile Zebra, or in fact a deadly Tiger, before making a discerning decision on what action is required. Nice.

LONE WOLF

The time is now (to bloom)

THE TIME IS NOW
(TO BLOOM)

Psychology continues to teach me many great things, as does life. In retrospect, I accept I've fucked up a shit load. It's important for me to understand I must take responsibility for my actions. I am accountable, and realise I reap what I sow. For me, it's imperative to have nothing but forgiveness, love, kindness, compassion and a whole lot of humility towards myself first and foremost, then outwardly towards others.

Today I must do things different. My first thought has to be… "What can I do for you?"…not…"What can I get from you?" That being said, there are days I just wanna hide away in the sanctuary of self indulgence. Without acceptance, tolerance and patience (I don't always get things right, I still fuck up) it's extremely difficult at best. As long as I'm happy, safe and not harming anyone, it's ok.

This mindset requires consistent, daily discipline, with a dedication to cultivate and nurture. No one is gonna do it for me. The reconnection to authenticity this attitude allows is sublime, and the freedom it brings is unparalleled. As long as I've got it, anything is possible.

Having learnt the art of stillness, I could tend to my garden and water my flowers, not focus on the weeds. As a result, my garden was in full bloom. With this knowledge and ability, I knew I had to keep on watering, and pass on where possible.

"Life had landed me in a position to be of service...and things were about to happen I could never of expected in a million years. "

S P O N T A (N E W) I T Y

There was a time when life was predictable. I'd always inadvertently end up doing the inevitable...kinda like a bystander watching the car crash happen. In other words, I was so disconnected from any sense of reality, that life played out regardless, and I just went along with whatever situation I found myself in. The outcome never really resulted in my favour. Life was very limiting. These days it's very different. Life still plays out, and I can still go along with whatever situation I find myself in (if I choose)...however, the lens with which I see life (and myself) has refocused. The difference is perspective. If you feel life is blurred or unattainable, maybe you too are experiencing the anxiety, confusion and fear I knew so well?

"Suffering leads to delusion, and delusion keeps us vehemently trying to control every aspect of our lives. "

When I got honest and reached out for support, one of the most fundamental teachings I learnt (apart from don't be a colossal-thunder-cunt), was to accept 'what is'. This meant letting go of control over and over. Be the log. Through repetition, I've learnt to accept the things I cannot change, realised I have the power to change the things I can, and gained the wisdom to know the difference between those two outcomes. With this mindset, my mentality went from zero to zen over a period of time, and here I am...perhaps at times I appear to have it dialled...but, I still struggle with life occasionally, because life can be a bitch. There is no way on earth I could of created new beginnings without overcoming my demons. In my experience, learning to relinquish problem behaviour, only became possible by facing adversity, and processing the pain of my past...only then could I make peace with suffering in the present. Anxiety naturally falls away, and delusion ceases to exist. Then we are free.

"Once we behold such treasures, we can be truly spontaneous. Adventurous. Unlimited."

Today, spontaneity equals magic. A supernatural ability to thrive. Is this marvel due to the fact I don't get mindfucked on chemicals anymore? Kind of a no brainer really. Is it also because (if I apply it) I have the ability to be free from the confines of my irrational, self critical mind and the tortuous thoughts it dictates? Errr, absolutely frickin'well yes.

Irrational impulsiveness, or 'spontanegativity'…always results in unnecessary drama. That in itself is addictive. We can feed on that shit all day long…or…we can take some positive action, get real, ask for help and realign our perspective to create a life we truly desire.

"Our own bullshit will always, ALWAYS try to sabotage this."

The power of sponta(new)ity brings a clarity of experience, and with it assurance. You have the ability to intuitively get closer to what feels right, instead of just blindly hoping for the best. You can also explore all the possibilities that arise, without the fear of misjudgement or uncertainty, even when the outcome is still not clear. These skills will allow you to follow the 'signs'…'signals'… 'synchronicities'…however you perceive it, and see where it takes you, with the comfort of knowing you always have a choice...and it's never wrong. Sounds bloody marvellous, right?

I was introduced to someone particularly significant in this whole story of mine. We'd known of each other for a while, however our paths never met. I guess you could say the stars had aligned and it was time. A mutual friend did the intro, and a few texts later I spoke to Polly for the very first time on the phone.

"I call her Polly, because right from the first moment we became aquatinted, I observed she had a fine appetite for making a pot of tea, peppermint tea."

In fact, "Polly put the kettle on"…and could take on the entire population of Morocco single-handed, drinking them all under the table without faltering. It is quite something, and a skill I believe she acquired from her former days as a hellraiser. Like myself, Polly had been a monster boozer, making the decision to change her lifestyle because it got so bad. Now she doesn't drink alcohol, or take any other drug for that matter. Peppermint tea total. Badass.

Polly was a celebrated best selling author, who'd been living overseas whilst working on her latest book. We'd spend hours talking on the phone about life, misadventures and all the hilarious mad shit we'd encountered in our lives. It was whilst exchanging these tales that Polly came out with…"Have you ever thought about writing a book?" Now, I must admit, I'd always fancied writing my memoirs in their entirety, having secretly written some stuff, including a part titled 'Lone Wolf', which told the story of how I'd met Danger Axe the punk that day. I'd had it stored on a memory stick but never felt compelled to do anything with it.

"Polly had awoken something deep within my soul. It ticked every box. Artistically, intellectually, therapeutically...I just knew I had to do it."

She proposed I submit 10,000 words for her to read, and she'd let me know her thoughts as to whether I could be a published writer. That seemed a hell of a lot of writing to do...but without hesitation, I sat and began to write. Two days later, I submitted 10,000 words to Polly. She rang as soon as she could in disbelief, declaring I had the art of capturing my story 'the way I tell it' down to a T. Her enthusiasm fuelled me with excitement, instilling the confidence and conviction to writing a book, this book, Lone Wolf.

"Thank you Polly, now go put the kettle on."

This had been one of the most significant 'synchronicities', and one I shall forever be grateful for accepting. The door had opened, and I wasn't about to let it slam in my face. The following weeks that ensued, I wrote 80,000 words in addition to the first draft of Lone Wolf. I always knew my ability to write so quickly (something Polly was stunned at) was due to the fact that not only was I clearly 'in flow', but also due to the fact I'd previously told my story a thousand times over in schools.

"I believe the energy I was now tapping into, was as if I had a bright neon sign above my head saying 'READY TO RECEIVE THE GOOD STUFF'...because that's what happened."

More opportunities arose. As if by magic, it just kept coming. Next up, I found myself being put forward for a work placement, as a freelance 'sober sensei' at a well established international treatment centre...a youth clinic specialising in mental health issues. The clinic made contact, and before I knew it I was assigned my first 'client', a young British fellow. He'd been expelled from a school not far from the one I attended. In the report, it stated he'd been thrown out for threatening to burn down the school, then lighting up a big fat doobie in front of the headmaster and defiantly blowing smoke in his face. I knew we'd get on.

Having completed a treatment program for addiction and behavioural issues, I was to assist in his ongoing recovery process once home. It blows my mind how willing some of these adolescent rebels are to redeem themselves in a way I failed to do until my 30s. I surely would of benefitted from such help if it were available to me then. It wasn't.

"Of course having the desire to change, and the financial means goes a long way, but still…"

Due to the nature of the clinic being international, I found myself being flown all over the world. Milan, New York, Paris…it was like Fashion Week all over again, but now I'm tending to hearts not hair. When I wasn't taking assignments, I'd immerse myself in art. Life could not of been better. The direction I now embodied had granted me an insurmountable sense of happiness, and with it the belief I could achieve anything. There's a strong sense of timelessness that comes with that essence. It seems strange to think I was once a nutty nervous wreck, so anxious, I'd gnaw obsessively at my finger nails like I was chompin' a rack of spare ribs. When the nails were done, I'd have the skin away for dessert, polishing the bone for the ensemble.

"I swear, if I could'a got my toes in my mouth I'd of munched on them too."

Now, let me be clear - My life had become (and still is) beyond my wildest dreams, but…I will ALWAYS have the odd curveball thrown at me. These 'inconveniences', or 'gifts', however we choose to perceive them, are for me, served as a timely reminder to keep us on our toes. I must never take anything for granted. Hmm…

dunno about you, that really does depend on where I'm at. Remember that old 'committee meeting' in my mind, those voices wanting me on the floor eating shit (and chewin' my toes)…if I'm to catch those snides red handed and stay on this path, self introspection, focus and balance is paramount. I've heard it said that maintaining a positive mental attitude, is no different to cleaning your teeth (or tuning in to that car radio, remember?) Think about it…there was a time you didn't have a friggin' scooby how to brush those pearly whites. Somewhere along the way, we were taught to do it first and last thing each day, every day. It's fair to say it may of been met with some resistance, however, after many days/weeks/months of continual scrubbing, we all naturally do it (don't we?), on autopilot, without having to give it any serious thought.

"Repetition. Effort. Discipline. Habit."

Now, if we were to apply that same principle (Dave!) to the upkeep of our noodle up top…perhaps our mindset may just be as clean and minty as our gnashers, no? We just gotta find that 'thing', a daily ritual of sorts…the cleaning of our teeth (metaphorically speaking of course). The stillness, the connection, the creativity, the good stuff…and apply it.

Note to self - Practice. Practice. Practice.

MIGHTY STRONG

One day whilst out minding my own business, I bumped into Johnny Big Bollocks. What struck me as completely obvious, was just how frickin' vulnerable he was in comparison to my new found strength. "Fuck man, my tormentor of yesteryear ain't got giant kahoonas after all!" His fragility exposed like a lone tree in the desert, and my empowerment was like the blazing sun shining down on his withered little branches. Neither of us acknowledged the past, we simply departed as swiftly as we'd met. What I noticed, was the immense feeling of gratitude, compassion and forgiveness that arose.

"Gratitude for who I'd become, compassion for his vulnerability, and forgiveness for the past."

Mighty strong are the wounded healers. Our weakness is now our unwavering strength, which undoubtably comes from being a survivor of our experience. We can overcome adversity with true grit resilience, because we have dared to know pain. We face it and move past it. It's what makes us courageous, unshakable like a mountain...and with that mindset anything is possible. This isn't an

exclusive club, where only the 'extra-super-special-fabulous' join…
it's for everyone, you just gotta get real and dare to dig deep and do
the work.

I've met many wounded healers on this path. Tony the DJ was
the catalyst who showed me what was possible. He spoke from his
heart, and that truth sucker-punched its way directly into my
consciousness at a time when nothing else could.

*"Every time I meet someone who's overcome adversity
I'm inspired, and that appreciation keeps getting
bigger."*

One such person I met seemed to surpass what I deemed possible.
I'd shared some of the early drafts of Lone Wolf with a friend of
mine. In his words he told me…"You've definitely found your
purpose in life." I knew he was right. He mentioned a friend of his
back in his native Australia, a woman called Sonya, and said I
needed to speak to her. So, with very little knowledge, other than
being told she'd overcome unimaginable suffering and tragedy, I
sent her a message.

We arranged to speak on a video call. I sat, listening intently
as she told her story. In February 2007, her beloved 15 year old
daughter Carly had been murdered by a 50 year old paedophile.
He'd posed online as an 18 year old musician, and over a period of

time had managed to lure her to a secluded beach. There, poor Carly had been brutally assaulted and killed. Sonya set up The Carly Ryan Foundation, to create awareness and educate children and parents on the dangers of the internet. She relentlessly works to expose the thousands of multiple identities paedophiles use to lure young children.

"It blew me away how someone could get past their own grief to be of service on this level."

Sonya wanted to tell her story in any way possible, because she had a true message of strength and hope. We discussed the possibility of doing a book together. She told me the 'story' was well known to the Australian press and media, which had been a huge burden and become a circus. She'd had countless offers to tell her story, none of which she entertained, as they all wanted the crime story.

"By the end of the call I just knew I had to help."

I got off the phone and the hairs on my arm were literally on the ceiling. I know this sounds nuts, but it was as if I'd just dialled into a new paradigm frequency...like I'd accessed divinity. I'd experienced this in mild form through meditation, more so with the Inipi, and at times speaking on behalf of Amy's legacy...moments of pure euphoric bliss, a refined presence that radiates through every cell in your being. To me, it's essentially the ultimate of connectivity and aliveness. The way I see it...when you're on the right path, 'in flow' and present, and in your heart, speaking truth and you embody it, not just for yourself but for something far greater...you tap into a pure channel of consciousness and a heightened sense of knowing is instilled...and when you're working on this level, there is no stopping it, because it's meant to be.

"Some seek this connection in psychedelics, others in religion or whatnot...it's untainted, straight from the heart synergy with a power greater than yourself."

In layman's terms..."The whole is greater than the sum of parts." It's why Sonya managed to introduce and pass a Law (Carly's Law) in State and Federal Government in Australia, when so many said she couldn't. When you're channeling an 'elevated-higher-power' frequency, shit fuckin' happens. That inner belief, it is a knowing that will always have your back, no matter what life throws at you. When you trust that higher consciousness, then everything always works out...and when you develop the evidence that this shit is real for you, then you become mighty strong beyond measure.

"The source, the flow, ya muddafeckin' mojo...whatever the funk you wanna call it, no human words can truly capture its essence...the power, energy or spirit of being."

Within days of that first contact I booked a flight to Australia. It was there we'd spend 10 days of insurmountable truth, profound emotions ranging from extreme admiration, gut wrenching empathy, and an abundance of radiant joy and love as pure as light.

"I knew it'd be an experience like no other, however, it truly surpassed anything I could have possibly imagined."

On meeting Sonya it was like meeting an old friend. There was an instant connection, one you might expect from a brother or sister. She is a light worker, a wounded healer, a badass maverick of a warrior. There is no human being I have met, or am likely to meet too soon, that attains the same level of acceptance, wisdom and pure unshakable equanimity as Sonya. Her openness, willingness and sheer strength and courage to help others is like nothing I'd seen before. It is with unparalleled humility and compassion, that her constant drive for selfless acts of love and kindness, continue to impact the lives of those who are fortunate enough to be touched by her magic.

The very essence of this magic I experienced on my stay, enabled me to capture the unimaginable circumstances she was forced to endure. That magic carried me through so I could relay, or rather transmit such unspeakable emotion into words. She is the real deal.

"I never thought I'd find myself writing my own book, let alone helping to write someone else's."

I now found myself on a quest to become an accomplished writer. I hadn't set out to do it, life had gifted me these opportunities and I chose to accept. I was ready. As I've said before, that crafty ego can derail any efforts to take such leaps of faith, and when you're tapping into the 'good stuff', you do not need to worry about the nitty gritty…the 'if's, how's? when's? and but's'. It's irrelevant…I'd learnt the only thing you need to focus on was the 'what?' and the 'why?', then let go of the outcome and trust.

Over the course of that following year, I'd swing by Australia (like you do) to fit in writing sessions with Sonya. Each time I'd learn knew incredible feats that she'd achieved. She was like Yoda, which is why I called her Soda. There was nothing she could not do. She'd learnt to meditate under the instruction of the truly great masters. Choosing not to be sedated on medication by doctors, who may I add attempted to prescribe enough 'downers' to KO an entire herd of elephants…instead, she trained her mind and heart with those who knew, which is how she survived the insurmountable grief at the time of Carly's murder.

"Meditation really can transcend all suffering."

Whilst overseas on my travels, I encountered yet another wounded healer, and another reason to broaden my mind further, only reinforcing my belief of the unknown. For me, this kinda shit seems to happen when you least expect it. For some time now massage had been (and still is) a staple go-to, helping not only with relaxation and stillness, but to iron out any knots in my back. I believed to be a combination of long-arse flights and work load. The last time I'd taken a 'lucky dip' massage, had been in the arse end of nowhere (I don't mean butt massage). It was a rather peculiar experience to say the least, because I was literally pummelled within an inch of my life, by what I can only describe as an incredibly large Sumo wrestler wearing giant nappies.

"To be fair, weirdly…I seemed to float outta there in a zen like state of euphoria."

Amongst a long list of mediocre looking options, there was one particular place that stood right out from the rest. It was a private practice run by a very aptly named Wendy Rose. What I immediately liked about Wendy when we first met, was her infectious energy. She had a very distinctive East Coast accent, yet looked somewhat mystical, like she'd been raised by Native Americans or some other off grid community. Put it this way, she didn't exactly embody your stereotypical masseuse from Essex. With a long mane all woven and heaped atop her head, she was dressed in what appeared to be a tapestry of handmade fabrics, with shapes, textures and colours all entwining to create a vision worthy of any cosmic mystic.

"If Jack Sparrow had a love child with Barbarella... Wendy would be the result."

Upon entering her studio, I felt as though I was in an old movie. It consisted of a large main reception/living room area, filled with vintage furniture, worldly artefacts and beautifully crafted chairs all made in the most incredible dark wood. Off from the main room were two treatment areas, the red room and the blue room. "Hmm, was this some kinda Matrix themed madness?" Without giving it any thought, I was drawn to the one on the left, the red room. "Oh well, let's see what rabbit hole I go down this time."

As far as I knew, I was booked in for an 'alternative' deep tissue massage, but you never really know what you're gonna get until shit happens. Wendy's profile clearly stated she was an intuitive energy worker, incorporating multi-disciplinary healing as an art form. As I lay there in preparation, the sound of sacred music began to make itself known, and I sensed things were about to get funky. Right on cue, an enchanted voice began to sing along to the ancient beats, chanting mantras in perfect harmony as I cast my mind back to Silva and the Inipi. Wendy was clearly 'channelling' something, and whilst 'working' on my right arm, she softly whispered words of a 'vision' she was having - a wolf with gills, swimming under water (?). She switched to my left side and received a vision of a tambourine.

"Grizzly bears in the Inipi...and now tambourines and a wolf with gills."

I couldn't really attempt to put into context what I experienced that day, nor give credit to what truly happens in such circumstances... simple words of bliss, connection, great mystery, wholeness and peace of mind will have to do. Once again, my curiosity had discovered more (or maybe not?) about the art of mysticism..this time, flat out on my back with the wonderful Miss Rose at the helm (easy tiger). Take it or leave it, believe or not...I think there's something rather intriguing about the unseen unknown.

After the treatment we got talking properly. Wendy was asking what I did for work...so I told her I helped people, especially adolescents with problem behaviour and addiction issues. We talked about wellbeing, spirituality, our past lives, travels and creativity. A fellow like-minded human being who simply understood, and had discovered their truth, just as I felt I had.

Before saying our goodbyes, I arranged to go back a few days later. It was on my return that I met Wendy's friend and colleague Rocky. Rocky had a face that told a story. Like Wendy, he was a 'healer', using a technique based on body alignment. I'd heard about this technique before. It is theorised our bodies can be extremely out of 'sync'...or alignment, due to trauma we experience in life, rendering our mental and emotional state dysfunctional. Makes perfect sense, right?

"Different techniques, names and reasoning...yet all points to the same cause and effect - pain and suffering."

I found myself back in the red room with Rocky. Having chatted for a while, he asked why I had LONE WOLF tattooed across my knuckles. I told him what it meant to me, about my past life and journey of self discovery through adversity. I asked Rocky why, or rather, how, he'd ended up doing this type of therapeutic healing… in response, he began to disclose some very personal information, a story of suffering stemming from childhood, and just like myself, was compelled to help others through an empathic compulsion to selflessly relieve the burden, because he truly knew what pain was like. The story Rocky went on to tell was one of brutality, neglect and immense sorrow. It went like this...

He was the youngest of three siblings, in an era known for its tough conditions. A post-war starkness, that in itself was barren enough, without the emotional absence and neglect of being subjected to the shortcomings of cold, hardened parents. It was one particular night Rocky recalled, when he was a mere child of only five years old. Along with his elder brother and sister, they shared a tiny bed in the box room they called a bedroom.

"In the darkness of night, he lay awake, scared… convinced there was something terrible outside the window."

As he cried out loud with tears streaming down his face, he could hear the distant staunch tone of his Mother's voice, commanding his reluctant Father to tend to their young boy's needs. To his horror, he could hear her insistence to urgently "Shut up!" the child's howling, declaring she could not stand another moments whining. Unable to control his emotions, he heard his Father shout - "If you do not stop crying, I'll really give you something to cry about!" Still unable to cease his upset…as feared, he heard the stomp of his Father's footsteps becoming increasingly louder as he came up the stairs. Rocky's eyes glazed over with a look of heartache, as he went on to describe how the man he called Dad, grabbed hold of the pillow from under his head, and proceeded to smother his face.

Rocky went on to tell me, that about two years ago when he'd met his brother, they confessed to each other the full extent of how that night had effected them. Processing the events, his brother confided to Rocky, that whilst lying there that night motionless pretending to be asleep, terrified of their Father's actions and what he might do next, he'd seen standing there at the foot of their bed, a Wolf. Clear and as real as the light of day, his brother said it was as if it'd been watching over them, keeping guard to ensure no harm would come to them.

"A Lone Wolf, the protector."

I suddenly realised why Rocky had decided to share this brutally honest story with me. I put my arms out wide and embraced Rocky to give him the biggest bear hug. We then proceeded to commence the treatment, which unbeknown to me would reveal (and conclude), there was still much healing to do.

Such synchronicities…'chance meetings', whether we choose to pass them off purely as coincidental or not, for whatever their meaning, remain to me, magical and nothing short of profound. At the very least, it is a blessing to meet such incredible people who have overcome immense suffering against the odds, and come out on top.

BOUNTY HUNTER
(OF THE LOST SOULS)

Having found myself becoming a 'sober-sensei-mentor' of sorts… on many assignments, I'd witness dynamics reminding me of childhood, triggers that always resulted in deeper realisations. Parent/adolescent engagement...aka acting as the 'buffer', mediating everyones needs and managing their expectations, would usually give rise to such 'delights'.

"Similar to when I first did talks in schools, I'd gain insights as much as offering them."

I'd developed my own style in doing this...I was clearly doing something right as the work kept coming, and just like everything

I've done in life, it was not only a tad unorthodox, it was on recommendation through word of mouth only. I'd worked out from the offset my best ally was always truth and integrity. There are of course situations where truth can cause harm, discerning between these moments takes skill and awareness which can only come with experience. You really gotta know your oranges from your apples to do this shit. It's full on frontline business, and if you think you can just wing it you're hugely mistaken. You gotta be creative...for me this meant drawing from everything I'd ever known.

"I've encountered many 'tricky' situations in life...and it still continues with mentoring these fellow renegades."

Let me give you a little taster of what I mean...

I'd been assigned a case to work on. The young fellow had been receiving treatment for behavioural issues, including substance abuse and severe depression. I was assisting in their ongoing recovery back home (the crime scene). The first few days couldn't of gone better, until it was decided the family would travel to their mountain home for the lead up to Christmas. Initially I did have concerns. Mountains are remote, not necessarily the best environment for someone who's not yet stable...however, getting out of the city and into clean air and nature is never a bad thing.

On the second day of being there, the fellow spiralled into an extremely dark place, resulting in a series of panic attacks, escalating to admissions of despair. As I aided their stability, the fellow confessed suicidal thoughts had crept back in. The parents and siblings were beside theirselves with anxiety, assuming a spell in treatment meant no more episodes.

"There's no reason you can't make a full recovery, however it takes time, continued effort and care"

Getting clean off mind altering substances is always gonna be key to making the best possible recovery (which they were), yet environment and stability is paramount too…which is why it can be a tad sketchy, placing ya fragile newbie arse up a mountain away from your staple comforts and familiarity. Again, there's no reason you can't do this, as long as you've got some guidance to fall back on.

Now, this is where intuition and creative perspective comes into play. I knew there were only two options on the table...

1 - Abort mission. Wave goodbye to Christmas in the mountains, and the entire family retreat back to the city.

or 2 - Stay put, and find a way to make it work.

The young fellow had tried to insist on returning alone to the city, but I knew (as did the worried parents) that wasn't an option. I also knew the fellow had a love interest. I'd met them briefly, and from what I could tell, they were 'solid'. They were also in recovery, from a sticky-icky screen addiction. Yep, that ol' chestnut! Throw into the mix a cheeky little coke habit, and you've got yourself one of the highest ranking gamers in the world.

What I was about to suggest to the fellow was always gonna be met with a big fat YES!…but understandably met with resistance by the parents, especially as they knew little about the young (ex) tech fiend. It was a calculated risk, but I said to the fellow…"If we can get your 'partner in crime' to stay with you, will that help?" Of course their whole demeanour shifted as they leapt at the chance to have their 'playmate' join them. Now, in early recovery this is deemed a complete no-go scenario. "Play now, pay later." Stay the fuck away from sex, love and all things deemed a distraction. Learn to sit with yourself and whatever you do, "DO NOT ACT OUT!"…buuut…

"This was just one of those situations where you gotta do what ya gotta do."

The way I saw it…"Fuck the rule book!"…the fellow was in crisis, having a meltdown, leading to catastrophic obsessive thoughts…

and in their own admittance threatening to do harm. Now, I'm not stupid, I know when someone's being an entitled little fucker who's stomping their feet defiantly to 'get attention'...and this wasn't it. In my mind, it was a definite safeguarding issue. So, I sat the parents down and laid it out clearly and calmly. Using the analogy of a heroin addict in crisis, sometimes they gotta use methadone to prevent withdrawals and 'sickness'...well, (ex) screen-demon was the methadone. They got it, and after talking it through as a family, it was agreed for them to come and stay.

There were of course conditions, like sleeping in separate rooms for starters (yeah right!). I facilitated a call to lay down those 'guidelines', to which they gladly (and respectfully) accepted. I departed on Christmas Eve, the day they arrived...and continued to check-in once I'd gone. I learnt the entire family, including the two lovebirds, enjoyed festive spirits with no further dramas...and even better, the last I heard they're still going strong.

"Sometimes it pays to take risks."

I'm often asked what I do for a living. I don't like labels or being boxed...maybe I've become an unconventional Guardian Angel of sorts, but a Bounty Hunter of the Lost Souls is more fitting. That's how it feels. A gun for hire, and like this example, my mission is not to drag their sorry arse back to prison, it's to get them out. Like myself, they've taken themselves (and loved ones) hostage in the prison of their mind...and in most cases the prison of addiction, control and sabotaging behaviour. Sometimes you've just gotta 'short circuit' the status quo, the obsessive thought process, the attachment...to distract and find a practical solution...and it's not always gonna be 'textbook' answers. You gotta think outside the box and draw from experience.

Most, if not all cases I've ever worked on are fairly typical in the way these fellows are wired. "Know yourself, know everyone." Given the world these young 'crazies' live in, it's no wonder they're hanging on by the skin of their teeth. There's a very high proportion of cases with savage screen (tech) addiction, then there's all the other shizer to deal with.

"The poison thorns of a misled youth...I know them so well."

I was starting to get cases of 'intervention' work. Therapists, psychiatrists and parents...who by their own admittance, couldn't quite gain the full honesty or trust of these young mavericks. In many cases, they were dealing with pure raging bulls, deviant to the core. They needed someone who could be a little more 'tactile' and on their level...more relatable perhaps...a shit load of tattoos and a car crash story goes a long way in this line of work. It's like a rite of passage, an instant connector which seems to gain the respect of the unsuspecting space cadet. I might say the same thing a parent or specialist's said a million times previously, and they'd listen. It's purely down to the fact I'm not playing a role, nor am I communicating to their 'illness'. I'm neutral...on their level.

Now, if you can understand and articulate what needs to be said, delivered in a skilful, unfaltering way...which for me is direct brutal honesty...it's like a bitch slap or a punch to the nose (metaphorically speaking of course)...and when you've got their undivided attention, simply dare to show your vulnerability...and in turn they get real. Throw into the mix a deadly intuitive instinct, so you can read them like a book, and you're gonna get results. That was my experience, and it was getting noticed.

"My workload increased, and unbeknown to me at that time, my sense of Zen was beginning to dwindle."

The following is a result of yet another layer, a hidden thorn I thought I'd extracted. Rocky had picked up on it when I was having that treatment. Through the synergy of assisting these young former wreckheads in their recovery to self discovery, I'd inadvertently been forced to face an issue that would not go away...

Let me explain...

When I replace meditation, stillness, relaxation, calm...the good stuff...for 'work'...I come unstuck. It's an eventuality, and one I now know I cannot afford to do. If I am to be of service and help others, I must never lose sight of 'the good stuff'...the 'cleaning of my teeth', the 'tuning in', my 'flow', and anything else that keeps me zen.

"Equanimity and balance is key, and I must always practice what I preach."

I had been served an ultimatum. A warrant for my ego's arrest, a conditional plea from someone close to me at that time. Polly. We'd been in a relationship for some time now. The moments we shared were wonderful, explorative and enlightening, however, it was also strained. Like a disease taking hold of its victim, a progressive, toxic energy had spread through my entire existence, suffocating me into submission. "Hang on a minute, haven't we been here before?" Yep, once again I'm waving a white flag...surrender was my only option. Polly was right, no matter how much I try to wiggle, side step or coerce my way out of the corner, it was there slap bang staring me in the face and unavoidable.

"Like a half-beat wrestler trying to think their way out of a full-nelson-headlock, it's no use. I'm Done."

Polly had witnessed me go from a good natured, calm and supportive friend and partner, into...as she put it 'Teen Hulk'. Ha! The irony! Jeez...there's me tending to all these teen rebels, and I'm quietly morphing into one of them! Spiritual grandiose can be a real bitch. Just acknowledging my part in all this malarkey was enough to take the power back. Now for some action.

Around the time I'd initially met Polly and we started dating, I was becoming more involved in the mentoring side of life. I'd originally taken a year out to travel, write music and be creative, immersing myself. I had space in my life to do tons of self nurturing. Meditative practice, country walks, everything was balanced and life was good. However, throw into the mix writing the story of your life, Soda's, and the increased workload...slowly but surely things got full on crazy. When you're dealing with other peoples trauma, it's hard not to get enmeshed. You've gotta find a way to 'zip up' and 'cut the cords'...which I hadn't yet learnt.

"Having created my own Utopia, I'd quietly regressed to a Dystopian battlefield...yet I hadn't seen it coming."

I know from my past experience that when I get caught up in a turbo-charged existence, my emotional and mental wheels don't just fall off, they catch fire and disintegrate in an almighty blaze of destruction. This was no different. Therapeutic support had always been a safe space for me, providing a little extra insight (and comfort)...and the inner peace that stillness provides, was the surest way to take immediate refuge from literally anything.

"The problem was I'd taken my foot off the gas, and had switched the focus to other stuff."

Having had one too many heated discussions with Polly, it seemed a visit to see a therapist may help, because deep down I knew something wasn't allowing me to settle. Having done some ground work on this stuff previously, I knew that sometimes we just need to remove ourselves from the centre of the very thing that is causing our grief...even if it is insanely difficult. Attending a handful of sessions reminded me of this, and really helped put into perspective the unhealthy cycle I'd been creating. Yep, that's right, I'd been creating. We can only truly be accountable for ourselves. It doesn't work pointing the finger and blaming everyone else, be it Polly, the postman or Bob next door. I'll be the first one to put my hand up and admit I'm guilty as charged. I don't always want to...but I've learnt I need to.

The thing with the lessons in life we learn, is that sometimes, if not often, we forget. I forget. So a continuation of learning and relearning is always a wise and virtuous act of humility. I don't know it all. Far from it. In fact, I know nothing in the grand scheme of things.

"So for me, it's bloody damn good to be the student as rewarding as it is to be the teacher...I must always have the beginners mind."

You've heard me bang on about ego shit loads...because the ego is a defiant (and persistent) muddafunka. A multifaceted diamond in the rough...depending on how you see it. Humility can allow us to actually own our shit once in a while, we can dare to laugh at our own stupidity, and even grow to accept it. Without humility, I will always defiantly defend my honour, pride, and 'imaginary' status...I will draw a line in the sand and demand "NO! I AM NOT TO BLAME HERE, THIS IS ALL YOUR DOING...ARGHHH!"

Sitting in session, I explain the full complexity, or rather the simple matter of fact..."I've been getting a tad 'irritable' sensei." Alas, there still seems to be a truck load of unresolved emotion underlying my once zen like state. With hindsight, stillness would of granted me two things had I been practicing.

Firstly - Self introspection. I can observe my behaviour with clarity.

and secondly - I can let go of certain emotions, such as anger. Very unlikely to be uptight when zen.

"So come on sensei, tell me what's behind all this trifle?" I'd been getting all bent out of shape, trying to mould my way of thinking into Polly's. I was so caught up in my own individual ideologies (needs/wants), I'd forgotten to allow each other to just be. Does that sound familiar to you?

I'd heard it said before that a chicken is a chicken and a duck is a duck. A chicken does not try to make a duck be a chicken...

"Hey duck, what's with the beak?...and fuck me that waddle, seriously?"

My actions were causing a reactive aversion from Polly. To her, I was a Tiger about to tear her to shreds, but really...I'm just a disgruntled Zebra, who's feeling a tad insecure and being mistaken for a Tiger. I believed my angst was coming from a place of frustration of not being heard, a desperate bid to be seen and understood. These old wounds of mine were upon me once more. My cries to be heard had been dismissed (or so I thought), and mismanaged. In all reality, they hadn't. It just felt that way. Here's what therapy revealed...

"For starters, you'll only ever get out of something what you put in. Therapy is no exception."

Past sessions gave me the evidence to be honest. So I was. It doesn't matter if you're talking to a therapist or friend, you'll remain as sick as your secrets. Be honest. Straight off the bat, the focus centred on my part. It served as no use whatsoever, pointing out every single thing I thought contributed to my annoyance (and inconvenience).

I was explaining my anger was valid, warranted, and indeed it was (to me). Unfortunately for Polly, she was on the receiving end. It's important I know that my emotions, ALL of them, are valid and perfectly ok. 'Unproductive' emotions can indeed be positive, like Joypain...and I can embrace every single one. There is nothing wrong with me, nor do I require fixing.

"Anger is a human emotion we all experience, it's how we regulate such emotion that is key."

In a nutshell, how to channel our emotions in a skilful, conscious and loving way. So what was really hiding behind this here green monster? 'Teen Hulk' had been reacting to life, and we needed to take a peek behind those big monstrous moods to get a clearer picture.

With an incline of work (and the nature of it), came an increased intensity in my being. There was also a significant trade off. I'd lost valuable 'me' time, something I treasured and wholeheartedly depended on like a sacred elixir. Stressed and at times very burnt out, not just emotionally but mentally, I'd reached tipping point and was teetering on the brink of sanity. I'm sure anyone who's in a full blown work commitment, married with kids, or perhaps engaged in an education program of sorts, can fully identify with what I'm saying here. How on earth do we maintain any sense of self, sanity or positive mental attitude, when we're strained?

"We can easily lose ourselves, and with it our plight to be happy. That simple joy of existence can evaporate without trace."

Work overload aside, underlying that was my still fragile, 'jagged-heart'. Was this heart of mine strong enough to withstand the complexities of intimacy? Hmm…perhaps not just yet. More than ever I longed to be in a deep and meaningful relationship with 'that special someone', but there still seemed to be a block. With hindsight, further alone time was indeed required, in order for me to focus on a deeper process of healing.

Something needed to change, so I began to realign the balance, reducing my workload, whilst reapplying the core principles I already knew to be proven. Meditative practice, nature and creativity. I also arranged to have one to one sessions with a Tai Chi master. Immediately I began to feel back in flow. It's like muscle memory. It doesn't forget. On an intellectual and psychological level, what I'd learnt and knew before, had come to light once more for me to see in all its entirety...I was in a vulnerable state of being, my inner child, the one that felt abandoned and hurt all those years ago. Little David was once again scared, exposed to the perils of life as it was unfolding. He was experiencing acute pangs of insecurity and needed a way out. Metaphorically speaking, my 7 year old David was hiding under the bed, scared of the dark and afraid to come out.

"More than ever, I now know the human psyche can react from a default setting once triggered, if it's not caught and processed."

This deep rooted wiring of the past conditioning can always kick in like a turbo-charged-jet plane, going from 0 to 6000 in a split second. Once those cylinders are wide open, it's all systems go! The alter ego can automatically dive straight back in to save the day. BOOM! Hulking-sulking Dave's gonna stomp his feet and fuck shit up! In all reality, all I need is a little reassuring from my very calming and supportive adult-self. The trouble had been, I was giving that part of me to others in need, and I had none left for myself.

This kid-teen-adult merry-go-round is a familiar staple in my ever so volatile past. It seems to come back whenever I feel fearful of a situation (Tiger)…and my immediate response is always…"Get me the fuck outta here, run away!" Polly had the delight of a rather timid 'kid-me', on return from his mission. However, this kid, morphed the guise of a 'teen-me', cue the green monster (the Badman), the angry snarling former version of myself, the teenager.

"There's nothing worse than been jacked full of superhero ego, with a depleted sense of self."

What I learnt from this episode, was that we in fact require a little downtime upon returning from 'battle'. Ideally at least 48 hours to be precise. That sounded wonderful, and something I really hadn't been practicing. Instead, I'd arrive at Polly's straight off a plane, jet lagged to fuck, emotionally, mentally and physically hungover from an intense block of work, having mirrored and morphed into some client who's just as fucked as I am.

I have been reminded once more - I must always make time for myself to 'just be'. To ground, be still, to rest, take refuge, reset and replenish. Only then can I be in alignment with my true nature and to others…be it colleagues, friends, family or 'that special someone'. Life has a habit of vacuuming us up and away from what's truly important…it's all too easy to lose ourselves. We drift. At first it doesn't appear we've strayed too far, if at all…but before we know it, we're way out yonder in the middle of no-man's-land. Or maybe that's just me?

Thank you Polly for pointing out I'd deviated from my path. It's ok to fuck up. It's ok to be fallible. I'm not a superhero, I'm a very human mere mortal…and I can be vulnerable as fuck at times. The pain of my past is there and can always reveal itself. Sometimes we're forced to face it without a choice, and if you're anything like me, it's uncomfortable to go there, but these challenging feelings are thrown at us, over and over…until we learn from them.

"They will not go away until we step up and take positive action."

Polly (as did self introspection) brilliantly pointed out that a failing relationship does not equate to a personal defilement, not for either participants. Polly is no more to blame as I am incompetent. Like a fine ship that enters turbulent waters, and goes down sinking to the depths of the deep dark ocean. This ship is a lost treasure, gone but never forgotten.

What I gained from this particular chapter of my life, is we can only endeavour to be the best version of ourselves. The same goes for any relationship we choose. It is not our job (or project) to fix another persons problems, and it certainly isn't theirs to attend to ours. Yes we can support and nurture the other, as much as we can the 'us', but we have to each take accountability and do the work individually to survive. Sometimes we drift because life (and our ego) gets in the way, but as long as we have a sense of what is right, our moral compass will always guide us back home safely to where we belong.

TO THE LANDS END

I was truly honoured to be asked by Soda to join the board of trustees and become a Legacy Advocate for the Carly Ryan Foundation. I accepted immediately. She was on a mission to implement Carly's Law globally. On her visit to the UK, I found myself back in London's Parliament. We sat with the Home Office for discussions on innovating online safeguarding measures, met with the Australian High Commission, and for me, the highlight was joining Baroness Floella Benjamin for afternoon tea in the House of Lords.

"Admittedly, I'd loved to of set the fire alarms off, however...it certainly wasn't appropriate that day."

Before she returned to Australia, we managed to work on more of the book. Due to our schedules, we both acknowledged it would be a work in progress. One thing I'm now clear on more than anything...I will never allow myself to lose sight of the equanimity in my life again. For me, it was lesson learnt.

Daily 'grounding' exercises were now a non negotiable. As was the 48 hour 'downtime' window. This post assignment aftercare ethic was invaluable to my wellbeing. To reinforce this dedication to the cause, I reintroduced specific affirmations to prompt the narrative of my mischievous mind to my advantage..."I am NOT my body (vanity/pain/sickness), I am NOT my thoughts (crazy arse bullshit), I am NOT my emotions (come rain or shine), I am NOT the story of my past" (let it go god damn you!)...and then, fuck it, daring to spice it up with a splash of cosmic-goodwill..."I AM a supersonic-muddafuckin-pure-ass-soul!"...and if I'm feeling extra-specially-fruity, sign off with a rather endearing..."I AM ENOUGH!" (say no more). Yeah I know right, pass the frickin' sick bucket. Well, personally...I'd rather have that dialogue playing through my thoughts each day, than the old chitter chatter bollocks, wouldn't you?

In a nutshell, be nice to yourself.

When I first studied the teachings by the bald one, 'Metta' practice always resonated. Metta means 'Loving-kindness' or 'Good will'. "May I be happy, may I be well, may I be free from suffering"… and…"May you be happy, may you be well, may you be free from suffering." With hindsight, I can see those intentions really did (and still do) cultivate a calmer response to myself, others and life. Daily, moment to moment awareness and dedication to practice such pleasantries is for me, vital.

Here's a tongue twister for ya…

"It's with those 'secret-sacred-sayings', that I set the intention to self heal this jagged heart of mine."

Cosmic-self-love and pleasantries aside…thank fook I'd crammed so much travel and adventure in so far…because unbeknown to me (and the entire population of the Planet), we were about to be hit by the mother of all clusterfucks, completely debunking any future plans to live this pirate life…MUDDAFUCKINCOVID.

Where were you when this all came about? I was in the UK minding my own business. To begin with it didn't really effect my plans…but things seemed to escalate, and just days before I was due to board a flight to Miami for an assignment in the Caribbean, the Trumpster announced only US citizens could gain entry. "Motherfunk!"

It was those weeks that ensued, that led me to a rather significant realisation...I'd outgrown the place I lived. The global world powers declared this here outlaw must be in lockdown (hmmm). "Fuck man, you tellin' me any sense of spontaneity has now gone?...and with it the freedom to just do what we want, when we want?" It was time to adapt.

"Whether we liked it or not, our liberty was being taken from us."

Those weeks on lockdown turned into months, and whilst the world was put on hold, it seemed the madness of the (people) pandemic spread, as authorities played out their own individual strategies as if it were a game of chess. Dunno bout you lot, but at times it seemed more like frickin' snakes and ladders. I quickly got my head around the idea to simply not focus on it, and be present in my own private sanctuary.

In essence, I was a frontline healthcare worker, which meant I maintained some sense of freedom throughout the dos and don'ts. Colleagues and other allies secured a safe passage on countless crusades to serve those in dire need. Suicide prevention became a very real issue...

"Isolation in lockdown can be anyones worst nightmare, especially if you've got severe mental health issues."

Lockdown strategies soon became a trend, as did the 'woke' movement. "Yep that's right people, hug some feckin' trees, help others in need and get creative." It appeared an army of self absorbed humanoids were finally beginning to realise they could be of service to the Planet and their fellow Earthlings. The biggest fuck up for most people I witnessed freaking out, was being caught up in the head, that and the savage screen consumption caused. It was time to be in the 'heart space', not the 'head space' more than ever. Pulling the plug on social media and unsubscribing from the mainstream years prior to this malarkey, served as a blessing. No unwanted misinformation, influence, fear, anxiety or screen addiction for me.

"I was hellbent in remaining in the heart space...nature was calling."

There were many blessings that came out of that time. I was forced to do what everyone else was made to do...STOP. Covid was the vehicle for the entire world's population to take stock, rethink and reshape. Now, of course not everyone was conscious enough to realise this, however...those that were, used the time wisely, and those that weren't...well, they simply continued to do what they'd always done. Business as usual. No doubt many people woke up momentarily, only to perhaps fall back asleep as soon as they'd forgotten why the fuck they'd awoke in the first place. Ego is a real bitch.

A strong sense of needing change was unavoidable, so I decided to go visit a friend in the West Country. I'd been many times, having contemplated moving there often.

"I'd yearned to be somewhere more island like, surrounded by the natural medicine of stillness and nature."

My acute sensitivity means life at such a rapid pace is not the answer, nor is consumerism, a self serving attitude or a million others things I could mention. Tried that, doesn't work. It's only when I shut the fuck up, slow the fuck down, and take time to actually reflect, that I can take stock of how I truly feel about myself, my surroundings, my connections to others, to nature, to the whole...then I can see (and feel) with clarity what my needs are, and meet them.

Whilst out west, I experienced an incredible 'ahaaa!' moment. It was to do with yet another synchronicity, dare I say it, a premonition I'd had years before. I've always seemed to have certain dreams, some extremely lucid, that would manifest into reality. This one was no different. Back when I was with the Amy Winehouse Foundation, I'd been working on a project in the infamous city of The Beatles…Liverpool. I was back home when I had the dream. The morning I awoke, I vividly remembered the name of a place 'Penrith'…it was ringing out loud and clear in my mind, so I immediately looked it up on a map. It sounded Scottish to me. Not far off…approx 100 miles north of Liverpool. No disrespect meant, when I say I just couldn't see a reason for me being there.

"On one hand I knew there was a reason I'd dreamt of Penrith, on the other, I had no clue why...so I kinda just left it there."

Back out west…one morning as I lay in bed reading a book of the local area, I suddenly had a flashback to that dream. BOOM! It was like a thunderbolt realisation, when the name of the place I was currently in jumped right off the page at me…'Penwith'. "Well fuckadoodledoo." I knew in that instant I was in the right place, 'Pen-frickin'-with'…NOT…'Pen-frickin'-rith'.

That very morning I decided to go browse a local town to see what properties were available. Call it a hunch, I just knew the right place would reveal itself…and sure enough later that day, the owner of an agency, despite having a day off, decided to show me around. Within a matter of days I agreed to take the property, and weeks later I was running a bath and unpacking my gear.

It had taken a shit load of courage and a strong sense of trusting the unknown to relocate so far away from everything I'd ever known. Friends, family and the old familiarity of my surroundings were now far far away. That place I'd resided in for over the past decade or so, had not only served as my first real home that I could call my own, it'd been my safe place, a sanctuary where I spent my early recovery from clusterfuckness. It's where I'd learnt to reconnect, be human again, to look after myself properly and begin to nurture my needs. It'd also been the place I had a certain attachment to, and it was incredibly hard (and emotional) to say goodbye.

"Once again I just had to take a leap and trust the net would appear beneath me."

Unbeknown to me, the West Country would be the setting for my true metamorphosis to take place. I knew in my heart I needed to be there, but it came with many challenges, and every one was like shedding another layer of skin.

I was situated at the most extreme point of the peninsula, literally on the Land's End. If my range was good enough, I believe

I could'a smashed a golf ball from the garden into the vast wild oceans of the North Atlantic. What this meant, was I was pretty damn remote. The postman actually congratulated me one wild Winters morning, for living in such isolation. When the storms hit, feckin' ell...seriously, you kinda half expected the neighbours dog to whizz past the window. I've never experienced anything like that before. Apart from Rupert my loyal cat companion, I was alone and disconnected physically from a lot of resources.

"I can now see it was all part of the plan...synchronicity will always grant you what you need, always."

We were all in the midst of the biggest global pandemic in history, and no fucker was socialising. I'd relocated to the wilderness in the worst possible conditions to make new connections. To be fair, I'd never of been able to jump ship and move somewhere so remote, if I hadn't already done the training. Us 'crazies' can be pretty darn resourceful, and my recovery to self discovery had armed me with the tools to cope. Although it took a little adjusting, I soon managed to adapt to life in the wilderness. My soul was calling for it...it knew it had to be somewhere sacred to do what was about to happen. I'd outlived the place I called the 'crime scene'...the town I'd ransacked in my former hellraising days. Those ghosts of the past were now just a memory, a story that once played out.

"For me, the metamorphosis process could only take place somewhere far far away."

Have you seen the film Cast Away? I first watched it when it came out at the cinema years ago. I remember me and Bumble arrived way too early, so we sat in his car outside and got really stoned on weed. (Spoiler alert)…the scene where the plane crash lands…fuck man, I nearly had a full blown panic attack! Jeez. On watching the movie this time round, I saw it in a whole new perspective. It made me reflect on the similarities of his own metamorphosis, to the one I was having. Granted he'd been a tad unfortunate to be shipwrecked on a remote island...mine was choice...but I could certainly relate.

"The resilience he displays is unparalleled. His human instinct to never give up and fight, is something to be admired."

I think we all embody, and can resonate on some level to that human will to survive no matter what. How we can struggle to adapt to the tough conditions of our environment. It makes you consider whether one could endure such extremities?…after all, is it just me, or are we all at times stranded alone, alienated and lost on our individual islands?

Opportunities for freedom come and go, perhaps serving as acts of the divine granted as a means to be free from the confines of our prisons. Not only our environmental ones, but our mental ones too. My own relative experience, shows me that we do indeed have these signs, opportunities, gifts...what I now know to be synchronicities...presented to us in life to serve and to enable us to be free and to go on to the next part of our lives, we just have to not only pay attention and notice them, but to readily accept.

"Fear is the biggest block. It will always try to fuck us over."

If we give in to fear, it will win every time. Those negative self defeating voices in our head, the committee meeting telling us every single reason why an escape plan will fail...it's there to trip us up, to derail us. I realised I had to overcome that irrational fear in order to accept these opportunities in life. Having the awareness, is enough to know it's the irrational fear controlling us, not so much what it is we think we're fearing.

We may lay in wait, assuming the winds will change in our favour, before boldly going into the unknown with only our hope for freedom to keep us alive. Are you laying in wait...clinging on to the turbulent conditions of the ocean of life? "Be the fuckin' log!"

It's enough to make anyone give up and turn back, but we must prevail, not allowing the fear or power of the 'ocean' to beat us.

"Holding on to our rafts for dear life, WE CAN break through the giant swells, finding ourselves in calmer waters."

When I first realised I'd finally broken free from the confines of 'the island' that remained my 'home' for all those years, I experienced an incredible sense of release, loss, grief, the severance of leaving a former self behind…no more a slave to the confines of time or convention. The transformation we can undergo, strips us of all those layers, literally to the other end of the human spectrum. There we can become the absolute opposite, far removed from our former selves and the institutions that made us.

"For some, a global pandemic such as COVID, granted this very same transformation."

The thing I relate to the most from this 'hero's journey' of being 'shipwrecked', other than unparalleled strength, is the sheer tenacity for survival. No matter how afraid, alienated, or alone we may feel, hang on for dear life and always refuse to give up. Using our innate determination and primal ability to construct a raft (metaphorically speaking), we CAN make a bid for freedom.

Anything is possible, if only we allow ourselves to grab it with both hands and fight. Even when we're out on the unpredictable and terrifying oceans on our raft, and we feel scared and alone, to just hold on to the hope that we will make it back to safety. Staying alive, survival, human resilience. Our need to be ok no matter what. The outcome really is dependent on what we focus on. That's been my experience. If we focus on the fear, then the fear always wins and keeps us a prisoner on our remote islands, disconnected, scared and alone without any hope of freedom.

"Paradoxically, we need fear, because its tension will force us to take action in the end (if we choose)."

If we focus on hope, freedom and refuge, we open up to the possibility of a life beyond isolation or limitation. If we begin to pay attention to the opportunities that arise, we can take action, building our rafts so we can find freedom…and no matter what, hold the fuck on! Like the underdog in Castaway, I survived simply by just breathing when I thought I had nothing else to lose. To me, that is not only a powerful realisation, but a true acceptance of surrendering to 'what is'…when we literally have nothing left.

"It's only when we let go and surrender, that we are granted what we need."

This was my experience when I hit rock bottom with addiction and mental health all those years ago…and now, way out west, at the Land's End. Getting to a place where I have nothing left, just me…facing myself head on…BOOM! That's where the magic starts.

THE END IS ALWAYS
THE BEGINNING

I was sitting in my home studio editing Lone Wolf, when I received the email from Lucy, sister of fallen brother Ben Raemers. Ben was a professional skateboarder who tragically took his own life. Another lost soul who found their existence too unbearable to continue.

No different to when I first heard of Amy's tragic demise, I was equally stunned, at what I can only imagine to be the deep sense of loss and suffering, that can only ripple outwardly amongst the loved ones from such a devastation. When Lucy asked me to help, there was no question - I'm in.

"Amy, Ben, Carly…I knew the end, however tragic, is always the beginning of their legacy to flourish."

Ben's family and loved ones had set up the Ben Raemers Foundation. Their mission…to end stigma surrounding mental health issues, providing awareness aimed at suicide prevention for the global skateboarding community and beyond. Anything I could do to help educate and raise awareness within that space was an absolute must for me, having had such a close relationship to both my own personal battle, and of course my affiliation to skating in general.

Having had long, in depth chats with Lucy, and Ben's cousin Chess…only then could I truly know the full complexities to the story and legacy of Ben. No different to anyone else I've ever engaged with on this level of understanding, no one can ever truly say they know what really happens in such circumstances, however, from my own experience of mental illness and adversity, I could absolutely relate. Different stories, but as always the emotional fallout, suffering and problematic behaviour remains very inline with my own and others I'd witnessed.

"I just knew if I could share insights, perhaps some experience where possible…incredible hope and positive change can come from that."

The way I see it, skateboarding can be your best friend, your ally, your confidant and saviour…it can also be your worst nightmare. I found my people (as did Ben), I found a way to escape reality (as did Ben). It was self expression, creativity and so much more. Community, fellowship, a posse of extraordinary souls, coming together united as one. However, there can be a very dark undertone to anything you depend on if your heads not right.

Now, I was no pro, neither was I idolised…but I sure as hell know, that when you become isolated within the space that once served you, shit becomes very unstable real quick…and if you don't have the means or resources to seek help, you're fucked. Throw into the mix the 'lifestyle' (and business) of skating (similar to music)… the pressure to 'perform', to 'post', to 'keep up appearances'…and let's be honest - if you're hellbent on partying and gettin' off ones noodle, it's really easy to loose yourself completely.

Anyway. It pains me to know family and close friends knew something was up, but that's the nature of the beast (addiction, trauma and mental illness)…very rarely are we granted such luxuries as power or influence over loved ones, and unless we find a way to truly get on top and harness the issues causing the destruction, there's always a risk of tragedy waiting in the shadows.

"Like countless others, Ben just could not get on top of the 'conditions' that had him in the grips of despair. Rest in peace brother."

These latest turn of events, gave me that extra passion and determination to spread the message of recovery more than ever. Like I said, the end is always the beginning, no matter how heartbreakingly awful that is…Ben's death was not in vain. Positive change can come from devastation. Collectively, we can always strive to prevent suffering. The Amy Winehouse Foundation, Carly Ryan Foundation and the Ben Raemers Foundation (like all organisations)…carry incredible messages of hope, and I just knew if my own personal message of hope in Lone Wolf could find one person still suffering and help them, then it had served its purpose. That was now my goal.

A huge amount of healing was made at the Land's End, in relation to myself primarily…and extending that, notably to my Dad. Over many calls, we developed a stronger bond than I'd ever known possible…and one I can say has helped heal this jagged heart of mine a little bit more, reinforcing a greater sense of peace from within. It wasn't just my beloved Dad. I don't know about anyone else, but the pandemic put all my relationships into perspective, especially being so far away from loved ones…absence really does make the heart grow stronger, and although those that mattered were hundreds (even thousands) of miles away…

"I felt more of a sense of connection to loved ones than ever before."

Laying in wait on a trip overseas, were two extremely profound experiences whilst accompanying a young fellow, who was staying in a remote part of the countryside. The first, took place having been invited to hike the nearby mountains by his parents friends, who were experienced explorers. I found myself in a familiar situation, up a sketchy mountain with a sudden realisation that it was frickin' high up. Led by the husband, we precariously crawled across a mountain ridge for about 20 metres, before it looked even remotely safe. I could hear his wife behind, calmly stating…"Do not look down"…to the sheer drop to our left. Shizer…I'd certainly been here before.

As I'm edging along the barely there ridge like Spider-Man, I noticed I was overcome with calmness. Now, don't get me wrong, my adrenaline was jacked, and I was certainly a tad perplexed to begin with…however…my breath, my heart rate, my demeanour…was in total acceptance and 'flow' of the situation. Gone was 'zero to imminent death' in a blink of an eye. Before I knew it, I'd reached safety and stood victorious, with an immense sense of achievement overlooking the splendour and incredible panoramic views. Go Spidey!

"Something had shifted. Last time I was up a mountain I'd experienced a full blown panic attack attempting a similar feat...but this was different."

Having gotten closer to overcoming my fear of heights (I've since jumped out of a plane at 15,000 feet), I was rewarded with an extraordinary visit to an inhabited castle owned by two local eccentric brothers. I was blown away as I walked around a maze of rooms filled with ancient artefacts and hidden treasures. I couldn't help but think it'd been the perfect metaphor for facing my fears. If I'd frozen, refusing to proceed along that dangerous ridge, I'd of surely been deprived such delights. It also made me realise I was becoming stronger within myself. Equanimity equals power... which means you're in 'flow' with a healthy ego in tow..."I'm the Badass!"

The very next day, the second and most profound experience took place. Me and the young fellow decided to go horse riding, at a nearby ranch. I was a complete rookie, previously having had a knack for spooking horses merely by looking at them. I was paired off with a beautiful white horse called Jesus. Having greeted the beauty, I could sense he was at ease with me, which only enhanced my confidence. I guess the pre-ride intimate gaze into each other's eyes, is kinda the equivalent of kicking the tyres before you burn rubber.

Anyway, off we trot and it's not long before I'm gaining a strong sense of wellbeing (partly for still being mounted atop of Jesus) As we gently rode across the sprawling meadows amongst the hillsides, with the glorious sunshine hitting my face, I had the sudden realisation...I was actually embodying the experience of that dream I'd had when I was young.

"Every single part of my reality lit up with the purest sensations of euphoria, tranquility and the joyful appreciation of being alive...just like the dream."

It was like the perfect ending to something that'd started right at the very beginning, way before I could of ever known it would end this way. Now, I'm not a religious man, but how apt was is it, for my four legged friend to be called Jesus on such an endeavour? Epiphanies don't come better than that...and just like the one I'd had the day before, I had to endure the dangers and pitfalls in order to overcome my fears and reach the glory. It was proof once again that my dreams, visions and aspirations always seemed to realise, especially when in accordance to the flow of life. It really is that simple - if you're tapping into the 'good stuff', the good stuff taps into you.

"The more evidence I gain through such experiences, the more faith embodied in myself, the universe and the totality of life."

Back to the Land's End, and I had to endure what I considered to be the harshest Winter I'd known. Storms, isolation and my car breaking down, all rendered me 'home alone' for a long period of time, which all served as the perfect storm to complete Lone Wolf. Using the mantra - 'Want to be here'...I battened down the hatches and cracked on with editing.

I was well on track to complete the final draft, when Captain flippin' Blunderclutz makes an unexpected cameo appearance...and I 'inadvertently' smash my wrist to pieces skating. How's your feckin' luck? I'd just got my car back on the road, and had decided to order a Thai takeaway. On route, I'd had the urge to go for a 'quick roll' in a nearby skatepark. Within minutes of shreddin' the deep end bowl I was spat out, eating shit on the all too familiar crusty 'crete. In true old-boy style, I say a cool and collected... "Yeah yeah"...to the young scooter crew that are looking down asking if I'm ok.

"You just know it's bad when you hear those ooofs and arrrs!"

I grab the board with my functioning right hand, and slowly make my way outta the bowl as if I'm perfectly ok. Now, usually the skater will always win...never let a slam have the last word, take another ride and make it count. I've broken bones, always getting back on to beat the slam...but this seemed to really take it outta me. Retreating back to my car, I inspect the damage. Yep. It was mash up, big time…and my left wrist, not only my 'charging' arm for skating, but writing, painting...fuck guitar, piano...I started to think the worse. The hospital wasn't far. First things first, and in true British Bulldog fashion, I go grab my Thai takeaway on route, holding back the grimaces of pain as I pay the waitress who's looking at me with an odd, bewildered look.

"I sat in the car and demolished the complimentary chilli crackers, before heading to the hospital."

Hallelujah for automatic cars. Once there, I stand behind a man in A&E who's complaining of an irritating insect bite to his left hand (for real)...I quietly think to myself..."Out the frickin' way you dweeb, my flippin' arms smashed to bits." Eventually I get seen and I'm given painkillers whilst I await an X-ray.

I couldn't help but think…"Am I not supposed to be past this kinda behaviour?!" Sitting in a hospital A&E clearly holds a lot of 'nostalgia' for me...perhaps for all the wrong reasons. I half-heartedly chuckle to myself at the sheer stupidity of it all, whilst trying not to fear the worse. To my horror, I get the X-ray back and a doc tells me it's well and truly fooked…I'm gonna need to see a specialist, expect surgery and to add insult to injury, he's gonna have to reset the bones immediately.

"Lovely, glad I'm not doing it on an empty stomach."

We proceed into a room where I'm told to sit on the bed, whilst another doc pins me back firmly. A nurse enters with a big arse canister of laughing gas and syringes, as they go about getting me ready for an arm wrestle. Three injections of anaesthetic later, I'm told to chug on the gas like Lord Vader, whilst they proceed to twist and pull my bones back into place like a medieval game of endurance. I was so out of it on gas, I felt my tongue drop out the side of my mouth as I nodded in and out of consciousness. I then entered an out of body state...looking down on the three musketeers, as they literally had a full blown work out yanking my bones back. I could hear the doc conducting the savage act of torture, panting heavily in my lug hole, whilst the dude pinning me down broke a sweat as he grappled my shoulders. All of a sudden I heard a

449

CRACK! and a POP!....as the bones went back in, followed by the warm sensation of a cast being placed over my wrist and hand.

"Blimey, what the hell? I only popped out for a Thai. Good job troops, even if it was a tad barbaric."

The following morning I was greeted with post torture pain. The points on my shoulders where I'd been grappled were significant, and although my entire wrist and hand seemed to be in place, there was a constant seething of agony. Call me mad, but from that waking moment, I knew I didn't wanna take those meds.

A week later I saw the specialist, who announced I'd need an op to reinforce the bones and joints, using a titanium plate affixed with screws. Before I knew it I'm lying on an operating table having nerve blockers injected into my shoulder. I'd never had an op before where I'm lying half present in consciousness, whilst some dude's opening you up on the other side of a dividing drape. I'm waffling on to these two junior nurses about this and that, and at the same time I can hear matey instructing his team throughout the procedure.

"I actually heard him correct a nurse for drilling a hole in the wrong place. Very clearly he snapped - "NO NO...NOT THERE, THERE!"

When it came to being stitched up, I heard the exact same nurse quietly whisper to the doc..."Look at his star tattoo, it's ruined"…to which he quipped..."That's the least of my worries." Charming. When the doc came around to have his post op chat, I couldn't help but ask - "Thanks doc, by the way...what the hell have you done to my tattoo?"...we both smiled.

That night, at approx 4am I had a panic attack, brought on by what I believed to be a blood clot in my hand, which appeared to be going purple. I called the emergency services and requested an ambulance, whilst an operator annoyingly insisted on running through a checklist of possible COVID symptoms. Eventually an ambulance turns up and I'm told there's no clot. I (begrudgingly) swallow a couple of Co-codamol, and shortly after fall asleep. When I awoke, and on strict instruction from the ambulance crew, I reluctantly continued to take the meds. On the second day, I made a (just about) conscious decision to stop…based purely on the fact I felt like a jellyhead…and set the intention to make a speedier recovery without meds.

"For me, they just cause my brain to shut down, which means I become drug fucked. In other words, I start operating on a lower frequency."

It's just an observation I've gained through my recovery from 'chemical enhancement'…and for me, meds are no different. When I'm clean I'm serene. When I abstain, I operate on a higher level of consciousness and my frequency is sharp and bright...and when I'm operating on that kind of energy, there's optimised balance and 'flow'…meaning anything is possible, including (self) healing at a more rapid pace.

Disclaimer - I am not saying do not take meds, or that meds do not have a purpose. Just because it works for me, doesn't mean it works for everyone. Go find out through your own experience what works for you.

Within two weeks of the op, I'm beginning to gain the strength to lift and pour kettles, after four weeks I'm picking a guitar up and beginning to play once more. I'm also driving again. I saw a consultant on the sixth week, who declared - "You've made an extraordinary recovery." They were gonna suggest physio, but could see I actually wouldn't need it.

"Once again, positive perspective. If you truly believe something is possible, it is."

I'd learnt years ago that whatever I think, will become my reality with necessary action. I now had extensive experience and evidence that proved this. I also knew that meditation (for me) has a purer, higher frequency than medication. So, if you're clean and serene, and plugging in to all things zen...BOOM! Good shit happens real quick, every time.

When I went back to the hospital to have my cast removed in exchange for a wrist brace, I finally got to see the star tattoo. I'd fallen out of love with that tattoo. It was an impulsive, drunken decision made late one night whilst hanging with our mate Bullet the tattooist. The nurse cutting off the cast was in fact the one I'd overheard in the op, stating to the doc that it was indeed ruined. We had a giggle over that, and when it was finally revealed, I couldn't help but laugh out loud. She was right, the star had a 4 inch scar running straight through the middle, which had severed it in half... sewn back together completely wonky.

"To me, and everyone I've showed it to, it seemed to be a symbolic metaphor for being perfectly imperfect."

I absolutely love my new version of the tattoo...it was a timely (and permanent) reminder for where I was at in the grand scheme of things. Another scar for life, with so much meaning to it than what lay on the surface. It was the symbol to encapsulate my true life metamorphosis...taking the old, destroying it, dissecting it, reinventing it, and putting it back together, allowing it to heal, becoming brand new...remaining perfectly imperfect.

From the very beginnings, I'd collected the battle scars...and over the years they'd remained a heavy burden, because I never knew the beauty in them. I always thought my scars defined me, but for all the wrong reasons. I had to come to know and understand my story, to find acceptance and make peace with it...to truly appreciate ALL that I am...but until then, it would dictate who I was. I had to go in search of something, anything to step out of that discomfort to find a release.

"My chemical romance allowed me to flirt with death, but luckily my self sabotaging ego got the bullet."

I could never really sit and be at ease, and I couldn't be on my own, yet I suffered in silence...a hopeless, dedicated member of the pity party. Escapism allowed me to constantly run from myself, that crippling sense of alienation and the thoughts in my head, and ultimately from life. I can't even imagine feeling like that now. I made it. I had hope. I found a glimmer of light. I found courage, my voice...I mustered the strength to boldly pull myself out from the void and into a new life of abundance...a faithful, dedicated member of the appreciation club.

Sometimes I can't quite believe the person I'm talking about in that old life was me. Underneath all the bullshit I was there, somewhere...a frightened little boy hoping that one day someone would save him. Unbeknown to me, the person who would eventually step forward to rescue him, would in fact be me.

"Giving up the fight and surrendering to my imperfections, learning to meet the battle scars with love not hatred...I found peace and it changed everything."

We can go through life searching, constantly looking to external sources, seeking that 'special person' or 'thing' that will fix us, to make us complete and whole again. That constant barrage of distraction to mislead us away from the real 'prize'. I gave it a damn good go, but alas nothing worked...cheap thrills and materialism failed me, as did false promises and lies.

For me, the 'good stuff' is no different to consumerism or the sticky-icky tentacles of chemical enhancement (if we're not careful)...it's really easy to lose ourselves in a quest to find 'that thing', the 'sweet spot', the elixir. Little did I know that all the while, that 'special thing' was my true authentic self, right here, right now, within...it'd been there all along, waiting patiently for me to arrive. It may of taken many years, and it certainly was a hell of a clusterfuck ride, but through sheer audacious determination not to be beat, my resilience won. It's been my experience, that just when we think we can't go on, we can, always...and it's at that very end point, where it feels the bleakest, that new beginnings can and will arise, if we dare to allow them to. We just gotta change those worn out habits and routines that no longer serve us, for something better...

"GET REAL. GET HELP. GET WELL."

I'm still a pirate at heart, a Lone Wolf yes, but certainly not a Lonely Wolf...seeking out new adventures wherever I go, however now, I run to, not from...and for me, that's the ultimate freedom money can't buy.

The end is always the beginning...

Appreciation. Gratitude. Love.

My beloved Mum, Dad, Bro, and all extended family and friends…
unconditional and timeless. Tony, you opened the doorway to what
was possible…forever, your dedicated brother. Chris, Barbara and
Christophe…your unparalleled support and wisdom granted me
tranquility. Matt and Bill…you provided the seeds. To all those
living against the stream…just for today. To all free thinkers,
shakers, movers and makers…keep disrupting the mainstream, we
need your inspiration for motivation and change. Polly…without
your encouragement this wouldn't be. Av, Barnaby, Dean, Harry,
Neen, Deadly, and George…for your mind, eyes and ears. Lastly - to
all the unseen guides, great masters and wise elders…may I continue
to remain your humble student. Forever thankful.

Oh and of course, not forgetting Rupert the cat…the best god damn
Zen teacher I ever had.

Be the log.